Bonnie Raitt

Bonnie Raitt

JUST IN THE NICK OF TIME

MARK BEGO

A BIRCH LANE PRESS BOOK
Published by Carol Publishing Group

Copyright © 1995 Mark Bego

Frontispiece: When Bonnie Raitt began her singing career, she was determined to become a blues singer like Muddy Waters and Sippie Wallace. (*Warner Brothers Records/ MJB Archives*)

A Birch Lane Press Book

Published by Carol Publishing Group

Birch Lane is a registered trademark of Carol Communications, Inc.

Editorial Offices: 600 Madison Avenue, New York, N.Y. 10022

Sales and Distribution Offices: 120 Enterprise Avenue,
    Secaucus, N.J. 07094

In Canada: Canadian Manda Group, One Atlantic Avenue, Suite 105,
    Toronto, Ontario M6K 3E7

Queries regarding rights and permissions should be addressed to Carol
    Publishing Group, 600 Madison Avenue, New York, N.Y. 10022

Carol Publishing Group books are available at special discounts for bulk purchases, sales promotion, fund-raising, or educational purposes. Special editions can be created to specifications. For details, contact: Special Sales Department, Carol Publishing Group, 120 Enterprise Avenue, Secaucus, N.J. 07094

Manufactured in the United States of America

10 9 8 7 6 5 4 3 2 1

Library of Congress Cataloging-in-Publication Data

Bego, Mark.
    Bonnie Raitt : just in the nick of time / Mark Bego.
        p.   cm.
    "A Birch Lane Press book."
    Includes index.
    ISBN 1-55972-315-7
    1. Raitt, Bonnie.   2. Singers—United States—Biography.
I. Title.
ML420.R278B66   1995
782.42164'092—dc20
    [B]   95-9357
                                             CIP
                                             MN

To Melissa Hill Porter:

In the summer of 1973, when I was a short order cook at Howard Johnson's and you were the ice-cream-counter girl, you said to me, "You've got to hear this new album—*Give It Up* by Bonnie Raitt." Thanx . . .

Gotcha!!!

CONTENTS

Acknowledgments

The author would like to thank the following people for their help and assistance: David Andrew, Joan Baez, Anne Bego, Peter Beudert, Hillel Black, Trippy Cunningham, Brad De-Meulenaere, Kara DeMeulenaere, Jim Depogny, Gino Falzarano, Peter Ferren, David Goldman, Sasha Goodman, Victoria Green Elliott, Jimmy Greenspoon, Peggy Lee, Virginia Lohle of Star File, Sindi Markoff, Sue McDonald, Debra Mitchell, Barbra Nagel, Dean Porter, Kim Reidman, Martha Reeves, Ken Reynolds, Ellen Rubin, Barbara Shelley, Mark Spector, and Mary Wilson.

FOREWORD
by Joan Baez

When I think about Bonnie Raitt, the first thing that comes to mind is that her reputation precedes her. Throughout her career she has consistently tried to promote other musicians—especially the older blues and rhythm and blues musicians, those folks who we tend to forget about. Her concern and devotion to them is consistent. I think that she is a generous woman.

I can recall the first couple of times I saw her. I remember walking out on stage once when she was singing. It was at Harvard, ten or fifteen years ago. It was some anniversary show, and they had a bunch of folksingers. Bonnie was one of them and I was one of them. I knew the song she was singing and, as a surprise, I walked out to sing it with her. As it turned out, this was not a good thing to do. She was terrified because it was me! And you know, I never really paid enough attention to that kind of thing, because there are not very many people who intimidate me.

But, that was a long time ago. Now, Bonnie has all of that confidence in the walking, and in the singing, and in the carriage of herself. It comes when you get to relax. You finally know that people *get it*. They *get it* about how wonderful you are.

It's interesting that Bonnie is just now receiving the recognition that she deserves. I felt a personal triumph when she finally got all of the Grammy Awards. So did we all, by the way, people who consider our music—folk music—to be more real than some of the other stuff that's out there. I faxed her, or telegramed her, at that time. I stay on top of people's successes, or I try to, if they are people I admire.

Bonnie Raitt is a principled person. People's personal convictions make principled people out of them. So, you might not want to be a principled person, because it's a pain in the ass with regard to your energy, and the things that you end up having to do. But, I think that in the long run, and usually in the short run, it's an appropriate way to live.

Like myself, she has Quaker heritage, and for us, that comes a little bit like second nature—to try and live a principled life. Since we're in this particular decade and era, you can't live a principled life unless you're engaged to something greater than career, because the people of the world are suffering, and I think Bonnie makes a genuine attempt to make it better.

Musically, it's very interesting that we are not in the same bag at all. Bonnie's much more bluesy than I am. It's always been her comfort zone. She has a low singing register, with belting and with blues. Very, very different from myself. I've struggled now for the last ten years. It's been like a thorough battle keeping the upper range. And as I listen to my fellow female artists, they don't do that for the most part or they weren't sopranos in the first place.

I was a puritanical puritan, whose interest was folk music. In fact, I never sang the blues. I didn't like the blues. It wasn't home to me at all, and never has been. I feel a little bit silly when I do sing the blues. But Bonnie, she was cut out for that. Her voice is called a "chest" voice; so musically, I certainly think she has been making the right choices. For me, the things I love the most that she does are ballads. They will always have that bluesy *smack* to them. I think that they are the most moving of her performances.

If I were to sum up Bonnie Raitt, how would I describe her? She's this tremendously gifted stringy redhead and she shows gratitude for people who got out there with the "gift." First of all, she kept her conviction-filled musical talent polished and used it well, and then, secondly, attempted to use it on people who had less.

The music business isn't for everybody. I'm here for the long haul. I wish that she wouldn't be anxious about it, because she *will* be in there for the long haul too.

When I think of Bonnie Raitt, I think she's pretty wonderful!

AUTHOR TO READER

My Encounters
With Bonnie

*B*onnie Raitt is the kind of person who looks you squarely in the eyes when she talks to you. She doesn't engage in idle cocktail party chat. If you are having a conversation with her, you have her undivided attention. I know this first-hand. When she is finished speaking to you, the impression that she leaves you with is indelible.

I first met her in January 1992 at a benefit concert at the Hollywood Palace Theater to raise money for a songwriter who had suffered a stroke and was without medical insurance. One of the star performers, Mary Wilson, introduced me to Bonnie backstage.

The next time I saw Bonnie was February 25, 1993, at the preawards cocktail party for the fourth annual Rhythm and Blues Foundation's Pioneer Awards on the mezzanine of the same theater. I had just begun preliminary work on the autobiography of Martha Reeves, *Dancing in the Street,* and I was attending the awards ceremony to see Martha Reeves and the Vandellas accept their Pioneer Awards.

While Martha talked with friends, I spotted Bonnie standing only a few feet away from me. Her red hair stood out in the crowd, and for a rare moment she was not engaged in a conversation. I seized the opportunity and walked up to reintroduce myself.

"I'm Mark Bego, and I met you briefly last January with Mary Wilson and Rita Coolidge at the fund-raising benefit for songwriter William 'Smitty' Smith."

"Oh yes, good to see you," she said, looking me straight in the eye.

"I'm the author of several books on rock and roll, and currently I'm working on Martha Reeves' autobiography."

"That's wonderful! Congratulations!" Bonnie said with genuine enthusiasm.

"Several publishers have been asking me what the possibilities were of you writing your autobiography. I'd love to help you do that."

Never once breaking her fixed gaze, she replied, "Well, you'll have to get in line. I have at least five different writer friends of mine bugging me to do just that. However, I'm not ready to do one yet. Writing my autobiography is still several years off."

Although her statement was firm, I asked, "Can I at least give you my business card in case you change your mind?"

"That would be great," she said.

She took my card and thanked me for my interest in writing her life story with her.

The year progressed swiftly, and I became preoccupied with work on Martha Reeves's fascinating life story. When Martha and I were finished working on the manuscript that became the bestseller *Dancing in the Street: Confessions of a Motown Diva*, it was again time to find a book subject.

I suggested several different possible rock star book subjects, and one publisher after another communicated the message: "Snag Bonnie Raitt for an autobiography and you can write your own deal." Every time someone asked me about my chances of working with Bonnie, I repeated the story, beginning with the words, "I already tried to talk her into it, and she isn't interested at this time. And—even if she did—at best I'm fifth or sixth in line to work with her."

That always left me in the position of asking one editor after another, "How about an 'unauthorized' biography *about* Bonnie?"

The answer was always, "No. Either convince Bonnie to work with you, or we're not interested." Frustratingly, the topic always seemed to be dropped right there.

In the 1990s, while Bonnie Raitt continued to rack up Grammy Award after Grammy Award, and one Platinum album after another, I knew that someone was eventually going to write Bonnie's story—with or without her cooperation. Why shouldn't it be me?

Finally—after Bonnie's third consecutive multi–Platinum album hit number 1—someone saw my point of view. It was September 1994, and I was in Seattle with Martha Reeves. We were on the last stop of a fourteen-city media tour to promote *Dancing in the Street,* when I received word that Hillel Black, the editorial director at Carol Publishing, wanted me to write a book about Bonnie—unauthorized.

Was I ruining my chances of ever working *with* Bonnie in any capacity by accepting this contract? Possibly, but it was a chance I had to take. After all, now that I had interested the company in publishing a book on Raitt, if I didn't accept this deal, they could simply proceed without me and hire a different writer for the same task. There was no way I could let that happen!

This isn't a book idea that just came to me one day out of the sky—it's one I've longed to write for many years. Ever since 1973, the first time I heard Bonnie's album, *Give It Up,* I've been in love with her and her expressive flair for blending traditional blues and folk music with rock and roll. I have attended every concert of hers I could get to. I've seen her at high points: headlining Lincoln Center in front of thousands of cheering fans, and at the famed MUSE concerts in 1979 in Madison Square Garden. I also saw her at a career low point: performing in a clearing in the woods in front of a couple hundred people at a 1987 folk festival at Croton-On-Hudson. And at her new zenith: at the Shrine Auditorium in Los Angeles during the 1995 Grammy Awards telecast, while millions watched. Whether she was singing to eighteen thousand cheering fans in Madison Square Garden, or in front of a bunch of campers sitting cross-legged in a forest, she was equally mesmerizing. The riveting quality of her singing and the enthusiasm of her performance was never altered by the size of her audience or the prestige of the setting.

Bonnie Raitt's story is an inspiring one of integrity, drive, conviction, and talent. It became my assignment to tell it with all of the excitement and drama fully intact.

My third face-to-face encounter with Bonnie came after I had already begun work on this book. It was Thursday, March 2, 1995, and it was a cold, rainy day in Los Angeles. It was one in the afternoon when I arrived at the Universal Hilton Hotel with one of my very best friends, Mary Wilson of the Supremes. Mary and I had attended the thirty-seventh annual Grammy Awards ceremony the night before, and tonight I was to be her date at the Rhythm and Blues Foundation's sixth annual Pioneer Awards presentation, honoring soul and jazz living legends for their musical contributions. This afternoon we had come to the press reception at the hotel's Club 555. Mary and I were instantly and warmly greeted by two of our closest mutual friends: Martha Reeves and Ken Reynolds, one of the event's publicists.

I found myself stunned by the company I was in. There were less than fifty people in the room, and it was a virtual "who's who" of the rhythm and blues world. The singing legends in the small cocktail lounge that afternoon included Fats

Domino, Little Richard, Cissy Houston, Darlene Love, Charles Brown, Martha Reeves, the Marvelettes, Inez and Charlie Foxx, Mary Wilson, Lloyd Price, Junior Walker, and Booker T. and the MG's.

Amid all of the flashes from journalists' cameras, cables and wires from television camera crews, and radio interviewers' recording equipment, a diminutive lady with a cascade of fiery red hair darted in and out of the throng of activity. She wore a sheer long-sleeve navy-blue blouse and jeans, and in the front of her red-orange hair there was a shock of steel gray—like fireworks in a sea of scarlet. It was unmistakably Bonnie Raitt, and she was truly in her element.

Although she had become as big a star as any of the rhythm and blues superstars in the room, it was clear that she was happy to take a backseat to all the R&B legends there. Although there are dozens of charities she devotes her time to, the Rhythm and Blues Foundation has recently become her focal point. With so many of the R&B legends of the forties, fifties, and sixties ripped-off, neglected, or conned out of their just and due royalties from records sold since then, it is the foundation's goal to return the respect and the money to these brilliant performers.

Watching Bonnie wind her way through the various groupings of singing legends, like a hostess making last-minute preparations at a party, it was clear that her focus was on all of the superstars gathered in that room that cold and rainy afternoon.

While I snapped photographs of Martha and Mary with their friends and peers, I wondered, Should I tell Bonnie Raitt that I am writing a book about her?

Mary had just finished a brief radio interview, and as she stood up, Bonnie suddenly crossed my path. "Can I get a picture with you and Mary Wilson?" I asked Bonnie.

"I'd love to," she said to me. She then turned and said, "Mary, you look fabulous!"

I snapped the photo and quickly handed a friend my camera. I asked, "Bonnie, do you mind if I have my picture taken with you, too?" She complied and then rushed off to take care of more business.

I walked over to Martha Reeves and told her that when the opportunity arose, I wanted to get a photo of her with Bonnie as well. Not long afterward, both Bonnie and Martha were in very close proximity. I knew that another photo opportunity had arisen.

"Bonnie, can I take a photo of you and Martha Reeves together?" I asked.

"I'd love to," she said. Then, pausing before she put her arm around Martha to pose for my camera, she took a step closer to me. Standing no more than five inches from my nose, she stared me straight in the eyes and said in an extremely intent voice, "What are you going to do with these photos?"

Before I could utter a word, Martha spoke up and said, "Mark publishes his photos in his books. He's a music industry journalist."

My dear friend Martha had saved me from shoving my own foot in my mouth.

Before I could utter a word, Bonnie said, "If you're a journalist, that's the one exception, because you can publicize the Rhythm and Blues Foundation. You'd be surprised how many photos I autograph for people backstage only to hear them say, 'Thank you, I paid $200 for that photo of you.' That same photo I posed for, for free. If the photo sold for $200 and the money went to the Rhythm and Blues Foundation, I wouldn't mind."

I assured her that I was a legitimate journalist, and that the photos would indeed be used to publicize the foundation.

The two ladies posed for my camera. Bonnie thanked Martha for posing with her and then turned to me with a smile. "I want copies of these!" she said.

"Where do I send them?" I asked.

"Send them to me in care of the Rhythm and Blues Foundation," she replied.

Before the press reception ended, many of the stars grouped together on the tiny stage of Club 555 for a once-in-a-lifetime gathering of talent. I quickly wedged my way into the crowd of TV and press photographers and took several of the pictures that appear in this book.

As the stars came down from the stage, Mary informed me that it was time to get moving. We had a full schedule of events before that evening's show, where she was going to be one of the celebrity presenters.

Seconds later, Bonnie looked my way, and I said to her, "I'll send you copies of these photos as well."

"Thank you," she said enthusiastically, "and *thank you* for writing all of those books!"

When Mary and I got into her car and left the hotel, I said to her, "I really don't know what to do. Should I tell Bonnie that I'm on assignment to write a book about her or not? She might get really upset."

Always one of my most level-headed friends, Mary Wilson said to me, "For once, keep your mouth shut. I know you're dying to tell Bonnie, but it'll only complicate matters, and you'll put her on the defensive. When she sees what a loving and respectful book you're going to write about her, you'll both end up happy with the finished product."

Then and there I knew exactly how I was going to proceed. The book that you now hold in your hands is the by-product of my three decades of admiration for one of the most loved and respected ladies in the music business today: the incredible Bonnie Raitt.

Not only do I hope that you enjoy reading it—I hope Bonnie does too.

1

You Got It

Since noon on January 21, 1990, a steady stream of limousines had been arriving at the Shrine Auditorium in Los Angeles for the music world's most exciting night of the year, the annual Grammy Awards. A phalanx of press photographers and TV camera crews surrounded every entrance, awaiting the arrival of celebrities, singing stars, producers, and record company executives.

A massive Byzantine theater in an unglamorous part of Los Angeles, the Shrine Auditorium was abuzz with energy. This was the one evening of the year when rock stars, jazz legends, classical musicians, and R&B idols all shared the same stage with equal billing.

For Bonnie Raitt, who was nominated for four of the top awards, this night would prove unforgettable. It would dramatically change her life.

Not only was she nominated for four high-profile Grammy Awards, she was also slated to perform live on the international telecast, seen by millions of music fans in over twenty countries around the world. She had been nominated for three

Grammy Awards in the 1980s, but she had never won one of the coveted trophies. Although the nominations had represented respect and recognition from her peers, the awards had always been presented to more commercially successful performers—not to Bonnie. On this particular occasion, Bonnie had arrived at the Shrine Auditorium early in the day.

With awards given in over fifty categories, many of the Grammys are presented in the early afternoon, hours before the TV cameras begin to roll. It was during that afternoon, amid the nonbroadcast awards presentations, that Bonnie and blues artist John Lee Hooker had won the Grammy Award for the Best Traditional Blues Recording, for their duet, "I'm in the Mood."

Bonnie was especially proud of the recognition that had been brought to the blues star. Lending her vocal and instrumental assistance to classic rhythm-and-blues stars of the past had become an on-going career endeavor, so this particular award meant much to her.

At 5:00 P.M., with comedian Gary Shandling hosting, the telecast began. In the middle of the three-hour show, working with her new band, Bonnie treated the television and studio audience with a performance of her new hit, "Thing Called Love." She gave the same kind of self-confident performance that had made her new album, *Nick of Time,* such an appealing hit. Bonnie not only displayed her commanding singing style, but her trademark slide-guitar playing as well. At the end of the number, the television cameras focused on her father, Broadway star John Raitt, who was applauding enthusiastically from the audience.

At the age of forty, Bonnie Raitt looked like a seasoned star that evening, not the hippie folk singer she had personified at the beginning of her career. Her mane of red-orange hair fell in curls around her shoulders with her signature lightning bolt of silver gray just above the left side of her forehead. Only the slightest bit of makeup touched her radiant face. She was dressed in a black satin minidress, a gold-and-black sequinned long-sleeve jacket with squared-off shoulders, and knee-high black suede boots. Never excessive in her stage appearance, she wore one ring on each hand and a pair of dangling gold earrings.

Seconds after the number was finished and the applause died down, rock singer Taylor Dane and heavy metal band Mötley Crüe were introduced by Shandling. Like Bonnie, the members of Mötley Crüe had just gone through substance abuse treatment.

Dane and the Crüe quartet announced the nominees for the category of Best Rock Performance, Female. (Per Grammy rules and regulations, whole albums can compete against single songs in the same category.) The first name they read belonged to Melissa Etheridge, who was seated in the audience. She was nominated for her song "Brave and Crazy." *Foreign Affair* by Tina Turner, "I Drove All Night" by Cyndi Lauper, and "Let's Stay Together" by Pat Benatar, were also nominated, but—for whatever reason—these three performers were not present.

Then Bonnie's *Nick of Time* album was announced. Her face filled up the TV monitors. She was standing backstage in front of a backdrop that was painted to look as though the Grammy-shaped symbol had been carved out of stone. Bonnie flashed a broad smile, as the auditorium audience clapped and cheered. As the cheering swelled, Bonnie blushed and smiled even more broadly; dimples formed in her cheeks. She was so truly surprised by the crowd's enthusiastic response that she took a shy step backward and looked away from the camera.

"And the award goes to," said Taylor Dane, pulling the

sealed white envelope open: "Okay! *Nick of Time* album, Bonnie Raitt!"

"Oh my God, oh my God!" Bonnie said in amazement, putting her hands to her forehead. While the song "Thing Called Love" played over the loudspeakers, Bonnie emerged from the wings with a look of astonishment on her face.

Taylor and the four members of Mötley Crüe all kissed Bonnie on the cheek while the crowd continued to cheer wildly. Looking on from the audience were three of her strongest supporters—her father; her producer, Don Was; and her new boyfriend, actor Michael O'Keefe.

Bonnie stepped up to the microphone. "I don't know what to say! This is a real miracle for me, after all this time. Thank you so much to the academy, and my peers for voting for me, and honoring me this way, and especially for nominating me in all those years when things weren't going so well. I'd like to thank first of all, my producer, Don Was; my engineer, Ed Cherney. I'm so amazed I can't even . . ."

She suddenly paused, her voice breaking, her eyes damp with tears. But she quickly composed herself and continued, smiling, "I'd like to thank the musicians and the songwriters and the crew in the studio and on the road who get this music to sound so good, and to get it out to you. I'd like to thank my friends at my new label, Capitol [Records], and especially I'd like to thank Joe Smith, David Berman, Tom Raleigh, and Tim Divine who had the courage to sign me. I really appreciate the job you guys did. I want to thank VH1 [Video Hits 1, a TV network] and radio for giving me a chance this year. To my managers, Danny Goldberg, Ron Stone, and Jim Birch, I love you so much; my lawyer Nat Weiss—thanks. And, especially close to my heart, I'd like to thank my mother and my father for their inspiration, and my family and friends for their love and support, and mostly I'd like to thank God for bringing me to this at a time when I could *truly* appreciate it. Thank you so much."

Not long afterward, Ella Fitzgerald and another second-generation pop star, Natalie Cole, walked out on stage to present the award for the year's best album. Ella wore a spangled black and silver dress, and Natalie Cole appeared in a beautiful ruffled black dress. They stood at the podium and proceeded to sing an impromptu chorus of Nat King Cole's "Straighten Up and Fly Right."

Then Natalie announced, "For the Album of the Year, the Grammy goes to the artist and to the album producer." The nominees were Don Henley's *The End of the Innocence,* Tom Petty's *Full Moon Fever,* the Fine Young Cannibals' *The Raw and the Cooked,* the Traveling Wilbury's *Volume One* and Bonnie's *Nick of Time.* While Natalie read off the nominees, and announced Raitt's album, Bonnie was seated in the audience, next to her date, Michael O'Keefe. Her freckled face again radiated when the audience applauded at the mention of her name.

"And now, the Album of the Year," announced Ella Fitzgerald. "Come on, Ella, open it," she said out loud to herself, trying to pull the seal loose on the envelope. Natalie leaned forward and pulled at the stubborn paper envelope for Fitzgerald. As she flipped up the envelope flap, Ella joked, "You know I'd do it all wrong."

The envelope opened at last. Fitzgerald announced, *"Nick of Time,* Bonnie Raitt; producer, Don Was!" Bonnie leapt from her seat, her mouth open in awe at what she was hearing. She slapped the palms of Don Was's hands in an enthusiastic victory gesture, and covered her eyes with her hand as if in shock at what she was seeing: the entire audience in the Shrine Auditorium on their feet giving her a standing ovation.

"I love you!" O'Keefe shouted to her amid the roar of the star-studded crowd. She hugged Don Was, and together they ascended the steps that led from the audience to the stage. As she did so, another famous redhead, Bette Midler, yelled, "That's right!" to Raitt's look of thrilled amazement. Natalie and Ella each kissed Bonnie, who clutched her third Grammy Award of the evening.

Taken aback, Bonnie stood in front of the microphone and said, "I can never get over this, as long as I live! Dad and Mom, this one's for you. And, to be given this by Ella Fitzgerald and Natalie Cole . . . I'm so transported right now . . . I thank everybody so much. It means so much to the kind of music that I do, it means that those of us that love R&B are gonna get a chance again. Thank you so much from the bottom of my heart. Thank you!"

Next, Don Was had his turn at the microphone: "I just want to thank Bonnie Raitt so much for setting an example to maintain your integrity, and maintain your audience, and just try to make a good record; people will respond to you—your peers, the audience out there. Thanks Bonnie."

Gesturing to her he announced, "Bonnie Raitt, ladies and gentlemen!" and the audience again applauded and cheered for the red-headed singer.

While Don Was spoke, Bonnie put her hand over her eyes to blot the tears that ran down her face. When Don finished speaking, they exchanged a congratulatory kiss. They were then led offstage by Natalie Cole, who was smiling broadly.

Several minutes later, it was time to award the Best Pop Vocal Performance, Female Grammy. Not only was Bonnie competing aganist Bette Midler's "Wind Beneath My Wings," Paula Abdul's "Straight Up," and Gloria Estefan's "Don't Want to Lose You," but she was also up against her longtime friend and rival Linda Ronstadt, and her "Cry Like a Rainstrom, Howl Like the Wind." All of the nominees were present that evening, which electrified the moment. Bonnie blushed and laughed as her name was announced.

Olivia Newton-John and comedian Sam Kinison were presenting the award. After the nominees were read, Kinison took the winner's envelope and ripped it into pieces, saying, "I can't—they're all friends of mine!"

Laughing, Newton-John announced, "Here's the real envelope!" Tearing the official envelope open she announced, "And the Grammy goes to, Bonnie Raitt, 'Nick of Time!'"

Bonnie's mouth was agape, her brown eyes popped wide open. She put her hands on her cheeks and held her face. She stood, and received another standing ovation. Natalie Cole jumped up from her seat in the row in front of Bonnie and gave her a big hug. Pop-jazz singer Anita Baker in the next row forward received a kiss on the cheek from Bonnie. Billy Joel, standing at his seat across the aisle in the front row, threw his arm around Raitt and kissed her on the mouth. Bonnie put her right hand to her chest, to feel her excited heart beating. On the way up the steps this time, she caught her shoe on the floor, and broke the high heel off. By the time she reached the microphone she was hobbling.

Clutching her Grammy Award in her right hand, she tossled her hair with her left, and said, "Broke my heel on the way up here!" Rolling her eyes, she continued "I'm so in shock, I don't know what to say. The women I've been nominated in the same category with are all some of my favorites. I'll accept this on behalf of them, because I can only take so much of this!" The crowd roared with laughter, and she continued, "Wake me up when this is over! Thank you—whoever is responsible. I'm sure it's not me! Thank you!"

She then leaned over and removed her shoes. While the audience laughed and applauded, she comically shook her broken high heels in her right hand and walked offstage in her stocking feet while the crowd cheered.

As Bonnie Raitt headed for the wings, she turned and waved her fourth Grammy Award of the evening in heartfelt appreciation.

Gary Shandling again took the microphone and said in a mock-serious tone, "For those of you who just tuned in, the updated score is—Bonnie Raitt: four, Denver Broncos: nothing!"

When Bette Midler's song "Wind Beneath My Wings" subsequently took the award as Record of the Year, Midler laughed, "I'm flabbergasted!" and then hollered toward the wings, "Bonnie Raitt, I got one, too!"

Backstage after the telecast, Bonnie posed for the press photographers and was showered with attention as the triumphant belle of the ball. "This is the first time in my life I've won anything, and I'm forty years old," she announced to the TV cameras. "I can't believe that it's real!" But *real* it was. With all that she had been through in the last twenty years, after that incomparable evening at thirty-second annual Grammy Awards presentation, Bonnie Raitt's life would never be the same.

While her fame has made her a household name, her years of heartbreak and rejection coupled with her hypnotic music, raise several provocative questions this book seeks to answer: What fuels her unwavering devotion to charity work? What lengths did she go to in her quest for the right formula for success? What roles did Jackson Browne, Bruce Springsteen, Linda Ronstadt, Sippie Wallace, John Lee Hooker, Aretha Franklin, Peter Asher, Dennis Quaid, and Whoopie Goldberg all play in Bonnie's adventurous life and career? How extensive were her drinking and drug habits in the 1970s and 1980s? Why did she finally turn her back on her rock and roll all-night partying life? How does she view her newfound late-blooming fame, and how does she view her future? Bonnie Raitt is one of the most fascinating women in the music business today. At one point in her life she was self-destructive, but she has ultimately emerged self-fulfilled. She has been unwavering in her convictions, and her every move in the past three decades has contributed toward her inspiring climb to the top.

2

Bonnie's Childhood

*B*onnie Raitt was born into a house filled with music. The middle child in a family of three youngsters, and the only girl, she was a self-proclaimed tomboy, who could compete with her brothers—Steve and David—when it came to playing baseball and climbing trees.

According to Bonnie, "From the time I was seven or eight, I was tomboy with a vengeance. When you are the one girl in a family of boys, and your dad relates to the boys well—well, I just couldn't stand the way girls got the second best of everything. They couldn't throw as far. They weren't paid as much. To me, it was the same as black people getting treated as second-class citizens. So I always stayed out and played longer and hit the ball farther and had tough hands and all that."

Their mother, Marjorie Haydock, is an accomplished musician. "My mother's a fantastic pianist," Bonnie explains, "and very early on, I was always admiring her ability to just sit down and play whatever came to her mind. She also accompanied my dad when he would do concerts. I grew up around him performing and was enamored of that whole lifestyle."

It was theater, in fact, that first brought Bonnie's parents together. They met in the 1940s when they were both appearing in a college alumni production of the play *The Vagabond King*. John Raitt was playing the title role, and Marge was the leading lady. Their's was a theatrical fairy tale of a romance.

To this day, Bonnie complains that her mother doesn't get her fair share of the credit when it comes to discussing her artistically gifted parents—who were also her earliest musical influences. That is undoubtedly because her father, John, went on to become a Broadway star, while her piano-playing mom abandoned her musical career to stay home with the children.

As Bonnie explains it, "She was a very talented pianist and, in fact, was my dad's accompanist and supported him when he was taking singing lessons. Then she stopped her career to work as a receptionist so he could continue to study singing. And then she had us kids, and there was always this feeling that maybe she could have been a star [too] if she hadn't."

Born on November 8, 1949, in Burbank, California, Bonnie Lynn Raitt is proud of her Scottish roots, and her West Coast upbringing. "I'm from Southern California," she proclaims, "actually the second generation born and raised here. It's hard to believe, but no matter where I am, people think I'm from the South, somehow, because I like rhythm and blues so much. I'm from Southern California—a recovering Los Angeles person!"

Bonnie shares her Scorpio birth date with several other strong women in show business. She says, "I love Katharine Hepburn—she has the same birthday I do, November 8. So do Rickie Lee Jones and Bonnie Bramlett."

It was in 1947, two years before Bonnie's birth, that John Raitt first thrilled Broadway audiences in the starring role of Billy Bigelow in Rodgers and Hammerstein's classic musical *Carousel.* He also played the lead in the touring company of Rodgers and Hammerstein's 1943 hit *Oklahoma,* (which Al-fred Drake had originated) and eventually reprised the role on Broadway as well. In the mid-fifties Raitt also starred in *The Pajama Game* on Broadway, and in several other Broadway shows, including *Kiss Me Kate* and *Annie Get Your Gun.*

However, when Hollywood purchased the rights to make movie versions of *Oklahoma* and *Carousel,* they didn't cast John Raitt in the roles he had played so successfully on the stage. They decided that they needed someone with "box-office appeal," and not a stage actor. Raitt was understandably unhappy when both starmaking roles went to movie actor Gordon MacRae.

Bonnie distinctly remembers her father's sense of disappointment over MacRae's getting all of the glory in the films *Oklahoma* (1955) and *Carousel* (1956). According to her, "I liked my dad's shows—it was the family business. I didn't spend a lot of time looking at other people's shows because I had a fair amount of loyalty to my dad. I didn't see the film versions of *Oklahoma!* and *Carousel* because my dad was in those roles—it seemed like being a traitor."

As it happened later with Bonnie, perseverance paid off for John Raitt. In 1957 he was cast opposite Doris Day in the film adaptation of Richard Adler and Jerry Ross's hit musical *The Pajama Game.* Finally allowed to recreate one of his trademark theater roles on the big screen, the movie proved a big hit for him.

Bonnie recalls being in awe of her father when she was a child. "From the time I was able to realize that he was a musician, I was just mesmerized by his talent."

The considerable musical talent that both of her parents displayed made for a unique home atmosphere in which to grow up. From an early age, they encouraged Bonnie to pursue music as well. As she explains it, "Having grown up with my dad performing for a living, it's kind of the family business for me."

She recalls, "We would go to his shows. There was lots of music in the house. And, all three of the kids—I have two brothers—we all sang. I was singing from the time I was two or three. It wasn't any deliberate, 'Okay, I'm going to teach you how to be musical.' There was no force-feeding."

However, John Raitt's consistent traveling and touring became a source of disappointment for young Bonnie. "He was gone a lot, and, as a kid, it used to break my heart, because I didn't understand. Now, of course, I understand because I'm on tour all the time myself. I don't have kids, and the reason is that it makes a real conflict. It would be great if I had a 'wife' to stay home with the kids, but it just doesn't work out that way."

Her parents' vast musical skills also proved slightly intimidating to young Bonnie. "I loved acting in school plays," she says. Yet, she's quick to explain, "I didn't think I could ever come near Dad."

Having a father who was not only extremely talented, but usually absent, caused a lot of discontentment within the house. "He wasn't around enough to be a real father," Bonnie laments. "He'd come home off the road and bring us presents. So naturally, as a little girl, I'd fall in love with him. My mother got a raw deal that way, because she was strict and had to be both the mother and father. I didn't get along with her at all. She's real strong, and I think there was a natural jealousy."

In similar fashion, her mother's keyboard proficiency represented both musical reinforcement as well as stiff in-house competition. After Bonnie's first attempts at piano playing, she told herself, "I'd never be as good on piano as my mother," and soon lost interest in it.

Instead of acting or the piano, Bonnie chose the guitar. Her first one was a $25 six-string Stella, which she received in 1957 as a Christmas present. She was eight years old. "I didn't take guitar lessons," she recalls, "but I was playing guitar along with everyone else in the country, in the folk-music revival of the late fifties and early sixties."

Another late fifties influence was the beatnik movement. Like Maynard G. Krebbs on TV's *Dobie Gillis*, beatniks were characterized by goatees, berets, black turtleneck sweaters, and bongo drums. It was the era of the beat poets, free-form jazz music, and poetry readings in coffeehouses.

Bonnie began emulating the beatnik look. "I took to wearing a peace symbol around my neck when I was eleven, around 1961" she explains. "It represented my whole belief! And, I used to wear olive-green tights and black turtlenecks and I had a pair of earrings—my mother wouldn't let me pierce my ears, but I had a pair of hoop earrings. I'd grow my hair real long so I *looked* like a beatnik."

From the time Bonnie was eight until she was fifteen, she and her brothers went to the same summer camp in the Adirondack Mountains of New York. It was known there that she was quite a gifted guitar player, and she was encouraged to perform in front of an audience. According to her, "When my dad was on tour, my two brothers and I went to summer camp in upstate New York. A lot of counselors were college students when the Kingston Trio, Odetta, Joan Baez, Bob Dylan, and Peter, Paul and Mary were coming out. Those being my role models, I promptly identified with whatever they were doing on guitar.

"My fondest memory of realizing that I was going to be able to do this pretty well, was being asked to play in front of people at my camp when I was ten. It became a hobby to learn songs from records; teach myself how to play them on guitar. With the piano, you have to take so much classical music that I didn't stick with it; because it was going to take me too long to be able to be a jazz pianist, or play like my mom."

The folk revival Bonnie refers to peaked in 1962 and 1963,

when Peter, Paul and Mary scored a string of Top Ten hits with "If I Had a Hammer," "Puff the Magic Dragon," "Blowin' in the Wind," and "Don't Think Twice It's Alright." During this same era, folk madonna Joan Baez also placed her version of "We Shall Overcome" on the charts.

Bonnie's siblings took to music as well. "My brother just drove me nuts practicing the drums while I was doing my homework," she recalls.

Bonnie distinctly remembers her adolescent metamorphosis with disdain. She changed from an adorable little girl into an awkward teenager. She recalls, "I got betrayed: I was a cute little freckle-faced kid who kept looking at Maureen O'Hara movies, that thought that was going to happen to me when I was, like twelve. Or, like Joan Baez—I was gonna get real asthenic and kind of a beatnik. And I just never did. I just got rounder and rounder, and more bangs. Like a lot of teenagers, I had a weight problem, a skin problem, I had braces. I felt betrayed!"

The freckles on her face were another source of discontent for young Bonnie. "I had a dream once where people were segregated—the spotty from the clear. And I saw these magazine ads: HIDE UGLY FRECKLES. I used to try and bleach them out with lemon juice and Tide. And then Doris Day came along and changed my life."

To escape from the dilemmas of adolescence, Bonnie retreated into her music. "That was my saving grace. I just sat in my room and played my guitar, and played all those sad ballads I learned off of the Joan Beaz records, and sang about unrequited love, and talked on the phone. I just couldn't wait to get older. I just could not wait to be a beatnik, to actually go to Selma and be in the Freedom Riders, and I was thirteen."

One of the things that upset her most as a young teenager was the fact that her father's occupation seemed to divide the family. John Raitt remembers, "When she was about thirteen years old, I was very much on the road in those days, and I came home just to take a shower and change clothes. She was crying in the bathroom, and when she came out, I said, 'What are you crying about?' And she said, 'You're never home. We don't have to have this big house. Why can't you be like other daddies.' I said, 'You'll find out some time that Daddy has to go where his talent is wanted, and you'll find that some day that that's what happens sometimes in life.' And she certainly has found that."

Her father's absence also caused friction between Bonnie and her mother. "I had a rough time with her when I was a teenager. She wasn't that happy, and I wasn't that happy," Bonnie remembers.

While John Raitt received curtain calls every night, Marjorie had the burden of raising her three children. According to Bonnie, "She had to be both mother and dad and be the disciplinarian. And it's a love-hate thing, where you want to emulate your mom, and on the other hand, you see her getting the short end of the stick—as it were—in the marriage, and as a parent. And it was a confusing time to raise kids in Southern California, where there are so many other kids who are overly spoiled and whose parents would just leave for Vegas and give them a bunch of money and let them run riot. My parents had old-time values and wouldn't let us run around. And we were pretty mad at them for not letting us be like other kids."

Although she grew up as the child of a movie star, Bonnie wasn't allowed the freedom to become a stereotypical Hollywood brat. When she looked back at her childhood a decade later, Bonnie would explain her insulated upbringing. "My old man wasn't plastic Hollywood, he was too square!"

The Raitt family made their home on Mulholland Drive, high in the Hollywood Hills, in Coldwater Canyon. Geographically, this put Bonnie in a socially disadvantaged position, since she lived at the top of the mountain. "I wasn't allowed to hang out, because I was always the first kid on the bus, and the last one off. It took me an hour to get to school every day. And by the time I'd get home, it'd be four, and for me to get back down the hill to play with my friends, I'd have to get somebody to drive me, and my parents weren't into it. That's how I got into just sitting in my room playing a guitar."

In spite of her affluent upbringing, Bonnie remembers the values she was taught about money. This trait has followed her throughout her career. She has always been a performer who planned her career around what seemed right for her beliefs and feelings, as opposed to making decisions based on strictly financial concerns. "My parents were Quakers *and* Scottish. They were both raised real poor, and we got a minimal allowance. We had to earn it if we wanted anything. I'd iron clothes if I needed to make extra money."

While she was growing up, none of the typical early sixties "California music" appealed to Bonnie. She had no interest in the Beach Boys, the Safaris, Jan and Dean, or Frankie Avalon. "When I was in junior high," she reflects, "the peer-group pressure was to like Jan and Dean. In the summer everybody would go to the beach and get tanned and learn how to surf. *Everybody* cut school. And I was redheaded and didn't get tanned and I lived in the canyon and couldn't get to the beach."

While her schoolmates listened to surfer tunes, other influences began to cause excitement in Bonnie Raitt's teenage world. In 1964 the Beatles tipped off "the British Invasion," and along with it came the Rolling Stones and the Dave Clark Five. At the same time, Motown music hit the radio airwaves like a tidal wave, and with it came Martha and the Vandellas, the Temptations, Mary Wells, the Supremes, the Four Tops, and the Marvelettes.

"The minute that I heard the Beatles and the Rolling Stones, that was my era!" Bonnie exclaims. "I could always tell the difference between Fats Domino and Little Richard, and some of

that other kind of pop music like Patti Paige and even Doris
Day—who I love, too. Somehow I could just tell the difference,
and as I got older, there was a big difference between surf music
and Motown, and Stax, and Wilson Pickett, and James Brown.
Ike and Tina Turner were really big at the time, although they
only used to film her from the waist up on the local dance show
here [Los Angeles]. But I thought she was just about 'it!' when
I was eleven. I dug the Supremes!"

Watching and listening to the great woman of rock and roll
contributed toward shaping Bonnie's broad musical horizons.
According to Bonnie, "I loved Joan Baez. I still do. She was a
Quaker, like I was, and she was a political activist and folksinger. And I thought she was so beautiful, and she was part
Scottish, and I'm Scottish. She was my hero. And, Tina Turner,
the Marvelettes, Martha Reeves . . . Aretha Franklin was my ab-
solute favorite."

The Quaker religion is a consistent thread that runs
throughout Bonnie's life. She says, "It's really one of the few
religions that encompasses the mysticism of Eastern religions
and is also very democratic. Because, anybody who has something to say can stand up and say it. I didn't grow up in a rigid
structure, and religion for me is more of a spiritual and social
leaning or influence."

The Quaker religion is strongly pacifist. This viewpoint
led Bonnie to become actively involved in the antiwar movement of the late sixties. The same sentiments also ran deeply
through the folk and protest music that Bonnie so loved. These
combined elements galvanized her conviction to become actively involved in peace rallies and marches, and to stand up for
her beliefs.

"I was going to save the world from the time I was eleven,"
Bonnie recalls. "That was the way I was raised. My parents were
pacifists during the Second World War, and Walt Raitt, my
Dad's brother, was the peace secretary of the American Friends

Service Committee, which is the social-activist arm of the Religious Society of Friends—the Quakers. My father also did a really great antiwar movie called *Which Way the Wind?* around 1963. So I just understood that you were to be of service to other people, and that people who just worked for their own aggrandizement were shallow. So from the time I was a kid, I wanted to do something for the good of other people. I mean, injustice really pisses me off. War and injustice are the things that caused me the most anger and crying in my life. And so I have to feel like I'm making a difference. I mean, music's great, but what's important is doing something meaningful with your life."

Bonnie looked on while her father's career changed and evolved. Away from the lights of Broadway, John Raitt began to travel around the country in touring companies and summer-stock theater productions. She recalls, "He wasn't washed up. He made more money off Broadway, but it seemed like the circuit was somehow not as glamorous as Broadway."

She would watch and wonder about the dichotomy of her father's career. On one hand, the family's Quaker religion preached the merits of the working class, and ending world hunger. On the other hand, her dad still had to play the Hollywood star scene. That meant a big car, an impressive address, and a lot of unnecessary glitz—all for show.

"To do what my dad did," she says, "you had to live in a house and drive a Lincoln. I always was very embarrassed when we came to Quaker meetings in a nice car, 'cause my parents both look larger than life. They're both ridiculously good looking. I wanted my parents to drive a VW and my mother to not set her hair. But she had to. I remember my mother explaining to me that it was very important, especially since my dad wasn't exactly on the top rung as a major star, to drive a car that made it look like you still were. . . . I could never let anybody control my life like he did."

Looking back she says, "Being a Quaker, 'Ban the Bomb' was a reality since I was six. I mean, at Quaker meetings at Christmastime we'd decorate trees with ornaments and dollar bills. We were getting money for Algerian refugees. And the whole thing was to learn about Christmas in other countries. I was real aware of the Third World getting ripped off, that kind of thing."

Obviously, from a very early age, Bonnie was infused with some very adult concepts about how the world was supposed to run. These ideas and ideals went into shaping the political activist that she became.

Did she have any role models who were a little less political in nature? "Kitty on *Gunsmoke* was always a hero of mine," Bonnie says. In her eyes, Amanda Blake as the hard-as-nails Miss Kitty, personified the ultimate liberated woman of her era in the Wild West. After all, Miss Kitty possessed flaming red hair, and did not have to marry Marshall Dillon to hold his attention or his love. Besides, she could stay up all night partying with the cowboys at her saloon. When Bonnie grew up she would closely emulate Miss Kitty. However, it wasn't the cowboys with whom Bonnie would surround herself, but the equally rough-and-rowdy boys in the band!

3

Bonnie Gets the Blues

Everyone owns a record album that will always remain special for one reason or another. For Bonnie Raitt, that album was the one that first introduced her to the blues. Like jazz, the blues is a unique musical form that can be directly traced to African-American musicians at the beginning of the twentieth century. Singers like Bessie Smith, Leadbelly, Ma Rainey, Alberta Hunter, Mississippi John Hurt, Sippie Wallace, and Muddy Waters, were among the blues pioneers. Their often sexual, usually down-hearted, and mournfully emotional music made the blues universally appealing. The blues vocalists of the 1920s and 1930s were the forerunners of the rock and roll stars of the 1950s—including Little Richard, Chuck Berry, and Fats Domino.

The magical album that lead Bonnie to the blues was called *Blues at Newport '63.* She recalls, "If I had to put a handle on what really changed my life in terms of exposing me to something, that was really the first time I'd ever heard blues played on the guitar. *Blues at Newport* had John Lee Hooker on it, and Reverend Gary Davis, John Hammond, Brownie McGhee,

Sonny Terry, and Mississippi John Hurt. I tell you, once you get exposed to blues, you can't get enough."

Listening to that album in her room, Bonnie would dream for hours about becoming a blues musician. She was especially impressed with white blues artist John Hammond Jr., who played the bottleneck slide guitar. According to Bonnie, "John Hammond was a major reason I wanted to go into music. To me he made it all right to take the older black styles and synthesize them into something new. It was clear to me that he was able to do it effectively."

She just loved the way the instrument sounded. "It has a strange kind of sound like a human voice. My grandfather had played Hawaiian lap steel when he was a Methodist minister, and he played hymns on lap steel, so I played with that silver bar when I was a kid."

It wasn't long before Bonnie could really play the guitar. Of her guitar evolution, she explains, "By the time I was ten, I taught myself how to play my grandfather's slide guitar. When I was eleven, I got enough money to get one of those red Guild gut-string guitars."

Once Bonnie had been exposed to the blues, her life would never be the same. "John Lee Hooker, Brownie McGee, Sonny Terry, Mississippi John Hurt, the great Son House—all those people were just unbelievable to me musically. I knew that I didn't sound like them—a little fourteen-year-old white girl. But I wanted to so badly that I played [them on the guitar] until my fingers bled."

The first blues song she taught herself was John Hurt's "Candy Man," which she had heard on that seminal Newport blues album. "It took me two weeks to learn that song," she recalls.

Bonnie was so taken by the blues that she could not wait to see a live blues performance. She distinctly remembers her first blues concert. "I saw Brownie McGhee and Sonny Terry at the Ashgrove, the local folk club. I took my dad, because I was only fourteen and I couldn't drive. He wore a turtleneck, and he had sideburns, because he was still playing Billy Bigelow [in the play *Carousel*], and it was really cool. I was hoping everybody would think he was my date."

Between the au courant folk music that she learned at the Quaker summer camp she and her brothers attended in the Adirondacks, and the crash course in blues music that the album *Blues at Newport '63* gave her, Bonnie Raitt now had a growing repertoire of songs that she would sing and play on her guitar. She was torn between emulating Joan Baez and Bessie Smith, so ultimately she mastered both folk music and the blues.

When she turned fifteen, Bonnie and her girlfriend Daphne showed up at the legendary L.A. folk club the Troubadour during one of the club's amateur "hootenanny" nights, and Bonnie made her unpaid nightclub debut. "We sang a combination of Scottish and Israeli songs," she recalls. "We were like a female Joe and Eddie. I thought Joe and Eddie were hot stuff!"

Bonnie attended University High School in Hollywood and, for a while, went steady with one of Jerry Lewis's sons. However, she didn't really fit into the whole surf and sun scene. She claims, "I always looked down on those kids in L.A. If I hadn't gone away in the summer[s], I would have become a real cheerleader, L.A.–Westwood kind of kid—gone to UCLA and majored in Spanish. That kind of stuff."

In 1965 Bonnie and her family moved from the West to the East Coast. She attended a Quaker high school in Poughkeepsie, New York, and concentrated on her music.

According to Bonnie, her first attempts at emulating John Hammond Jr.'s bottleneck slide guitar came when she was sixteen or seventeen. She had played with the hollow metal bar on her grandfather's Hawaiian lap steel guitar, and used that technique on her own gut-strung Guild guitar. While most steel-guitar players put the metal bar on their ring or little fingers, Bonnie found that her middle finger gave her the most dexterity. It is now known as her trademark playing style.

After she graduated from high school, Bonnie enrolled at an Ivy League women's college, Radcliffe, in Cambridge, Massachusetts. She had long been fascinated with Africa, specifically with the colorful art and culture of Tanzania. When she began college in 1967, she majored in African studies. "I didn't want to work in America. I just said, 'Forget it!' The country was falling apart in the sixties. It was just a lot of hedonistic rock music. It went from the beautiful days of Selma and SNCC, when white and black people were working together in the South . . . then Watts blew up, and all of a sudden Black Power came about, and there wasn't anything pleasant about being a white person working in America."

On the weekends she would hang out in the local blues and jazz clubs near campus. Soon her interest in music eclipsed her academic pursuits.

While performing in music clubs in the Cambridge area, Bonnie met a talent agent and blues promoter named Dick Waterman. He had started out as a photojournalist, capturing blues musicians on film, and segued into a manager-agent's role. He started to secure concert dates to lure several of the great blues artists of the twenties, thirties, and forties out of retirement or obscurity, and back into the spotlights. When Bonnie met him, Waterman was actively working at resurrecting the careers of such legends as Skip James and Mississippi Fred McDowell. At the time, Dick Waterman was thirty-three, and Bonnie was eighteen.

Bonnie was also playing guitar in small Cambridge clubs. "I used to sing protest music in parks, and I thought Joan Baez was just about God," Bonnie recalls of this developmental era of her life. "I always had two sides of me. One wanted to sing

Bob Dylan protest songs and get good grades, and the other wanted to wear leather jackets and get laid."

Bonnie began dating Dick Waterman. She recalls, "We were just sort of vague friends. Then for a while . . . I think he liked redheads or something."

It wasn't long before Bonnie began performing on a more professional basis. She recalls, "I was taking a break from college, and someone suggested I play a club because it was a good way to make some money and have some fun. Once you get paid for doing something you love to do anyway, it's pretty hard to turn around and go back to school. I haven't had to do it yet!"

Bonnie soon became the promoter's protégé, and girlfriend. According to Bonnie, "[Dick Waterman] was really instrumental in my career. He rediscovered Son House, and managed a lot of the Delta and Chicago Blues players, like Buddy Guy and Junior Wells. I was able to travel around and meet them, because I was friends with Dick." Living with Waterman, Bonnie totally immersed herself in the blues world.

Her transformation from college student to full-time blues singer was swift, but unintentional. What had started as a one-semester sabbatical blossomed into a lifelong break from the world of academia. "I never expected to have a career in music," Bonnie insists. "But I thought, Geez, if I want to take a semester off from college and support myself by making fifty dollars here and there, well . . . It was hilarious to me that it went over."

She was in love with show business, and there was no turning back. She was amazed that she could actually make money at something she so deeply enjoyed. As she explains it, "When I made $100 a night singing for half an hour, that was enough. I was nineteen and I was making more money in one night than a lot of people make working two or three days all day."

Through her association with Dick Waterman, Bonnie soon

became friends with several of her blues idols, and Waterman began booking her as an opening act for Arthur "Big Boy" Crudup, Junior Wells, and Buddy Guy, among others. She was nineteen when she first met and befriended blues star John Lee Hooker. He has remained one of her oldest and dearest friends. Playing at places like Club 47 in the Cambridge music scene, she also met another lifelong soul mate, Jackson Browne. During these formative years, Bonnie also crossed paths with and appeared on concert stages with two other folk hopefuls, Cat Stevens and James Taylor.

As a teenage girl, she totally immersed herself in the nocturnal life of a blues singer. This hard-living new lifestyle also included a quick education in all of the excesses that go along with the business—especially liquor. Bonnie not only found herself appearing as opening act, but serving as alcohol dispenser to several of her heroes as well. If she allowed them to drink too much before a show, the show might not go on. And, if she didn't allow them to drink at all, the show definitely would not go on as scheduled.

"I carried the booze bottles for all those guys," she recalls. "Like, I knew that Fred McDowell could have two of these gins before he went on; and an hour before the show, Son House could have his bottle of vodka. And if he had any more, he would forget the words. And if he had any less, he would forget the words. So I was like the nurse. And some of them could handle it better than others. But if you just gave somebody a bottle in the dressing room, they'd be passing it around, and everybody would be completely 'faced' by the time they were supposed to go on."

While college students her age were busy dropping acid and playing their Beatles albums backward—searching for hidden meanings to the jumbled lyrics—Bonnie was partying all night with black blues performers old enough to be her grandfather. What did her conservative Quaker mom and dad think of that?

According to Bonnie, "I was hangin' out with seventy-year-old blues guys who drank at ten in the morning. My parents were a *little* concerned!"

Musically, it was Bonnie's intention to become as good as the blues performers she was opening shows for, and as respected as Muddy Waters. "I wanted to be the female Muddy," she said.

In 1968, eighteen-year-old Bonnie Raitt had the opportunity to travel to Europe with two girlfriends. While there she went shopping in a London record store called Dobell's, which was known for their blues selections. Browsing through the bins by chance she happened to pick up another album that would prove significant in her life. It was by a blues singer from the 1920s who went by the stage name of Sippie Wallace. Bonnie distinctly remembers, "I saw the rhinestone glasses and the tiger-striped vest, and said to myself, This woman really knows how to dress!"

Sippie had recorded the album Bonnie purchased in London while she was on a 1966 European tour, billed as the American Folk Blues Festival. That tour included Little Brother Montgomery, Junior Wells, Roosevelt Sykes, Wallace, and several other blues masters. Sippie's performance was recorded and released by Storyville Records of Copenhagen, Denmark. Both Montgomery and Sykes accompanied Sippie on the album. By cruising through the bins of a record store, Bonnie had acquired a lifelong musical influence.

Sippie's sexual-innuendo-filled songs really blew Bonnie away. She had never heard a woman sing about sex as frankly and amusingly as Wallace did. Bonnie was especially impressed with "You Got to Know How" and "Women Be Wise." Raitt would have a profound influence on Sippie's life as well.

Born in Houston in 1898, Beulah Thomas was nicknamed Sippie, because most of her teeth did not appear until she was more than three years old. She could not eat much solid food and had to sip everything she consumed. In 1923 her first recording, "Up the Country," became a big hit. That song sold over 100,000 copies, and marked the beginning of a bright career—as a songwriter and recording artist, and as an attraction on the vaudeville circuit across the country. Four years later she moved to Detroit and met her second husband, gambler Matt Wallace. By the time of the Depression, Sippie had recorded forty-eight songs and had quite a following. She began recording again in the 1940s, but by the 1960s her career was little more than a footnote in blues history. It was Bonnie Raitt's interest in the singer that would eventually bring Sippie Wallace back to prominence.

"I'd never heard a voice like that in my entire life," Raitt recalls. "I liked Bessie Smith, but I wasn't a big fan of *classic* blues, and Sippie was somehow much more *raw.*"

When Bonnie was nineteen, another lifelong "friend" would join her life: the electric guitar. "I certainly started out at a time where there weren't a lot of women playing electric guitar," she explains. "I started out in 1969, and, at that time, I don't think there were very many women instrumentalists leading bands. Then, of course, I sang too, but it used to be that if you were going to be a woman musician, you had to look a certain way, and take your shirt off a lot, and get a kind of sleazy agent, and basically play parties for show, because no one ever took these bands seriously."

Early on, Bonnie began discounting the confining labels that music was constantly given. She was as passionate about R&B music as she was about the blues. Bonnie says, "While the purists separate Chicago and Delta blues from rhythm and blues, to me it's just funky music. Muddy Waters gets to me the same way Wilson Pickett does!"

Around the same time that Bonnie traveled to Europe, Dick Waterman moved to Philadelphia. When she returned from her European holiday, she began commuting from Boston to see him.

Bonnie recalls, "It only cost eight dollars student standby to fly to Philly, so twice a month I'd fly down there. That's when I started hanging out. I would skip school a lot. We would take off to lots of little blues festivals Dick would book. And I think I went to almost every gig."

Dick Waterman remembers the reactions of the elder statesmen of the blues when they met Bonnie and discovered that she was a blues singer as well. "Sort of amusement," Waterman recalls. "They thought her interest in the blues was some kind of freakish quirk. But she's proud that Buddy and Muddy and Junior and Wolf now regard her as a genuine peer, not 'She plays good for a white person, or a girl,' but, 'She plays good.' "

Bonnie made the decision to quit Radcliffe during the second semester of her sophomore year. "It was getting silly, I really wanted to be with Dick more than I wanted to go to school."

Around this same time, Bonnie also began to work with the Quaker organization, the American Friends Service Committee in Philadelphia. It appeared less and less likely that she would ever return to the college life of writing term papers, and attending morning classes. The night-owl lifestyle of blues singers was more to her liking. She recalls, "It was better than typing and I liked the hours."

One night, at a club called the Second Fret in Philadelphia, Bonnie saw another girl singer up on stage, and thought to herself that she could perform as well. She decided to audition for the club. The fact that Dick Waterman knew the owners of the club was a definite "plus." The owners liked her singing style, and she landed a spot opening for a local band called the Sweet Stavin' Chain. She was offered 10 percent of the money taken at the door that night, and earned $54. Her set went over so well that she was then offered a four-night booking of her own.

Her stage repertoire included songs by James Taylor and Elton John, along with blues numbers like "Walking Blues" and "Women Be Wise." She remembers, "In the beginning, at my first gig, both of my parents were there, and I sang this Willie Dixon song that Howlin' Wolf had done, called 'I'm Built for Comfort Not for Speed.' I was eighteen, in a little folk-coffee-house in Philadelphia. That was the first time I realized, 'I'm really going to have to think twice about them being in the audience!'"

When Bonnie turned nineteen, her parents divorced after over twenty years of marriage. The demands of her father's career had pulled the marriage apart. Marjorie would settle on the East Coast, and John would live in California. The breakup came when Bonnie and her two brothers had left the family nest, so the divorce did not prove as traumatic as it might have been.

Meanwhile, Dick Waterman had booked Bonnie at a club called the Main Point, where she opened for her bottleneck-guitar idol, John Hammond. She recalls, "It was for $200 for the four nights and I was in the middle of my set when he walked in with a leather coat on with the [collar] points sticking up, with his hair all greased back—holding this guitar, and then he sat and watched. I think I was the closest to . . . I *came* for the entire set, in whatever spiritual way you do that."

At the Second Fret, Bonnie became friends with a quartet called the Edison Electric Band. Their bass player was six feet tall with a long black mane of curly hair. He went by the name of Freebo. Freebo had been a football player in high school, and while attending West Pennsylvania State University became the tuba player in the marching band until, says Bonnie, "the mid-sixties when everybody found marijuana and got weird."

When his band broke up, Bonnie offered Freebo a job as her bass player, and he accepted. She was making $300 a night at this point, so she could afford to musically augment her set. Over the next two years, Bonnie—backed by Freebo—consistently played gigs up and down the East Coast. She says, "On stage we sat next to each other with a little Matthews Freedom amp, which runs on forty flashlight batteries, or you can plug it in." Of all of the musicians who Bonnie has played with in her career, it was Freebo who was with her the longest, appearing on all seven of the albums she recorded during the decade of the seventies.

One of the mainstays of Bonnie's career in those days was playing gigs on college campuses. Traveling with Freebo, and Bonnie's dog, Prune, they would stay in college dormitories, or they would share hotel rooms. It was a hand-to-mouth existence, but Bonnie was doing what she loved, so it was all worthwhile.

Either as a headliner, or as the opening act for such top blues artists as Taj Mahal and Mississippi Fred McDowell, Bonnie began to gain a small but devoted following for her blend of folk, rock, and blues songs. Playing gigs at the Main Point in Philadelphia, and at the Philadelphia Folk Festival, led to her debut at the Gaslight in New York City.

It wasn't long before she had garnered some good reviews and came to the attention to several different record labels. In the spring of 1971, Bonnie Raitt was offered a recording contract with Warner Brothers Records, and began to assemble material for her debut album.

Although she was thrilled at the opportunity, her anti-establishment views made her question her own motives. "I was very uncomfortable going with a big company," she claims, "and I thought it was immoral—politically, to be a leftist, to be trying to be a star."

While she didn't set out to become a star, she realized that if she was going to continue as a singer, she could use the financial support that a recording deal would bring her. Besides, the tour support and the advertising would help her continue the career she loved.

Signing with Warner Brothers Records seemed like the ideal move for her. Dick Waterman negotiated the contract, which was structured to allow her a wide path of artistic freedom. And, at that time, Warners was the label that folk-rock singer-songwriters Joni Mitchell, James Taylor, and Randy Newman were all signed to.

The *Bonnie Raitt* album is an understated classic. Not only was it the launching pad for one of the most brilliant careers in the music business, it served as the prototype for most of Bonnie's albums in the 1970s: a combination of pure blues, a rock classic, a Motown number, a few gems from new songwriters, and a Bonnie original or two.

Instead of trying to emulate the elaborately funky Philadelphia sound, or the slick productions of the New York City recording studios, Bonnie chose to record her first album in the most rural setting she could find: the garage of an abandoned summer camp on the shore of Lake Minnetonka, Minnesota. Recorded on a four-track recorder, in a musical commune-like setting, Bonnie gathered together one of the oddest conglomerations of musicians she could find. It included professional blues musicians Junior Wells and A. C. Reed, a local bar band called the Bumblebees, and her own core band, which included Willie Murphy on piano, Peter Bell on electric guitar, Douglas "Toad" Spurgeon on trombone, and Freebo on bass. Bonnie played both the acoustic and slide guitars on the album, and Willie Murphy produced it.

Also on hand was Bonnie's brother, Steve. Bonnie says, "Steve, who is two years older than me, lives in Minnesota. He moved there when I did my first album. And he's mixed sound and produced records for Willie and the Bees, and the Lamont Cranston Band." Steve Raitt is also heard on one of the album's cuts, "I Ain't Blue," providing the percussive sound of a stick on a plastic pitcher. Such touches provide the album with much of its simplistic charm.

Bonnie and company arrived at the summer camp–studio, in August 1971, and began to create the music that would launch her recording career. Located thirty miles west of Minneapolis, on Enchanted Island, the studio was called Sweet Jane, Ltd. Studios. The back-to-nature commune atmosphere contributed to the "home grown" sound of this uncluttered and appealing debut disk. Bonnie was only twenty-one at the time.

The guest appearances by the two veteran blues players was an extra treat. According to Bonnie, "The two special additions were Junior Wells and A. C. Reed, who drove up from Chicago to see if I really was going to do this after all, and maybe slip in a little fishing on the side."

From a control board located in a loft in the camp's large garage, Dave and Sylvia Ray adjusted the sound levels, and captured on a four-track tape machine the musical proceedings that unraveled below them. (In the 1960s, Dave had been a member of the trio Koerner, Ray & Glover.)

The repertoire was quite varied. It included contemporary rock (Steven Stills's "Bluebird"), traditional blues (Tommy Johnson's "Big Road" and Robert Johnson's "Walking Blues"), sixties pop-blues (Lenny Welch's 1963 hit "Since I Fell for You"), Motown (the Marvelettes' "Danger Heartbreak Dead Ahead"), new folk compositions (Paul Seibel's "Any Day Woman" and John Koerner's "I Ain't Blue"), a pair of compositions by Bonnie ("Thank You" and "Finest Lovin' Man"), plus two down-and-dirty Sippie Wallace gems ("Mighty Tight Woman" and "Women Be Wise.")

On the subject of this first album, Bonnie looks back with fondness and humor. "I can't believe how young I sound—and I thought I was so tough. I'll never forget Junior and A. C.'s faces when they pulled up to the garage we called our studio, out in the middle of nowhere. Talk about 'going back to the country!' "

According to Bonnie, "We recorded live on four tracks because we wanted a more spontaneous and natural feeling in the music—a feeling often sacrificed when the musicians know they can overdub their part on a separate track until it's perfect. It also reflects the difference between music made among friends living together in the country and the kind squeezed out trying to beat city traffic and studio clocks."

Photographed in a rustic setting, Bonnie appeared much older on the album's cover than her twenty-one years. Sitting next to a rough-hewn end table in a cabin, she projects the image of a worldly-wise woman with the blues. On the table next to her are a dirty ashtray, a half-finished long-neck bottle of Black Label beer, and a bouquet of dried weeds in an empty Cutty Sark scotch whiskey bottle. Seated under an antique ceiling lampshade, she looks like she has had a rough night of drinking and wailing the blues.

Although the songs came from very different sources, they were unified by Bonnie's sincere singing, and the unmistakeable blues attitude she projected. To take a sixties pop hit by the Marvelettes and include it on the same album as a 1920s blues number like "Mighty Tight Woman" and make it all seamlessly meld together is quite an accomplishment. On her very first album, Bonnie proved that she instinctively knew the sassiness of jazz and blues, the funk of rhythm and blues, the integrity of folk, and the energy of rock and roll.

"Bluebird" appropriately kicks off the album with the harmonic feeling of an all-acoustic jam session. Although her young voice is high and girlish, Bonnie sings with authority and style. The unpolished direct-to-tape approach effectively propels this bright folk ballad.

Sippie Wallace's "Mighty Tight Woman" is a down and

dirty, bawdy blues number. Sounding like a singer and her band in a speakeasy of the 1920s, Bonnie is the narrator of the song, a prostitute advertising herself to her next potential man. As though the sexual image of being desirably "tight" doesn't cast clear enough allusions, Bonnie sings of throwing herself down on her knees, begging "take me please." John Beach's ragtime piano carries the tune, and Junior Wells's harmonica solo gives it a perfect touch of blues authenticity.

Not since the 1920s had the sexual climate of America been so free and relaxed. This all-but-forgotten blues classic that Bonnie discovered on the album she found in London was perfectly suited to the sexual revolution of the 1970s. It was an excellent choice, and Raitt didn't miss a beat on this one, sounding like she was singing with a seductive wink in her eye.

"Thank You," which Bonnie wrote, is a nice, simple ballad that shows off her lilting voice. The cut features a real rarity: Raitt accompanying herself on the piano. Maurice Jacox's flute behind her makes this song a fresh change of pace.

On her second composition on the album, "Finest Lovin' Man," Bonnie pulled out the big guns, including both Junior and A. C. on the track. The result is bona fide blues à la Bonnie, and one of the most effective numbers on the album.

Bonnie is also in her element on the blues chestnuts "Big Road" and "Walking Blues." "Big Road" has Raitt presiding over Freebo's bawdy tuba playing and Junior's "harp," while the beat on "Walking Blues" is carried by Peter Bell's hamboning (slapping his thighs). Both of these songs find Bonnie in Muddy Waters–wannabe heaven, and she obviously had a ball recording them.

Taking the Marvelettes' "Danger Heartbreak Dead Ahead," and giving it a folk-rock spin was a perfect pop foray for this varied album. Bonnie also makes the pining ballad, "Since I Fell For You" all her own. This song soars with a jazzy sax solo from A. C. Reed. These two numbers set up a career-long pattern for Bonnie, who is always able to give a new twist to the pop and rock hits she records.

"I Ain't Blue" is a sweet ballad that features some fascinating percussion sounds, provided by a shuttlecock in a cup, a stick and a plastic pitcher, and someone playing a shingle. Obviously, Bonnie and the boys were getting heavily into their summer-camp surroundings when they developed these makeshift instruments!

The album ends with another Sippie Wallace blues number, "Women Be Wise," into which Bonnie breathes new life. With its ragtime piano sound and Raitt's most "been there, done that" world-weariness vocal interpretation, this lusty blues song is turned into a musical treat. In the lyrics, Bonnie advises women not to advertise their man's sexual talents to their girlfriends, or they'll steal him away for themselves!

This album represents Bonnie at her most blues oriented and is a well-crafted audio outing. Through it, her growing cult of fans suddenly became aware of some of the best and most fun blues numbers of a bygone era. Although the *Bonnie Raitt* album was well received, it didn't sell many copies at the time of its release and never appeared on *Billboard* magazine's album charts.

The CD version of this album now available allows Bonnie's new fans to listen to, and discover where her musical roots lie. She viewed and cast herself as a folk-oriented blues singer.

Looking back on her career, Bonnie remarked, "I just think that I'm 'blues based.' I don't want to call myself a blues artist. I'm not a mainstream—I suppose I'm a mainstream artist now—but I still find it hard to believe. As long as you are true to what you really hear in your heart, and musical sensibility—which I've got to do—I'm the one out there singing the songs every night, and I've got to hear every single note."

After this first album was released, Bonnie's popularity began to grow on the club circuit. Word-of-mouth enlarged her circle of fans. At first she was startled by the audience's reaction. She was getting a better response, and drawing larger crowds than some of her blues idols who were still on the circuit.

At the time she said analytically, "I can appreciate—and it's too bad—that the audience understands the music of Fred McDowell better through me than through the real thing. If I were better they'd like me less. My taste is funkier than I can bring off. I know it seems like a hype for me to sing the blues. But they speak to me. The blues is pain. Maybe because the problems of the middle class aren't real, like how to buy food or pay the rent, we suffer real pain from divine decadence."

When *Newsweek* wrote about Bonnie Raitt in 1972, it predicted her "impending stardom," and spoke of her "passion and innocence" as a performer. It also stated, "It's startling to hear her sing the exuberant blues of Robert Johnson or Mississippi John Hurt, even when transposed to her own softer style. She has the bluesman's manner of self-communication, when she sings in a folk-husky voice, rich in impurity."

Although she was still on the ground floor of her musical career, Bonnie had begun to gain a small but loyal following. Not only did she appeal to avant garde blues and folk-rock fans, but from the very beginning, she found that she was viewed as a musician's musician. She would invite musician friends to come up onto the stage from the audience, to join her in a song or two. She explained at the time, "I don't like being separate from the people who come to hear me." Her stage performances were actively emulating the summer-camp feeling of her debut album. They became part love-in, part concert. Word was spreading that Bonnie had the blues. She had 'em bad—and that was *good!*

4

You Got to Know How

*T*ouring across the country and performing in small rock and folk clubs, Bonnie proceeded to win hearts and fans. One of the keys to her early success was the fact that she really knew how to connect with her audiences. Her concerts were intimate events that projected the feeling of a living-room performance. It was clear to anyone who saw her perform in the early seventies, that Bonnie Raitt was a star in the making. Public notoriety, however, made her nervous. As much as she loved singing and performing on stage, she strongly resisted the lure of mainstream fame.

"I don't want to be a star," she vehemently stated in 1972. Then twenty-two years old, she rationalized, "Nobody likes a stubborn, independent woman. I'm not shaking my ass to be famous!"

She was very vocal about preferring small clubs to concert halls and was very critical of the music business as she had come to know it. "Fame is a drag!" she exclaimed. "Back in the sixties, there were clubs for singers with small loyal audiences. Today the clubs want performers who are backed by the big-money promotion of record companies. So you have to record. You have a hit if you're lucky, but if you don't get another one, you're finished. Record companies want new faces. It's like planned obsolescence. What a waste!"

Bonnie Raitt set a pattern for resisting mainstream promotion. She wanted to maintain the comfortable homegrown feeling that had infused her career from the beginning. "I hate personality cults," she said. "I want people to enjoy me as they would their friends. I need the feedback from that kind of audience. You get a lot of love."

Love is exactly what she got when she wheeled into Ann Arbor, Michigan, in 1972 to appear at the annual Ann Arbor Blues and Jazz Festival and met her idol Sippie Wallace for the first time. Sippie had stopped publicly performing jazz in 1937, and her vocal appearances had been relegated to singing gospel in church. After a two-decade hiatus from show business, she was coaxed out of retirement in 1965 by a Detroit electrical contractor and blues fan named Ron Harwood. He became her manager, and, thanks to him, Sippie had a much-acclaimed career revival. In 1969 Sippie had suffered a stroke. According to Harwood, "It was six months before she could walk or talk, but the first thing she did was to play the piano."

When Bonnie was booked at the Ann Arbor festival, she asked the event's promoters to invite Sippie to perform as well. Still confined to a wheelchair, Sippie came to hear Bonnie rehearse her composition "Women Be Wise." According to Ron Harwood, "[Sippie] was so deeply moved that she agreed to join with her in a duet onstage."

The duet version of "Woman Be Wise" that Raitt and Wallace sang that day in Michigan's most famous college town was recorded. It can be found on the Atlantic Records' album *The Ann Arbor Blues and Jazz Festival 1972*.

Bonnie and Sippie formed an instantaneous bond. According to Raitt, "It's a connection that transcends age and space. She's more my own grandma than my natural grand-mother."

"I love Bonnie!" Sippie said with mutual affection.

When it came time to select material for her second album, Bonnie again chose to record a Sippie Wallace classic, this time covering the song "You Got to Know How." Bonnie called on the same basic formula she had used on her debut disk: some-thing old, something new, some things borrowed, and several of them blues.

The *Give It Up* album, however, was recorded using a dif-ferent producer in a different locale, and it had a smoother, more polished sound. Bonnie had taken the *Bonnie Raitt* album and gone a step further toward refining all of her vocal strong points. Overall, she sounds more up-front and confident on this album, which is acknowledged as one of the best albums of her career.

Give It Up was recorded in June 1972 at Bearsville Studios, near Woodstock, New York. It was produced by Michael Cus-cuna and included several top-notch area musicians. John Hall, who had just formed the group Orleans, played the electric gui-tar on the album, and Freebo played everything from the tuba to the electric and bass guitar. The legendary Paul Butterfield made a guest appearance on one of the cuts, and local horn player John Payne is heard on sax and trombone.

"This album was made primarily with musicians from the Woodstock area," said Michael Cuscuna at the time. "Like Bonnie and Freebo, Lou Terriciano (a fine singer as well as pi-anist) and John Payne are based in Cambridge."

Kicking off the exciting proceedings of this wonderfully di-verse album is the boisterous rag and roll of Bonnie's own com-position, "Give It Up or Let Me Go." The song sounds like it is being performed by a festive street fair band, with Bonnie shouting the ad-lib "shake it, don't break it" midnumber. This song also gave Freebo a chance to show off his acclaimed tuba playing.

According to Bonnie, "In the tradition of Sippie, Ruth Brown, and Aretha, this was my interpretation of their classic 'I'm Not Taking It Anymore' attitude. It's still one of my all-time favorite tracks, and you can bet it was just as much fun to be there as it sounds."

She slows down the pace for the pensive ballad "Nothing Seems to Matter." Another Bonnie Raitt composition, the song is clearly about the end of a love affair. It coincides with the cooling of Bonnie's romance with Dick Waterman. Although he would continue to book and manage her, the spark of love was fading.

Bonnie took Rudy Clarke's "If You Gotta Make a Fool of Somebody," and turned it into an effectively wailing jazz-blues lament. It had originally been a 1961 hit for James Ray, and the musical track on Bonnie's version has an apropos country twang to it. Next she swung into the bumping and thumping "Love Me Like a Man," where she commands that she wants to be "rocked" by a man—like her backbone was *his* own. It's a percolating hot and nasty affair, with Bonnie's sumptuous slide-guitar playing at exotic full tilt. This sexy blues romp signaled the fact that Bonnie Raitt was musically coming into her own.

Speaking of that song, Bonnie explains, "One of the best modern blues songs ever written, and another that I couldn't imagine a set without. It was written, as was 'I Feel the Same,' by one of my earliest friends and influences, Chris Smither. We lived a block from each other in Cambridge back then and spent a lot of afternoons swapping songs and guitar licks."

Joel Zoss's "Too Long at the Fair" is the most delicate and understated song that Bonnie recorded in the 1970s. The lyrics are about reaching the end of one's rope. Bonnie infuses the number with folk pathos and a beautiful simplicity. The song has the same bittersweet quality that her nineties hit, "I Can't Make You Love Me," possesses.

Bonnie's cover of Jackson Browne's "Under the Falling Sky" is another rhytmically exciting rock and roll affair, which includes Paul Butterfield on the harmonica. This is another cut that sounds like it was sheer fun to record in the studio. Not only did Bonnie excel with this tune by Jackson, but she also would include him in the growing circle of lifelong friends born out of her career.

"First in a long line of Jackson's songs I've recorded," Bonnie says. "This was my first so-called rocker. It features Freebo and his former Edison Electric bandmates: Mark Jordan on keys and T. J. Tindall on guitar—all of us blown away by Butterfield's incredible harp [harmonica] playing. There was no one like him."

Sippie Wallace's "You Got to Know How" is the album's true classic. The stage performing that she'd done over the last two years had smoothed out some of the hesitancy in Bonnie's voice that characterized her first album. On this jazz-ragtime cut, she sounds especially confident and in control. She puts a vigor and verve into this song about having the sexual skills to make "it" last all night. A song comprised of bawdy, nasty, 1920s blues at its best, this composition remains one of Raitt's signature songs.

Next she rocks out on her composition, "You Told Me Baby." A rollicking come-on about being ready for love, this is Bonnie's first recorded song on which she shows off her skills on the electric guitar.

"Love Has No Pride," Eric Kaz and Libby Titus's song about not being afraid to ask for what you want, finds Bonnie on the piano *and* acoustic guitar. Her only accompaniment is Freebo playing his trademark Fender fretless bass. This plaintive ballad is the perfect way to end a wonderfully warm and rich album.

"Love Has No Pride" has special meaning for Bonnie. She explains, "Throughout my twenties, this one was a kind of signature song for me and my audiences . . . truly one of the most heartbreaking I've ever heard. I remember being devastated at the time I sang this by a lover who'd chosen to just take off. Seems like I spent a year of gigs trying to sing him back."

One of the strongest and most loved albums of Bonnie's career, *Give It Up*, provided an exciting gamut of emotions, from sexy come-ons to heartbroken laments. This recording became the first of Bonnie's albums to enter the charts in *Billboard* magazine. Although it only made it to number 138, and sold approximately 250,000 copies at the time of its release, her career was well on its way.

When she was asked at the time about her penchant for digging up older blues material to perform and record, Bonnie said, "I'm a vehicle. Not for me or Elton John or Carole King, but for the old songs people ought to know or the new ones that haven't had a fair hearing."

Looking back on her first two albums from the perspective of the 1990s, Bonnie claims, "I feel close to *Give It Up* [1972] and the first album, but it's impossible for me to listen to them for pleasure because I sound so young. I sound like Mickey Mouse!"

One longtime friend who came into Bonnie's life through this album was John Hall. He was later to find fame with the Woodstock-based group called Orleans. Hall played the electric guitar on "Too Long at the Fair" and "You Told Me Baby," and added background vocals on "I Know." He had worked with Taj Mahal, and wrote the song "Half Moon" for Janis Joplin's final album, *Pearl* (1971). Another member of Orleans,

Wells Kelly, played drums on Bonnie's *Give It Up* album as well.

The one song that didn't make it to this album was a scheduled recording of Fred McDowell's "Kokomo," on which McDowell was to perform a duet version of the song with Bonnie. It was her intention to introduce the legendary bluesman to a whole new audience.

Dick Waterman says, "She [has] never spoken about Fred's death of cancer in the summer of 1972 when she was doing her second album in Woodstock, but it hit her really hard. It was almost as if she was angry that they just didn't have a little more time—she could have done it for them. As her popularity was climbing and helping them was a real motivation, those men just ran out of days."

Fortunately, it was not too late for Bonnie to help Sippie Wallace, and that became one of her personal missions. This sense of helping out the pioneers of popular music is a strong thread that runs through Bonnie's life today. Her vast respect for the musicians of yesteryear continues with her work with the Rhythm and Blues Foundation.

When *Give It Up* was released in September of 1972, Bonnie wrote on it, "This album is dedicated to the people of North Vietnam, and the loving memory of a dear friend, Fred McDowell."

In 1973 Bonnie headed back to the West Coast. She recalls, "I moved to L.A. to be with [rock group] Little Feat. I fell in love with somebody and liked the climate here better. In Cambridge I was too well-known. I couldn't walk down the street without being recognized and I was drinking too much. It was just a big untogether scene for me."

Her own fame was beginning to restrict her life in Cambridge, so she packed her bags for the Hollywood Hills. "I really liked the East Coast scene, and then I met Lowell George [of Little Feat]," Bonnie said in 1988. "I heard their album

Sailin' Shoes, and went crazy. I got in my truck and drove to California and resettled here to work with Lowell. I'd have to say Little Feat was the biggest influence. Whether or not I do their songs. Musically, they're my favorite band."

The man she fell in love with was Garry George, an employee of Warner Brothers Records when she met him. Judging by his photo with Bonnie in a 1975 issue of *Rolling Stone,* he was quite the partyer. His lined and tired-looking face staring back from the magazine page wordlessly tells of many a late night party with Raitt and Little Feat. "I used to be sad, but now I'm happy," Bonnie said of her relationship with George at the time.

However, she never spoke in detail about the nature of their relationship or her feelings for him. For many years she steadfastly kept her private life out of press interviews. In this way, she managed to remain somewhat of a mystery.

The rock and roll party scene of the mid-seventies was in full swing when Bonnie moved back to Los Angeles. Thanks to the social drug of that decade, cocaine, and it's speed-like quality, the drinking and partying could go on way past dawn. On the subject of drinking and doing coke, or "blow," Bonnie looks back and says, "You know, late at night one made the other one more. . . . You were really able to drink if you did blow, but not all the time. And it's hard on the throat. But I think alcohol was the one of choice. I was never a pothead or into psychedelics. I was around these old blues guys, and they were alcoholics. And I prided myself in not liking acid rock and all that I wanted to be the female version of Muddy Waters or Fred McDowell. There was a romance about drinking and doing blues. These blues guys have been professional drinkers for years, and I wanted to prove that I could hold my liquor with them. I bought into that whole lifestyle. I thought Keith Richards was cool—that he was really dangerous."

A bawdy participant at any social event she attended, Bonnie was quoted as walking into one gathering and announcing, "I don't want to see any faces at this party I haven't sat on!" *ME!*

During this era, Bonnie became very close with the band Little Feat, which had a long history of playing together, then breaking up. Also signed to Warner Brothers Records, Little Feat recorded two albums around the era Bonnie became chummy with them. At the time, Little Feat consisted of Bill Payne on keyboards, Lowell George on guitar and vocals, Sam Clayton on congas, Paul Barrère on guitar, Kenny Gradney on bass, and drummer Richard Hayward. Her close friendship with Payne and the other surviving members of the band continues to this day.

When Little Feat recorded their third album, *Dixie Chicken,* in 1973, Bonnie was on hand to lend her background vocals on the album. Right after they completed the album, the band broke up. Bill Payne briefly joined the Doobie Brothers, then subsequently left in the middle of their tour schedule and joined Bonnie's band.

Since Lowell George of Little Feat had been producing the group's albums—and he was now without a group—Bonnie decided he should be the producer of her next album, *Takin' My Time.* Besides, Bonnie was having a great time partying with him. Unfortunately, the resulting album tracks were lackluster, and John Hall had to be brought in to the rescue, and to record the album all over again.

Bonnie recalls, *Takin' My Time* is one of my favorite records to listen to, although I started out with Lowell George producing it and he and I got too close to be able to have any objectivity about it. That's a problem when you're a woman and you get involved with the people you work with—and I don't just mean romantically. It becomes too emotional. It's hard to have a strong woman telling the man her ideas when, in fact, the man wants to take over the situation. So that album had a lot of heartache in it. At the time it was a difficult one to make, but now I like it."

The *Takin' My Time* album was recorded in June and July of 1973. It opens with Bonnie's bright and snappy rock rendering of Martha Reeves and the Vandellas' 1965 smash "You've Been in Love Too Long." The cut features John Hall's jolting electric guitar, with Hall and Bonnie overdubbing the Vandellas' chorus lines. Bonnie growls with emotion on this peppy rendition of the Motown classic.

Joel Zoss provided "I Gave My Love a Candle," which—like "Too Long at the Fair"—is a beautifully crafted ballad that Bonnie sings with heartfelt emotion. Jolting the pace into another stratosphere, the next song, "Let Me in" is a wild rock-and-roll-ragtime-polka of a song, complete with Freebo's tuba—plus the trombone, flugelhorn, and sax. This is another of Bonnie's cuts that conjures up images of the tape player catching a fun studio party in progress.

Mose Allison's "Everybody's Cryin' Mercy," is a jazz-blues lament, which carries with it the feeling of a smoky jazz club around midnight. On this song, Bonnie can be heard putting new emotional shadings on her still-developing singing style. "Cry Like a Rainstorm" is a composition that Linda Ronstadt would later cover. This folk version of the Eric Kaz ballad is one of the album's finest moments.

"Wah She Go Do" is Bonnie's Calypso-reggae number. It is an amusing Caribbean pastiche in which Bonnie sings about the merits of having two men in her life: a husband, and a lover for the times when the husband is too tired to make love. This is the perfect vehicle for Raitt to make her feminist opinions known in a most amusing fashion.

"I Feel the Same" is pure blues, penned by Chris Smither. Highlighting Lowell George's electric slide-guitar solo, Bonnie sounds great on this well-executed number. Continuing on her bent of supporting new up-and-coming singer-songwriters, Bonnie tackles another beautiful folk song by Jackson Browne, "I Thought I Was a Child," which features her acoustic guitar playing. The song and this performance seem to be out of the Joni Mitchell mode, which is about not wanting to let go of a love affair.

A medley of Mississippi Fred McDowell's "Write Me a Few of Your Lines" and "Kokomo Blues," supplanted the duet with him that was never completed. With a hand-clapping rhythm section, and Bonnie on the bottleneck electric guitar, this is a smokin' blues classic that McDowell himself would have been proud of. This recording is a fitting tribute to a trailblazing blues legend.

Randy Newman's "Guilty," finishes off the album with fitting blues fervor. Bonnie sings of having some whiskey from the bartender, and cocaine from one of her friends, and wallowing in the blues. The cause of her blues, according to the lyrics of the song, is being too deeply in love. This was Bonnie's first real raspy-voiced blues number, and it is a preview of coming attractions.

Bonnie agrees that the song "Guilty" was a high point of vocal emotion on the *Takin' My Time* album. "I remember the first time Michael Cuscuna played me this song at his apartment in New York. It was before Randy had even recorded it, and I knew even then that it would strike a chord—deeper than even I knew at the time. As I sometimes say in my shows when I do it now: 'Man, I'm glad I don't have to feel like this all the time anymore!'"

Takin' My Time was released in October 1973. Bonnie continued to tour, preforming in rock clubs and concert venues across America—almost nonstop. The album climbed to number 87 on the charts. This was to be her pattern for several years: tour, record, tour, record, tour, record.

Like her father had done throughout the years in his "bus

and truck" road shows, Bonnie had adapted to the perform-pack-unpack-perform lifestyle of a concert star. It was often tiring, but it had become her passion.

Album by album, concert by concert, she was becoming very well known in music circles. At the same time, other female singers were making bigger names for themselves. Carly Simon, Carole King, Joni Mitchell, Melanie, Maria Muldaur, and Linda Ronstadt were all recording rock-folk albums at the time, and slowly and progressively, Bonnie was establishing herself without the benefit of hit singles. At the age of twenty-three, she had become a cult artist whose albums were sparsely produced and carried with them the sound and feeling that they were the products of really great jam sessions between friends.

Bonnie, along with David Crosby, Gregg Allman, Don Henley, and Joni Mitchell, were featured on Jackson Browne's 1973 album, *For Every Man*. Bonnie can be heard singing harmony vocal on the folk ballad "The Times You've Come."

According to Bonnie's contract with Warner Brothers Records, in 1974 she only had $10,000 allotted to record her next album. Since she had recorded the *Takin' My Time* album two times, it cost twice as much as it should have, so the company began to limit her expenditures. They agreed to advance her more money to put into her fourth album, but only on the condition that she would hire a producer with a hit-making track record.

This was the album that caused Bonnie the most grief. She decided to go with Jerry Ragovoy as the producer because she liked his track record. He had written two songs for Janis Joplin's *Pearl* album, "Cry Baby" and "Get It While You Can," so he had rock credibility. He was also known for his R&B productions, which included Dionne Warwick and the Spinners' "Then Came You."

Almost immediately, Bonnie and Jerry Ragovoy began

feuding over song choices and stylistic concerns. In Ragovoy's mind, Bonnie's career was bogged down in the blues, and he wanted to polish her sound. Raitt recalls, "It was too slick, but I learned a lot. I learned that I really needed a producer."

From the very first moment the needle hit the grooves on *Streetlights*, there was no question that this was a new sound for Bonnie. First of all, this is the *only* Bonnie Raitt album on which she doesn't play the bottleneck slide guitar on any of the cuts, and, in fact, she plays acoustic guitar on only three songs. Ragovoy wanted her to concentrate on being the star singer and to leave the instrumental tracks to New York City's hottest session musicians.

Recorded at the Hit Factory studios in Manhattan during the summer of 1974, *Streetlights* contains a pop sleekness. Gone was the street-fair-summer-camp-Woodstock-commune sound of her first three albums.

The freewheeling "let's have a party and make some music" kind of feeling no longer existed. This was clearly Bonnie's R&B album—and it's a great album—but it was a very different approach for her.

According to Freebo, this was her make-it-or-break-it album. "The environment changed her singing," he recalls. "She was in a professional world with *Streetlights*, and had to act like one. She was being told, 'Come on, Bonnie, be a professional, don't find excuses from the bottle, don't cop out on your friends. There you are, you know, get down!' And she did."

One has to keep in mind the fact that Bonnie had already recorded three critically acclaimed albums of blues-rock. When she recorded *Streetlights*, she was still just a rebellious twenty-three-year-old singer. Reluctantly, Bonnie handed over the steering wheel to Jerry Ragovoy.

The album opened with three songs from three of the most well-respected singer-songwriters in the music business: Joni Mitchell, James Taylor, and John Prine. First up was Joni's

"That Song About the Midway." On Mitchell's 1969 version, from her album *Clouds,* it is a simple poetic ballad accompanied by a lone guitar.

Bonnie's version begins the same way, putting the emphasis on her beautifully expressive voice. Slowly, strings, horns, drums, and percussion come up from behind her. The music cushions Bonnie's singing and never gets in the way. This song remains one of her most beautiful early folk ballad performances.

James Taylor's "Rainy Day Man" receives a similar approach, with Bonnie's singing nicely set off by full orchestration. The musicians on this cut, and on most of the album, included David Spinozza on guitar, Leroy Pendarvis on keyboards, Steve Gadd on drums, and percussion wizard Ralph MacDonald. These were the very same musicians used by Carly Simon, James Taylor, Bette Midler, and Paul Simon on their Gold and Platinum albums during this era. Obviously, Warner Brothers Records hoped that some of their alchemy would rub off on Bonnie.

John Prine's folk-blues-rock song "Angel From Montgomery" has become one of Bonnie's most popular signature numbers. She has since recorded this same song twice, live in concert. On this studio version, Bonnie delivers a fabulously lamenting, poignant performance. This song tells the story of an old woman looking back on her life. On this particular recording Bonnie weaves a spell with the lyrics of Prine's beautiful ballad.

"I Got Plenty" is an R&B ballad, which finds Raitt singing with an exciting chorus that includes Sharon Redd and Tasha Thomas—two of the most respected backup singers in the business. Sharon Redd was one of Bette Midler's backup trio, the Harlettes. After finishing this album, Tasha Thomas headed for Broadway, starring as Auntie Em in the Tony Award–winning musical *The Wiz.*

"What Is Success" is one of Bonnie's favorite cuts on the album. According to Raitt, "This is a classic, yet relatively unknown song from one of my all-time favorites, New Orleans legend Allen Toussaint. Allen, the Meters, Little Feat, and I were all part of the close-knit Warner's family in the early seventies—good friends as well as mutual fans. Allen's songs seem to spring like some exotic hothouse flower from his intensely personal and very spiritual view of the world."

Later that year, Toussaint was about to score a huge hit with the singing trio LaBelle. Their steamy version of his composition "Lady Marmalade" went to number 1 only months after Bonnie worked with him. This is one of her funkiest and most soulful recordings.

"Ain't Nobody Home" was written by Jerry Ragovoy, and it features a percolating instrumental track that Bonnie soars on while fronting. Soulful and upbeat, it offers a full horn section, and shows off some of Bonnie's strongest singing up to that point in time.

She sounds especially sassy and self-confident on David Lasley and Allee Willis's "Got You on My Mind," which is a soulful medium tempo song propelled by Ralph MacDonald's lively percussion touches.

"You've Got to Be Ready for Love (If You Wanna Be Mine)" is pure seventies soul music. Leroy Pendarvis's bouncy piano work is especially catchy, and similar to his keyboards on Ashford and Simpson's *I Wanna Be Selfish* album, which he recorded that same year. This was the era when disco-tempo songs were just beginning to become popular, and it seemed like all of the music that was coming out of New York City around this time had up-tempo disco touches added to them. This song takes Bonnie the closest to doing a disco number. There's really a very nice Philadelphia soul approach to the track, and Bonnie's voice sounds strong and vibrant on it. Listening to the beat of this song, you can just tell that this is one over which Raitt and Ragovoy must have wrangled.

Streetlights was Bonnie's one "big city" album, in the same sense that the *Bonnie Raitt* album was her "summer camp" album. Although distinctively different in approach, Bonnie's emotional singing is equally enjoyable—in different contexts—on both records.

"To an extent, I like all my records," Bonnie explains. "I make sure of that or else I don't put them out. I think it's terribly irresponsible to put out something that you think is junk. *Streetlights* was the one done under the most duress. It was meant to be an 'uptown' soul album, but the strings and the horns and some of the material were just not what I was into at the time. But I liked working with Jerry Ragovoy."

When the album was released in September 1974, it went to number 80 in *Billboard.* Slowly, album by album, Bonnie was scoring progressively higher and higher chart figures. Her legion of fans was growing.

In the liner notes of *Streetlights,* Bonnie thanked several people, claiming that "without [them] I could never have bitten the Big Apple all summer and lived to eat the worm."

Recording *Streetlights* had been a crash course in recording a professional-sounding album. Bonnie's era of recording "home grown" LPs was officially over. Her first three albums had a certain naive quality to them, and an innocent charm. From *Streetlights* on, Bonnie was viewed as a professional singer, and not just a cult-followed folksinger.

Bonnie acquiesced, and delivered her *Streetlights* album the way her record company wanted. The sound on this album was more accessible to pop and rock record buyers, and—in spite of her reticence—it moved her a step further up the mountain toward mainstream stardom. She accepted this new direction in her career, in part because it put her in a better position to help the blues singers she so loved. In 1974 Bonnie flew Sippie Wallace to her concerts in Washington, D.C., and Boston, where Wallace joined her on stage and performed. Sippie's showstopper was her emotional version of "Amazing Grace."

Bonnie had struck upon a formula for building an audience for herself, in concert, as well as for her albums. The albums provided her with new material, gave her a platform to promote herself, and, in turn, the record company gave her financial tour support and advertising. She became known as a performer whose fame was spread more by word-of-mouth than by radio airplay. She was also known as an album artist. There weren't any hit singles in her career at this point, nor was there an attempt to create any. Bonnie was not interested in chasing Top Forty radio exposure, and she proved that she didn't need to do so to draw audiences to her shows. From the very beginning, Bonnie's devoted fans were known to come back to see her in concert time and time again. And, when they did, they brought their friends.

She was still at the phase of her career where she was playing small clubs and concerts at colleges. Soon she would have to make the transition to playing large concert halls, simply to meet the demand for her music. Bonnie Raitt was about to join the big leagues.

5

Home Plate

ith her first three albums, Bonnie had been deliberately loose and uncommercial. With *Streetlights* she had been forced to be—in her opinion—too slick. With her next album, *Home Plate*, she was aiming at a point somewhere in between those two marks. And with her next three albums, both commercially and artistically, she was going to hit consecutive home runs.

Right after she finished the tour that followed the release of *Streetlights*, Bonnie returned to Los Angeles, where she began work on her fifth album for Warner Brothers Records. The previous year in New York City, she had learned the merits of having a professional record producer in the studio with her, overseeing all of the details, making suggestions, and carrying some of the creative weight.

The man she chose to direct the new project was veteran rock and roll producer, Paul Rothchild. While director of recording at Elektra Records in the 1960s, Rothchild was responsible for producing several of that label's best-known singer-songwriters. Among them were Tom Rush, Tim Buckley, and Phil Ochs. Rothchild then moved on to electric music when he signed the Paul Butterfield Blues Band to the label. In the folk-rock realm—he had a hand in turning David Crosby, Stephen Stills, and Graham Nash into a trio.

In 1966 Rothchild went into the recording studio with a new rock band that had just been signed to Elektra. He produced their debut album, which was released in January 1967. They turned out to be one of the most influential bands of the era: The Doors. Suddenly, Paul was looked to as the perfect record producer to bridge the gap between folk, rock, and blues.

In September 1970 Rothchild began producing Janis Joplin's landmark final album, *Pearl.* When Joplin died on October 4, the existing tapes were used to assemble her lasting epitaph of an LP. Hugely successful, it spent nine consecutive weeks at number 1 on the album charts.

Janis Joplin and Bonnie Raitt had much in common. They were both white women who grew up loving the blues. While Bonnie embraced John Lee Hooker and Sippie Wallace, Janis was enamored with Bessie Smith. And, like Bonnie, the first time Janis was able to find herself in the financial position to pay tribute to her idol, she immediately did so. Fortunately, Bonnie was able to help Sippie's career while she was still alive. Bessie Smith had passed away in 1937. On August 8, 1970, Janis purchased a headstone for Bessie Smith's grave at Mount Lawn Cemetary in Philadelphia. It had been minimally marked for the thirty-three years since Smith's death, and Janis was thrilled to finally give Bessie her due respect.

Bonnie could not escape parallels to Joplin's *Pearl* album. Several of the most important people in her life—three different producers—all had played roles in the creation of that LP: John Hall, Jerry Ragovoy, and now Paul Rothchild.

In chosing Paul to produce her *Home Plate* album, Bonnie

soon realized that she had made a wise decision. He had come highly recommended. According to Ray Manzarek of the Doors, "Paul was an intellectual, a mystic, and an artist. He took all the anxiety out of recording and was absolutely brilliant at setting an atmosphere, mood, and sense of security for an artist. He allowed the collective unconscious of the Doors to flow free. He was the fifth Door."

Paul Rothchild liked the idea of giving Bonnie Raitt's next album a new sound. It coincided with his own philosophy for spontaneity in the recording studio. He said, "Managers always say that: 'You've got to be consistent.' Campbell's Soup is consistent. The list of consistent is endless, and it is what it is: lowest common denominator, average, consistent. I would much rather have somebody take a whole lot of chances, fail big, or blow the mind big!"

Something interesting and monumental happened between the recording of Bonnie's fourth and fifth albums. Torchy female rockers were suddenly "in." Like Bonnie, Linda Ronstadt had recorded four solo albums that were a mixture of folk, rock, and other divergent styles. Linda, too, had recorded with a close circle of friends, and loved to bounce from "party down" rock and roll numbers to heartbreaking ballads.

In 1972, when she recorded her *Linda Ronstadt* album, she assembled a band for herself consisting of Glenn Frey, Don Henley, Randy Meisner, and Bernie Leadon. After the album was completed, the band decided to stay together as a group. They called themselves the Eagles.

In the beginning of 1975, Ronstadt's *Heart Like a Wheel* LP became a sensation. Overnight she turned into the hottest female singer in the business. She sang a combination of country, rock, blues, and soul, and all of a sudden she went from the kind of cult success that Bonnie Raitt was enjoying to multi-million-selling Top Ten and number 1 albums. A stream of

Grammy Awards were soon to follow. There was no question that Warner Brothers Records began to view Bonnie as their answer to Linda Ronstadt.

Far from rivals, Linda and Bonnie were close friends. Ronstadt and Raitt ran in the same Los Angeles music circles in the 1970s and were both friends with Lowell George and Little Feat.

While Linda was in her unbeatable triple-Platinum sales phase in the 1970s, she confessed that the person she most wanted to sound like was Bonnie. "I hate the sound of my voice," Linda said. "I never listen to my records. I like to sing, but I don't like to hear myself. Most people are like that. If I could do what Bonnie Raitt could do, I'd be out bragging on myself day and night. Because she sings effortlessly, she never makes a mistake. She plays great guitar and she's very funny. I know she has an inferiority complex too. I want to shake her sometimes!"

For the next five years, it would be predicted that Raitt's career was about to catch fire, and she too would become as hot as Ronstadt. This is not to say that Bonnie ever consciously attempted to emulate Linda. She has never once stopped being true to her own nature. But among the female rockers of the late seventies, Ronstadt and Raitt had the most in common.

In a way, this kind of success was exactly what Bonnie didn't want to happen, and she admitted that she was afraid of the upper stratosphere of stardom and the constraints it puts on performers. "I don't want to be a pop singer like Linda," she said. "I love her stuff, but people tend to lump women together. They assume, wrongly, that we're all after the same things. I mean, everyone wants to be liked, to be successful, but that's not why I have horns playing on *Home Plate*. I don't care whether I go down in history as a major performer. I don't spend that much time on it. All I ever want to do is make people have a good time. I don't care if I'm significant as long as I get to live and be happy."

Meanwhile, back in Los Angeles in the summer of 1975, Bonnie began to work on her new album with Paul Rothchild producing. Among the guest musicians who assisted in the creation of this excellent album were Emmylou Harris, Jackson Browne, J. D. Souther, John Sebastian, John Hall, Bill Payne, Tom Waits, and Bonnie's band members Freebo and Will McFarlane. She was in an all-star setting on this album, and it showed.

The album begins with another Allen Toussaint original, "What Do You Want the Boy to Do?" The instrumental tracks are lively and multilayered and the backgrounds are soulful and exciting. Bonnie sounds stronger and more assured than on any of her previous albums. From the very start she sounds like she is really into communicating the lyrics, and relaxed about having a competent crew of professionals around her. This is one of her best uptempo cuts from the seventies.

Bouncy and thumping, John and Johanna Hall's "Good Enough" continues the upbeat and rhythmic pace on this song about being good enough—both in and out of bed. Soulful and shakin', it chugs along at an exciting pace with tasty background vocals and jamming instrumentals.

"Run Like a Thief" takes as its subject sleeping with a best friend's lover. An electric blues-rock ballad by John David Souther, it gives Bonnie a chance to drive a song home with her rich and impassioned vocals. Likewise, "Fool Yourself" is a blues rocker with Raitt dishing out musical advice to the lovelorn.

"My First Night Alone Without You" is a sublime ballad that is one of the standout tracks on the album, with Bonnie providing solo vocals on this ode to another love affair turned sour. The tone is jazzy, Jai Winding's piano is commanding, the singing is intense, and the performance is decidedly blue.

"I heard this song on an old Ray Charles album (always a big influence on me) and just had to cut it. It's such a perfect blend of music and desolation—one of the saddest torch songs ever," she says.

Finally, after an entire album's absence, "Sugar Mama" reunites Bonnie and Slide—guitar, that is. Part of the song is carried by Raitt's rough-edged singing, and part of the recording highlights her electric slide playing. She explains: "One of the reasons I like to play slide guitar, what drew me to it in the first place, was the fact that it sounded like a human voice crying— it was very evocative. Especially when you're singing about something that's so intensely personal that you have to stop singing and play instead. It takes over for the voice. It's a complimentary way of saying something that you could no longer sing, because it was too emotional."

She worked her slide playing to the max on "Sugar Mama." "I got this song from one of my favorite bands from the early seventies, Delbert and Glen, featuring Texas roadhouse king Delbert McClinton and his partner, Glen Clark. The band sprung from the fertile musical spawning ground of Ft. Worth, Texas. Jerry Williams, Stevie Ray and Jimmy Vaughan, and Lou Ann Barton are a few more offshoots. That pungent mix of country, R&B, and blues—all run through that special Texas sieve—is what 'roots' music is all about."

"I'm Blowin' Away" is a sweet, lamenting ballad, that perfectly suited Bonnie's voice. "They all know I need songs," she said about her musician friends. "Eric [Kaz] wrote 'I'm Blowin' Away' for me—I think. After he wrote the first line about, 'I've been romanced, wined, and danced/Crazy nights and wild times,' he called me up and said, 'I've got a song for you.' " A perfect vocal choice.

The album ends with the drunken-sounding revelry of "Your Sweet and Shiny Eyes." An off-the-wall drinking song, it sounds like it was recorded at an all-night tequila fete. With a disharmonious chorus behind her, Bonnie sings of celebrating her birthday in a bar while drinking margaritas. The song was a quirky but fun way to end a festive and well-balanced album, which is still considered one of her very best.

Everyone connected with the project was convinced that Bonnie was about to have a real career breakthrough. Even the cover photo of Bonnie, dressed in a baseball outfit and sliding into a cartoon home plate, was accessible and friendly looking. Echoing what many critics at the time felt, Freebo stated, "The biggest growth is in her confidence in her voice. A lot of it came out in *Home Plate.*"

At the time that *Home Plate* was released, Bonnie was completely happy with it. She said, "It combines all the good things on the first albums, like the group feeling—everybody putting in input, a producer taking some of the load off me, providing a structure within which I can be funky, with a band that's professional, so we got the songs sometimes in three takes instead of twenty, because we'd be prepared. And I also think this the first one where my voice is out, recorded better. It isn't necessarily true that I'll never do any old acoustic blues or play guitar, but it represents a time capsule of one particular change that I went through, and I think it's a change for the better."

According to the official Warner Brothers Records press "bio" that was sent to music industry journalists, Bonnie Raitt had become a colorful character. The last paragraph of the 1975 four-page biography read, "Between albums and extensive concert tours, Bonnie and her notorious band perform benefit concerts as often as possible to raise funds for community health services, listener sponsored radio stations, political causes, and underdog concert promoters. After a few bars rest, she has been heard to tell a salty joke or two in mixed company."

Like Patsy Cline before her, Bonnie Raitt had a reputation for preferring to hang out with the boys in the band, and drink and tell dirty stories. She was also the first to admit it. In her first cover story in *Rolling Stone* magazine, Bonnie confessed, "I don't think before I talk. In terms of true freedom, you should just be able to be what you are. And that just naturally comes out of my mouth. Me and my brothers' friends were always a group—I was the only girl and I probably started to make off-color jokes as a way to get in with the guys. And ever since I can remember, it's been me and a bunch of guys. I really like cracking up with my friends and foolin' around with the guys. It's a release of tension."

She was also known for her social drinking. "By the midseventies, I started running and stopped drinking bourbon," Bonnie says. "I was drinking wine and beer. And then eventually I drank tequila. I was part of the seventies tequila circuit in L.A. We were proud to drink tequila and stay up all night. That was a lifestyle we all espoused and loved. Nobody that was around the Eagles, Little Feat, or me, or Jackson Browne's band is going to say we got a lot of sleep when we were in our twenties."

She explained at the time *Home Plate* was released, "In Cambridge I had a lot of nights of getting drunk—but not sloppy drunk, and I wouldn't get hung over. But last year [1974], on tour, the work schedule was so hard and I was drinking, and I started to get hung over in the morning—that comes with getting older, not getting exercise, and not having good food. And, I'd be sloppy onstage. So this year I've stopped bourbon, and those nights are few and far between. Onstage I just have wine and club soda."

When she was asked if she did recreational drugs, she replied, "Nothing much: a toot 'n' a toke."

The *Home Plate* album was released in September 1975, and twenty-five-year-old Bonnie Raitt immediately headed out on the concert circuit. This was the most important album of her career so far, and she had to take it to the people. Although it didn't knock Linda Ronstadt's *Prisoner in Disguise* out of the Top Five on *Billboard* magazine's album chart, it became Bonnie's biggest hit album to date, peaking at number 43. In spite of her squeamishness about stardom, it was beginning to happen.

Bonnie and her top-notch band went out on the road and promoted the album in concert, playing over one hundred nights a year. Her concerts that autumn included performances in Los Angeles, New York City, Nashville, and everywhere in between.

At her concert in Santa Monica that fall, she was joined on stage by several friends and admirers for the encore. They included Joni Mitchell, J. D. Souther, and Jackson Browne. After she listened to the audio tape of the show several weeks later, she remarked, "This was like the best show of my life!"

She played several dates with John Prine and Tom Waits on the bill as her opening acts. Suddenly she was a headliner, and it felt great. However, she remained the same "team player" kind of gal she had been when she was a struggling opening act.

She had a ball touring with Waits and Prine. When the three of them rolled into Nashville, they played at the Grand Ole Opry.

Of Prine, Bonnie joked at the time, "His face is so cute. He's got no bones, just like me. We're like the Pillsbury dough twins. It's like an instant affair whenever we're around each other—but he's married and I have Garry, so I'm glad we don't see each other that often, but we're cut from the same stock."

While rumors of affairs circulated in the music world, Bonnie claimed to be devoted to Garry George. He favored the same kind of music-infused partying lifestyle that Bonnie led, and was basically along for the ride. Bonnie was steadfastly devoted to her career and touring schedule, and Garry was happy to share her with her music and her musician buddies.

On November 9, 1975, Bonnie played the most prestigious

concert of her career—to date. She headlined Lincoln Center's Avery Fisher Hall in New York City, with Waits and Prine warming up the stage for her. At that same time, her father, John Raitt was starring on Broadway at the St. James Theater, in the revue *American Musical* (also known as "American Jubilee"), with Tammy Grimes and Lillian Gish. Fortunately, John Raitt's show was not running on Sunday nights, so he was able to catch his daughter's show uptown.

Bonnie Raitt was fabulous on stage that evening. I was in the audience and remember it quite distinctly. (In fact, I still have the ticket stubs.) I was so convinced that I would one day write a book about Bonnie Raitt, that I even took notes that night: "I had a good time making this last record," she said from the stage of Avery Fisher Hall. "My producer, Paul Rothchild is here. I found a bunch of musicians that I've long been in admiration of, and they all contributed songs."

She also mentioned that she had just celebrated her twenty-sixth birthday the night before. "Speaking of birthdays," she said, "We played with Sippie Wallace on her seventy-seventh birthday in Ann Arbor. This is a little something me and the girls worked up," she declared, introducing the next number.

Leading into "Angel of Montgomery," she announced, "We played the Grand Ole Opry a couple of weeks ago with John Prine," It was a cold and breezy night in Manhattan, and Bonnie warmed the cavernous hall to the point where the atmosphere more closely resembled a blues and rock love-in than a concert. I had been in love with Bonnie's music since *Give It Up*, and I was delighted to find that she was as exciting live as her recordings led one to believe she would be.

Her proud father, John Raitt, was in the audience that night. He was also present at the after-concert party that was held for her at Sardi's, the Broadway area's legendary eatery. At Sardi's he commented of his now-famous daughter, "She watched me struggle for years. I'd like to think that she learned something about dignity and integrity."

Although she was now playing prestigious gigs in places like Lincoln Center, it didn't put a damper on any of Bonnie's on-tour levity. She enjoyed being on the road—just her and the boys in her band.

Deborah Mitchell, who is currently an editor at *Vanity Fair* magazine, recalls seeing Bonnie and the band out for some preshow recreation: "It was spring of 1976, and she played a date at Bryn Mawr College. It was during the day, somehow, when I saw her on campus. As I recall, they played an afternoon show, and there was an evening one. Bryn Mawr is a very beautiful college—it means 'big hill' in Welsh. The swimming pool there has this ornate fish that the water spouts out of. It's very Gothic, with all of these beautiful stone buildings with little arches. There's Pembrooke Arch, and all of these architectural appointments.

"I was walking across campus, and I saw Bonnie and a bunch of the guys from the band on roller skates. These were the old-fashioned roller skates with the silver metal wheels—the kind you had to strap on your shoes—before the days of roller blades! I remember seeing Bonnie and the guys skating around the campus. It was really kind of adorable. She wasn't that great a skater as I recall. I remember her skating while holding onto the guys in the band, and them holding onto her. It was very cute to see, and they were having a lot of fun! They were all laughing, and there were kids all around—students having a good time with them. It was so adorable. The show that night was great! I was a big fan of hers. I know I played that album that has 'Guilty' on it—'I'm guilty'—I played that album: *Home Plate,* constantly that semester."

In May of that year, Bonnie went on tour with her buddies, Little Feat. They had again reunited, and had become quite a respected and eclectic rock and roll band since their 1974 album, *Feats Don't Fail Me Now* had gone Gold. Raitt had added her background vocals to some of the tracks to that album, along with Emmylou Harris. Besides, there was always a party wherever Little Feat landed.

During that tour, on May 26, 1976, radio station KSAN in San Francisco broadcast Bonnie's show at the Great American Music Hall, live on the air. This was especially magical for Bonnie, because Sippie Wallace joined her on stage for a couple of numbers. The Raitt-Wallace duet version of "Woman Be Wise" was especially nice, and later appeared on the 1990 album *The Bonnie Raitt Collection.* Bonnie was later to say of Sippie, "Our friendship on and off stage remains one of the highlights of my life."

Bonnie was so busy on the road promoting her *Home Plate* album, that 1976 became the first year in five that she didn't release a new album. When she did return to the studio, it was with Paul Rothchild at the helm again. This time around, he plotted her course directly into what was to ultimately become her biggest selling album of the 1970s—*Sweet Forgiveness.*

Bonnie began recording the tracks for *Sweet Forgiveness* in late 1976 and finished it in the beginning of 1977. Adding two more musicians to her touring-recording lineup she now had her own solid band of four musicians to accompany her wherever she played. In addition to Freebo on bass and Will McFarlane on guitar, she had Dennis Whitted on drums and Jef Labes on keyboards. She had been so pleased with the results of her *Home Plate* album that she was confidently relaxed to have Rothchild as her producer. Another product of the California rock scene, it was also recorded in Los Angeles.

Her list of guest musicians included Michael McDonald of the Doobie Brothers; John David Souther; Bill Payne; and Norton Buffalo, who played the harmonica on the song "Run-

away." She again chose songs from some of her favorite tried-
and-true songwriters: Jackson Browne, Eric Kaz, Bill Payne,
and Paul Siebel.

Album by album, Bonnie Raitt was becoming more and
more a mainstream rock and roll artist. Released in the spring
of 1977, *Sweet Forgiveness* took her to a new plateau of fame
and musical respect.

Opening with the stripped-down rocker "About to Make
Me Leave Home," Bonnie was in strong voice, and her trademark slide guitar emotionally kicked off the tasty proceedings.
However, it was the second cut that really became a milestone
in her career. It was a cover of Del Shannon's 1961 number–1
rocker, "Runaway." Everyone who heard that particular song
knew that Bonnie had hit a new high-water mark. Sassy, startling, and arousingly peppy, with this particular cut, Bonnie
Raitt was finally to be acknowledged as a full-fledged rocker.

According to Bonnie, her friends were always turning her
on to new and obscure songs. "About to Make Me Leave
Home" was one of these. "I was already a big fan of the great
Memphis soul production team of Willie Mitchell and Al Green
when a friend—Bonnie Simmons—turned me on to another
great Hi Records artist, Syl Johnson. I got this song from one
of his albums, and it's definitely one of the swampiest tracks
I've recorded. Playing it live is like pulling the choke out on my
set . . . definitely in my Top Ten!"

Bonnie recalled the evolution of recording her sizzling version of Del Shannon's signature song, "I was fooling around in
the studio with the guitar hook to Al Green's 'Love and Happiness' while working on *Home Plate,* and the song 'Runaway'
just popped into my head. I played it through in that Al Green
groove and vowed right there to put it on the next record."

Mark Jordan, of Freebo's old Philadelphia group, the Edison Electric Band, contributed the beautiful ballad "Two

Lives." Paul Siebel, who was one of Bonnie's favorite un-known-if-it-wasn't-for-her songwriters, gave her the touching ode to a barroom character by the name of "Louise." In the lyrics of this plaintive song, Bonnie sings of how Louise's body was found dead in her room. Dave Grisman's intricate mandolin work midsong is especially moving. This is one of Bonnie's most effective and moody ballad performances.

"Always one of my favorite Paul Siebel songs," says Bonnie of "Louise," adding, "I love the open Tex-Mex feel of this arrangement. The mandolins, guitars, and Freebo's fretless bass just seem to gently blow the song along."

In addition to Mary Travers of Peter, Paul and Mary ("Doctor My Eyes"), Bonnie is one of the few soloists to try to interpret Jackson Browne's seventies compositions. With "My Opening Farewell," Raitt excells on her third Browne cover. Her singing in this one again proves her a master storyteller. A sad ballad about being tongue-tied over finding a way to say "goodbye," she again takes a sad lament and draws the listener into the spell of her singing.

"Three Time Loser" rekindles the fire of "Runaway," with Bonnie's searing singing and slide-guitar performance. Again, she proved that she could rock and roll with the best of them. Slowing the pace down to the medium-tempo blues of Bill Payne's "Takin' My Time," Bonnie lets McFarlane have a hand at the slide and concentrates on her fiery and gravelly vocals. Finally, she tugs at the heartstrings with Karla Bonoff's ballad "Home." With J. D. Souther's harmony vocals backing her on the chorus and David Grisman on mandolin, Bonnie again shows that she is a vocalist for all emotional modes.

Sweet Forgiveness was one of Bonnie's most varied, centered, and focused albums. She proved that she was poised and ready for her leap into the major leagues of the late seventies contemporary rock scene. Warner Brothers knew that they had a brilliant album in the making, and quickly prepared to release Raitt's first hit single, "Runaway."

Raitt herself had mixed emotions about even going after the "singles" market. It was diametrically opposed to what her early career was all about, but she reluctantly went along with the marketing and promotion of it. To say that "Runaway" was an unqualified smash would be an exaggeration. However, rock radio stations immediately embraced it, and it made it to number 57 on the *Billboard* singles chart. "Runaway" gave Bonnie a recognizable hit to play in her concerts.

Robert Christgau prophetically wrote in the *Village Voice* that year that " 'Runaway' should become Bonnie's first hit single ever—not the smash hit she feared (and coveted), but an AM breakthrough neverless—makes perfect sense: rock and roll nostalgia is an accepted way to getting a 'girl singer' on the charts, as Bonnie's friend and rival Linda Ronstadt has proved more than once."

As she had in the past, Bonnie immediately hit the concert trail after her new album was completed. Due to the chart success of "Runaway," and her critically acclaimed concert performances across the United States, the *Sweet Forgiveness* album was ultimately to be certified Gold—for 500,000 copies sold. Peaking at number 25 on the album chart, it became the new zenith in her eclectic recording career.

Bonnie used her newfound rock celebrity status to further her own original cause: the promotion and revitalization of the careers of blues stars from a bygone era. In the spring of 1977, when she returned to Manhattan for her second headlining date at Avery Fisher Hall, she did not choose to have the stage warmed up for her by another rock and roll act. Instead, she brought along two of her blues heroes: Sippie Wallace and barrelhouse-blues-piano man "Little Brother" Montgomery.

Held on Monday evening, March 28, 1977, that Avery

Fisher Hall concert was infused with the love and respect that Raitt lavished on Sippie Wallace. The sight and sound of Bonnie Raitt singing duet versions of "You Got to Know How" and "Women Be Wise" with Sippie Wallace herself, was an unforgettable experience for me to have witnessed.

6

The Glow of Success

In 1977 and 1978, at the age of twenty-seven, Bonnie Raitt was happily riding the success of her first Gold album. She was known in musical circles as a hot act, who consistently delivered. She was exciting, energetic, rhythmic, and rocking. Through the middle years of the decade, she had gathered thousands of devoted fans who have stuck with her.

With her strong rock and roll woman-warrior image, and her songs of triumph and heartbreak, she found that the majority of her fans were female.

Bonnie said, "I get letters from women saying, 'Your music got me through,' or 'You were a real inspiration for me and my music and I really appreciate how strong you are.' Mostly what I get now is, 'You make me proud you're up there. You're one of the first women that I'm not jealous of,' instead of saying, 'I hate you 'cause my old man's in love with you.' I get all my response from women. I don't get any letters from guys. And, a lot of gay women write letters: 'You're one of my favorites.'"

Years before Melissa Etheridge arrived on the scene, when the question was posed to Bonnie that if she was gay, would she address that subject matter in her songs, she replied, "I think I'm the kind of personality that would."

In addition to her growing legion of fans, she also became a favorite of the rock press. In a 1977 cover story on Bonnie in the *Village Voice*, Robert Christgau wrote:

> I consider Bonnie Raitt the best interpretive singer this side of Rod Stewart, her only competition among rock and rollers. I also think she's the most interesting woman artist in rock and roll.
>
> At various times I've felt more passionate about Joy of Cooking, Bette Midler, Joni Mitchell, but Bonnie's the one I come back to. Aretha Franklin is obviously a genius and Bonnie probably isn't, but it's Bonnie's records I play for pleasure and renewal. . . . It seems odd to call Bonnie's audience a cult because her music is so mainstream. But she inspires a commitment that fits no other pattern, and for once some of that commitment is reciprocated. That's why she's always tried to hold the line on her ticket prices, which only recently rose to the low standard of $6.50.

While Bonnie kept busy climbing her own personal career ladder, she not only had several top-name performers appearing on her albums, but she also lent her services to several of her friends as well. The two acts that benefited the most from her "guest vocals" during the 1970s were Jackson Browne and Little Feat.

She can be heard on Jackson's 1976 album *The Pretender*, singing in the background of the song "Here Come Those Tears Again." Browne has remained one of Bonnie's most frequently utilized songwriter friends and has provided her with consistently good songs to record. He has also remained one of her closest pals.

The same can be said of her relationship with the group Little Feat, and the group's individual members. Not only is Bill Payne on most of Raitt's seventies albums after *Takin' My Time,* but she can be heard on their albums *Time Loves a Hero* (1977) and *Down on the Farm* (1979). Little Feat's cult-worshipped albums are notorious for having the most cryptic and nonspecific liner notes in the business. Usually Bonnie was part of a background singing chorus with several of the band's other friends.

In addition to those two albums, Little Feat also released a Gold two-record set called *Waiting for Columbus.* During the recording of these LPs, group leader Lowell George had also come up with his own solo album deal. His *Thanks, I'll Eat It Here,* one of the longest-to-record, and most over-budget albums in Warner Brothers history, was ultimately released in early 1979. Bonnie was featured on that album as well. In the rambling liner notes that accompany that recording, those thanked for their contributions to the album include Raitt; J. D. Souther; John Phillips (the Mamas and Papas); Bill Payne; Jeff Porcaro (Toto); and Jimmy Greenspoon, Floyd Sneed, and Danny Hutton (Three Dog Night).

According to Lowell George, "It seems like it's taken years to make this record—probably because I started two and one half years ago—and during that period of time I undoubtedly forgot a number of people who were of great assistance." When it came time to credit those people he could remember, he prefaced his list with the command, "This is what we call the Musician Blindfold Test. Try to match the player with his sphere."

Three Dog Night's keyboard player, Jimmy Greenspoon, suggests that the lack of memory about the *Thanks I'll Eat It Here* sessions is in direct correlation to the amount of booze and drugs consumed during the recording process. Greenspoon also remembers Bonnie Raitt floating in and out of these sessions, and singing on several of the songs.

He especially recalls the drugged out days and nights he spent working on Lowell's only solo album, along with a hard-core partying crew—including Bonnie. Greenspoon relates, "Lowell enlisted myself, and everybody in the world to do the album. Literally everyone: Nicky Hopkins, Jeff Porcaro, Floyd [Sneed] was on it. There were some cuts that never made it to the record—Bonnie Raitt, of course, David Crosby came down, and it took like two years, because Lowell liked to work and party, and everybody was partying so much. It was literally a two-year project! If 'something' ran out in the studio, Lowell and I would go up the hill and get some more 'stuff,' [drugs] and he'd get a case of cognac, and he'd drop it off, and we'd go up and score some more coke. We'd get back and he'd say, 'Okay, where were we?' and I'd say, 'We were in the second verse.' And, he'd go, 'Okay, great. NEXT!'

"It was stupid! It was party central, and all of those people were party animals. In fact, at one point we left Nicky Hopkins slumped over the piano and went to get another case of cognac, and he was still passed out when we returned, so we just recorded without him. Everybody was still in the studio, recording, and singing, and playing, and he'd be slumped over the keyboards—out cold! I remember, Bonnie and David came in the control room, and were just looking around going, 'What are all of these people doing? This is amazing!'"

Greenspoon confirms that hours and hours of tape were recorded, but most of it never made the album. As for the songs featuring Raitt, he says, "She sang backgrounds. I don't know if it made the final cut, because there were eight or ten songs that didn't come out on the actual album that Warners released. 'China White,' and 'Rocket in My Pocket,' and a lot of great songs there. Someone told me that they were going to release all the unreleased songs, but I've never seen it. It was supposed to be a boxed-set of Lowell George and Little Feat and all of his A list friends: Lowell and Bonnie and David Crosby, but it's somewhere in Warners' archives."

Jimmy has a special memory of Bonnie: "She was sweet, nice, and professional. She would come in, sing, play, laugh, sit down, and listen to the playbacks, and leave—unlike the rest of us who would come in, leave, get more 'stuff,' come back, laugh, leave and come back again, and then pass out! We took over Sunset Sound studios for a number of months and months and months. I left to go on the road with Three Dog Night and came back, and Lowell was still in the studio working on the album!"

Describing the cross-pollination of the stars of the California rock scene in the late sixties and early seventies, *Time* magazine reported in a 1977 cover story on Linda Ronstadt,

> Colonies of rock musicians were forming in the Los Angeles subdivisions of Laurel Canyon, Echo Park, and Venice. Glenn Frey drifted in from Royal Oak, Michigan. Don Henley was a North Texas State English major before he decided to move west. They eventually formed the supergroup the Eagles. Before long everyone knew Jackson Browne and Bonnie Raitt, who had grown up around L.A. Neil Young, Joni Mitchell, and Stephen Stills lived near the top of Laurel Canyon, Frank Zappa in an old Tom Mix house a short walk away.

In explaining the communal feeling of the L.A. music scene, Linda Ronstadt recalled, "We were all learning about drugs, philosophy, and music. Everything was exciting."

Meanwhile, Linda's career was skyrocketing. While Bonnie Raitt had created two extremely good albums with Paul Rothchild, Linda Ronstadt had been using producer Peter

Asher, and in 1977 became the first female singer in history to have four million-selling Platinum albums in a row. (By 1980 her total was seven consecutive Platinum albums!)

After the *Sweet Forgiveness* album was released and went Gold, it was obvious to everyone that Raitt's next album was going to shoot to the top of the charts, like Ronstadt's were doing. This prediction seemed so evident that other record labels were actively seeking to steal Bonnie away from Warner Brothers.

As Bonnie explains it, "After 'Runaway,' it looked like I was going to have a hit record if I worked with Peter Asher. This was in, like, 1978, and Columbia Records was trying to sign me. There was this big Columbia-Warner war going on at the time. James Taylor had just left Warner Brothers and made a big album for Columbia [*JT* 1977, produced by Peter Asher, including the number–4 hit "Handy Man."] And then, Warners signed Paul Simon away from Columbia. And they didn't want me to have a hit record for Columbia—no matter what! So, I renegotiated my contract, and they basically matched Columbia's offer. Frankly the deal was a really big deal." Now that Warner Brothers was spending even more money for Bonnie's albums, the race and pressure to transform her into a highly successful star was intensified.

Explaining how she chose Peter Asher as her next producer, Bonnie says, "Peter and I have the same lawyer, and I would run into him, James Taylor, and Linda Ronstadt socially. When my records would come out and not be hits, Linda and James would say, 'It's too bad you can't get a better sound for the radio, work with someone more professional.'"

In a December 1977 issue of *Rolling Stone* Peter Asher, and his star acts—Linda Ronstadt and James Taylor—were the subject of a cover story heralding Asher as "The Producer of the Year." In the context of one of the two articles about him in that issue, Asher was asked about future projects. "There are a few people that I greatly admire and know I would like to work with," he said. When the name Jackson Browne was mentioned, he replied, "That would be one. Bonnie Raitt. But, who knows whether I would be a practical possibility, either from their point of view or from mine? There are people, I think, whose careers could be better organized. I hate it when I go and see a show, if it's somebody good, but the set's wrong or the band is no good or the sound is horrible or something—I hate that."

Bonnie read the article and started to think about the possibility of working with Asher. She said, "I've always respected Peter's work, but until I read in *Rolling Stone* that he was interested in producing me, the thought had never crossed my mind. We sat down and talked and I told him I was frustrated that my records didn't sound more live, and he said, 'Yeah, I want to make it live too. Everybody thinks I'm Mr. Slick. I want to prove to people that I know what rock and roll is.' I felt that he saw what made me special to him and he tried to bring it out."

In the 1960s, Peter Asher was one half of the British rock duo Peter and Gordon. Their biggest hits as a team included "A World Without Love" (1964), "I Go to Pieces" (1965), and "Lady Godiva" (1966). After the duo broke up in the late sixties, Peter moved into the producing end of the business. His sister, Jane Asher, dated Paul McCartney at the height of Beatlemania, so Peter was well acquainted with the Beatles in their heyday. When the Beatles formed Apple Records in 1968, Peter became the A&R director. The first act he signed to the label was James Taylor.

Peter's success with Linda and James during this era had made him the hottest producer around. Bonnie recalls, "I was a little intimidated to be working with someone of his personal power and position in the music business. But, it wasn't like I was selling out. I knew I'd have control over the songs, and he couldn't make me do something I didn't want to do."

Having Peter produce her seventh album seemed such a natural choice. However, it also carried a certain stigma with it: the shadow of Linda Ronstadt. "I knew I was going to take a lot of flak for *The Glow*, that people in the business were going to say that Peter was trying to turn me into Linda Ronstadt," she admitted. "But what it really was, was that Peter wanted to show people that he could make a funky record."

To find material for *The Glow*, Bonnie went through a mountain of old 45's, record albums, and songwriter demo tapes. She explained, "It gets harder and harder to find songs. Either I'm going to have to start writing more or find some new songwriters." She began toying with the idea of writing songs again. She had not written any new songs in seven years—since the *Give It Up* album in 1972.

In between the albums *Sweet Forgiveness* and *The Glow* Bonnie was diagnosed as having nodes on her vocal cords. This is a common affliction for singers, often caused when they over-use their voices. With a specialist operating on her, she went into the hospital and had them removed. While she was recuperating, she wasn't allowed to speak—let alone sing—for two weeks.

It was during her recovery that she wrote "Standing by the Same Old Love." She recalls, "I couldn't sing. I couldn't even talk. Friends were calling me up just for the pleasure of being able to know that, for once, I couldn't talk back. One afternoon, I wrote the song in my head. It was two weeks before I was able to sing it for anybody else."

Referring to her five-year song-writer's block, Bonnie explained, "I guess it's a combination of laziness and lack of desire. I don't spend any time at it. I don't play guitar or piano for recreational purposes. I'm not a songwriter. I'm not a poet like Jackson [Browne]. I'm just not that good at it. Maybe I'd be better if I worked at it more. But, as it is, I don't have enough time to do the things I enjoy. I don't think music should be the beginning and end of existence. I'd like to do different things: study anthropology, take up painting, or flying. I don't want to be one-dimensional."

On April 26, 1979, twenty-nine-year-old Bonnie Raitt arrived at the Sound Factory recording studios in Los Angeles and began work on her album *The Glow*. That same month, Bill Payne announced that Little Feat was officially disbanded, and Warner Brothers released Lowell George's long-awaited *Thanks I'll Eat It Here* album.

Two months later, on June 28, Lowell played to a sold-out house in Washington, D.C., and the next day died in his Arlington, Virginia, hotel room. At the age of thirty-four, he had suffered a heart attack, brought on by his rampant drug abuse. Bonnie was devastated.

July 12, 1979, was the final date of recording for *The Glow*. On the thirtieth of the month she was seen on Dinah Shore's top-rated talk show, along with several of her singing buddies, the Doobie Brothers, and Jackson Browne. The special ninety-minute version of *Dinah!* was devoted to the upcoming MUSE concerts in New York City, to bring about awareness of the dangers of nuclear power.

In August, Bonnie was among the friends, fans, and comrades of Lowell George to perform at a benefit-tribute concert at the Great Western Forum in Los Angeles. Bonnie, Jackson Browne, Linda Ronstadt, Little Feat, Nicolette Larson, Emmylou Harris, and the Tower of Power Horns performed, raising $230,000 for Lowell's family. The audience was also star-studded, as members of Van Halen and California Governor Jerry Brown were on hand for the event.

Bonnie sang an emotional rendition of "Here Come Those Tears Again" with Jackson and several of the members of Little Feat. Bonnie, Little Feat, and each of the soloists performed sets of five or six songs with the same house band, which Bill

Payne had assembled for the event. Ronstadt, Larson, and Harris appeared as an all-star trio, and Bonnie's singing soared on Lowell George's "Rock and Roll Doctor." After she was finished performing, she recalled, "People would call out for this one when Lowell was onstage, and Lowell would tell them 'Rock and roll doctor? You're looking at him, sucker!' "

Linda Ronstadt was in tears when she performed her sorrow-filled version of Lowell's drug ode, "Willin'." Her recording of that song on her *Heart Like a Wheel* album had been the general public's first introduction to his music. Then Bonnie and the entire ensemble rejoined Linda and the band for "Dixie Chicken," complete with a celebrity kick line.

As Bill Payne said after the concert, "This really wasn't done for money or grandstanding. The reason we were up there is because Lowell George brought us together during his life. He wasn't as well-known as some of the people who were up there that night, but he'd influenced each and every one of us."

When Bonnie released her album *The Glow,* she wrote in its liner notes, "I'd like to dedicate this album to the spirit of a very special friend, Lowell George."

At this point in her career, Bonnie was still a cult rock figure. She was neither a major star, nor an acknowledged hitmaker. The general public still was unaware of her. When she joined up with the Doobie Brothers, Jackson Browne, James Taylor, Carly Simon, and Crosby, Stills and Nash to form the political activist group Musicians United for Safe Energy (MUSE), with the exception of Bonnie, they were all multimillion-selling artists. She was their buddy and comrade, and a respected musician. Although she had a legion of devoted fans herself, she did not possess their superstar status. But she was to benefit from their combined fame.

The lead-up to the MUSE concerts, which were to be held at Madison Square Garden at the end of September, had begun on July 30, on Dinah Shore's TV show. The program's announcer proclaimed: "Today: the number-one singing group in the nation—the Doobie Brothers, with their hits 'Minute by Minute' and 'What a Fool Believes.' Singer-songwriter of 'Running on Empty' fame—Jackson Browne. Beautiful folk-rock singer Bonnie Raitt joins in a song with the Doobies and Jackson Browne."

After the Doobie Brothers sang their huge hit, "Minute by Minute," Dinah Shore sat down with the group, introduced the individual members of the band, and chatted for several minutes. Then, Dinah and the Doobies introduced their mutual friend, Bonnie Raitt.

Dinah said, "We're going to introduce a lady now, who grew up with music—an entirely different kind of music than what she sings. As a matter of fact, she's been on the show with her father—who is into an entirely different kind of music, as I said. And she was really embarrassed the first time she came on, because she didn't want to sing the kind of music that would upset him, but at the same time, she didn't want to not be true to herself. She's a pretty great gal, and, [to Doobie Brother Patrick Simmons] Patrick, why don't you introduce her?" Simmons took his cue and said, "She . . . don't need much introduction, because everybody knows . . . Bonnie Raitt."

After Bonnie walked out on stage, the following conversation took place:

Dinah: Where did you-all first meet?
Bonnie: Should I tell?
The Doobies: (in unison) Yeah!
Bonnie: We're on the same record label, Warner Brothers Records. I've been a fan of you guys ever since I first started making records, you'd already been rolling along.
Dinah: You met in Cincinnati?
Bonnie: Oh, yeah, that's true!

Dinah: Under what circumstances?

Bonnie: Oh, I forgot all about that.

It was a showcase . . .

(This leads to a conversation about Bonnie and The Doobies "getting vague" together at a Holiday Inn bar after the concert.)

Dinah: When was the first time you sang with The Doobie Brothers?

Bonnie: Actually, I think right before New Year's Eve up in Sacramento. We were doing a benefit for Solar Cal, which is a piece of legislation we're trying to get passed here in California to promote a publicly controlled solar industry and I just jumped on stage and sang "Listen to the Music." There's a lot more guys in this band than in mine, so . . .

Dinah: You have another friend backstage, would you introduce him?

Bonnie: A man who also needs no introduction, one of my best friends, and I think the best songwriter this country has produced so far, Jackson Browne!

The Dinah Shore show was an open platform for Bonnie and her musician friends to express their increasingly more vocal political views. The Vietnam War was over, and the sexual revolution was already a reality. The war was now on to eliminate nuclear weapons and nuclear power. The near-meltdown at Three Mile Island in Pennsylvania had been a battle-cry against the promotion of nuclear power. This disaster provoked one of the most hotly debated issues of the late 1970s and early 1980s. Bonnie actively began battling against nuclear energy, while promoting the use of solar energy.

On the program that day, the Doobies, Jackson Browne, and Bonnie Raitt sang their version of John Hall's song "Power," which labels nuclear-produced electrical power as "poison." It was the beginning of Bonnie's use of her career to publicize her political views. Since the broadcast of this show, her political causes have been discussed on her television appearances, just as much as her music. It set a precedent that continues to this day.

Introducing the song "Power," Jackson Browne explained, "This is a song that Bonnie and I have sung together several times at various rallies and events recently, in the last year, year-and-a-half. I first heard it at Seabrook, New Hampshire, when John [Hall] and I were both playing at the occupation of the Seabrook, New Hampshire, nuclear plant . . . demonstrating against it. And it's become somewhat of an anthem to the antinuclear-power movement, and it's a song that we chose to sing today, because Bonnie, and John Hall, and the Doobies, James Taylor, Graham Nash, and I will be playing at Madison Square Garden this fall—in September—and it's a song that we'll probably be playing together."

The rousing version of "Power" that followed drew a huge round of applause from the studio audience on Dinah Shore's show that day.

Bonnie later explained, "I first became aware of how dangerous the nuclear industry had become when I read about Karen Silkwood's death back in 1974. Sometime later the Supporters of Silkwood approached me about doing a benefit to raise funds for the family's case against the Kerr-McGee plutonium company, which they believed was responsible for her death. Ironically, tickets to a concert Jackson Browne and I were giving a few days later in Oklahoma City were found in her car when she died. But, the kicker for me has been the attempt to license the Diablo Canyon power plant just a few hours upwind of where I live in Los Angeles. When it became known that the plant was about two miles from the Hosgri earthquake fault, I knew there was no other choice but to get involved. I read all I could and the more I found out, the more frightened and angry I became. Stopping nuclear power is not just another cause; it's a necessity. What good is music if you don't have anyplace to play it, or anyone to play it to?"

The MUSE Concerts for a Non-Nuclear Future were held September 19–23, 1979, at Madison Square Garden, culminating in a huge rally on one of the landfill plots in lower Manhattan, where Battery Park City now sits.

According to my notes taken that evening at the opening-night concert, John Hall began the show at 7:30 P.M. with a twenty-minute spot. "Bonnie Raitt comes out and does a number with him ['Good Enough']. She performs her set, and at the end of it she is joined by Jackson Browne." My watch had quarter past midnight when the Doobie Brothers came out and did "Take Me in Your Arms," the beginning of a full set. "Then the whole cast [including Bonnie] comes out on stage, John Hall does the final announcements, [Doobies' producer] Ted Templeman in the background, all singing 'Taking It to the Streets,' with Phoebe Snow, and the song 'Power.' 12:55 A.M., the show ends."

On the resulting documentary concert movie soundtrack album, *No Nukes: From the MUSE Concerts for a Non-Nuclear Future*, Bonnie can be heard with the Doobie Brothers, Carly Simon, John Hall, Jackson Browne, Graham Nash, Rosemary Butler, and (unbilled) Phoebe Snow on those two songs. Bonnie's songs "Runaway" and "Angel From Montgomery" are also included on the three-record album set that was released only weeks after the concert, in December 1979. Amid the five-evening series of concerts, the varied lineup included Bruce Springsteen and The E Street Band, Gil Scott-Heron, Chaka Khan, Poco, Raydio, Jesse Colin Young, Sweet Honey in the Rock, and Crosby, Stills and Nash.

At a press conference held that week at the Statler Hilton Hotel, across Seventh Avenue from Madison Square Garden,

Bonnie verbally attacked one reporter who accused the musicians of being "too powerful or too pushy."

"Artists traditionally have been in a position to get public attention," Bonnie declared. "Now, if the media had reported accurately about the dangers of nuclear power . . . if they hadn't consistently misestimated crowd sizes at antinuclear demonstrations . . . Our responsibility is to focus media attention. If just the movement people had been here today, you probably wouldn't have even covered this!" According to a press release by Elektra-Asylum Records, "the MUSE concerts attracted nearly 100,000 paying fans to Madison Square Garden in what may be the biggest series of benefits ever held in this country. The shows, all of them more than four hours long, were recorded by the twenty-four-track remote unit of New York's Record Plant with a rotating corps of engineers. This [recording] yielded about twenty hours of music, and that was only the beginning. The MUSE artists then had to evaluate their tracks and decide, with some consultation, which songs and performances should be included on the record. Once the choices were made, those tracks had to be mixed and sequenced to give *No Nukes* a smooth flow and coherence. The main burden for assembling the record however fell most heavily on MUSE board members Jackson Browne, Graham Nash, John Hall, and Bonnie Raitt."

The album went to number 19 on the charts, and became the first LP on which Raitt appeared that would break the Top twenty.

The antinuclear cause received a boost when *Rolling Stone* magazine put several of the MUSE concert stars on the cover of its November 15, 1979, issue. The seven rockers on the cover were Bonnie, Bruce Springsteen, Carly Simon, James Taylor, Jackson Browne, Graham Nash, and John Hall.

With all of this high-profile activity centering around Bonnie in the final six months of 1979, the scene was set for the October release of her seventh LP. In Warner Brothers' eyes, it was now or never for Raitt.

It was so obvious to them that *The Glow* would catapult Bonnie Raitt into major-league stardom, so every detail of the album was carefully planned. Warner Brothers would market Bonnie in exactly the same way that Elektra-Asylum Records did Linda Ronstadt. *The Glow* features the most glamorous album cover of her nine original Warner Brothers albums. The portrait of Bonnie on the cover was photographed by Jim Shea, who had just photographed Ronstadt for her *Living in the USA* album. The package even had the same "look" as Linda's albums. It was designed by Kosh—the graphic artist who had just won a Grammy Award for Best Album Package for Ronstadt's *Simple Dreams.*

James Taylor's and Linda Ronstadt's albums also had full lyrics printed inside of the package, so this became Bonnie's first and only album to publish the songs she sang while at Warner Brothers. Here it was: The big push was on. If she was going to become a huge star, this was her chance.

From the beautiful look of the album, to the music contained on it, *The Glow* is a truly wonderful album. It has all of the elements that give each of Bonnie's albums their charm: sad ballads, raucous rock and roll, slide-guitar blues, and passionate singing. Seasoned with bourbon, tequila, and years of partying, her voice had gained a nice raspyness to it. She was singing in a lower register than she did on her first albums, and it seemed to be better suited to those three-in-the-morning-drown-your-sorrows kind of drinking songs that she so loved.

The album opens with a ferocious version of Sam and Dave's 1968 soul hit "I Thank You." Kick-ass drums, wailing guitars, a full-throttle vocal performance by Bonnie, and this album is instantly off and running. She sings the R&B classic with gutsy rock energy. This time, she had a winner on her hands.

"Your Good Thing (Is About to End)" is a masterpiece of soulful singing and top-notch music. David Sanborn's breathtaking saxophone solo in the middle of this song takes it to a jazzy height. At one point Raitt's voice and Sanborn's sax are engaged in an outlandishly hot duet. This song is one of her best single performances of the seventies, and of her recording career.

"Standin' by the Same Old Love" was Bonnie's first new composition in four albums. A jumping blues rocker, it provides a potent showcase for her voice and her slide guitar. Beginning with pounding drums and Bonnie's scorching vocal, it's a rocker of major-league proportions. According to Bonnie, "It's about a woman who's talking about her sexuality with the man she lives with."

Jackson Browne's "Sleep's Dark and Silent Gate" is a somber blues-rock ballad. Again, Browne proves a perfect songwriter for Bonnie to interpret. Bonnie sounds focused, and totally connected with the lyrics of this bittersweet ballad.

The title cut, "The Glow," takes the folk-blues mood a step further into the smoky jazz-club kind of mode. Accompanied by the jazz trio of Bob Magnusson on bass, John Guerin on drums, and Don Grolnick on piano, Bonnie turns this number into a beautiful ballad about drowning one's sorrows in a cocktail glass.

As Bonnie described it, "['The Glow'] is about staying up till three in the morning, drinking—that kinda theme." It was a subject she was quite familiar with.

"This song was a real stretch for me and I'm really proud of how it came out," Bonnie said. "The writer, Veyler Hildebrand, played bass with my pal Danny O'Keefe for years, and with me briefly around this time. He played me this song one day and I was so blown away I had no choice but to record it. One of the most starkly honest songs about feeling this particular way,"

Again mining the exciting R&B catalog of Motown hits, Bonnie whipped into Mary Wells's 1961 smash "Bye Bye Baby." With Rick Morotta's jangling Motor City–style percussion and a steller harmonica solo by Paul Butterfield, this was another fitting tribute to the great Motown divas.

Reaching even further back into rock and roll's archives, Bonnie next sang Little Richard's 1957 hit "The Girl Can't Help It." Little Richard originally performed this sexy song in the 1956 Jayne Mansfield rock and roll film of the same name. Here, it becomes Raitt's sizzling "The Boy Can't Help It." The center of the song effectively turns into a National Steel Slide Guitar solo for her, and she works it! This is another of the album's top numbers.

"(I Could Have Been Your) Best Old Friend" is a blues number, in which Bonnie again uses her slide guitar to express her emotional depths. This cut is the only song on the album that includes her trusty bass player, Freebo. To date, this is his last studio recording on one of Raitt's solo albums. Bonnie's voice is shown off at its most gravelly. She had finally grown into the very adult blues singing she had been performing since she was a teenager.

Rolling into Robert Palmer's "You're Gonna Get What's Coming," she gives this hot cut her strongest rock and roll performance to this date. Raucous and sung with high voltage energy, Raitt opened up the flood gates and proved that she could totally rock out with the best of them.

The album ends with the blues ballad "(Goin') Wild for You Baby." Carried by Bill Payne's electric piano and Oberheim synthesizer, Bonnie pours her heart out on this song of devastation and the depression of desertion. Waddy Wachtel makes his guitar sing on this fitting blues closing to *The Glow,* one of Bonnie's all-time best albums.

Discussing the album, Bonnie explained, "I think 'Goin' Wild for You Baby' is my favorite. . . . It's got a quiet soulfulness to it, and some of the deepest words I've ever sung. It gets me every time I hear and sing it."

She was also careful about keeping some sense of a live studio performance in her singing. "We tried not to make *The Glow* slick. I did all the vocals on the first or second take, but there must be some reason why people didn't take to it—'the vibes' or something. The combination of Peter and I looked promising, even though it was surprising, since I try hard *not* to have a polished veneer."

Utilizing some of the best musicians who had graced James Taylor's and Linda Ronstadt's multi–Platinum albums, the sound was brilliant. Don Grolnick on the piano and Waddy Wachtel, along with recording engineer Val Garay, were all staples on Linda's albums. Even background singer Kenny Edwards, who had performed with Linda in the sixties group the Stone Poneys [sic], sang background on several of the cuts on *The Glow.*

However, unlike Taylor's and Ronstadt's almost concurrent releases, Raitt's was far less successful in sales, airplay, and chart figures. The album peaked on the charts at number 30— five points lower than *Sweet Forgiveness,* and, sadly, it failed to sell enough copies to be certified Gold. The album's one hit single, the rocker "You're Gonna Get What's Coming" only made it to number 73 in *Billboard.*

The one bright spot came in January 1980, when Bonnie received her first Grammy nomination for "You're Gonna Get What's Coming." It was one of the competitors for the newly created category Best Rock Vocal Performance, Female. However, the award went to Donna Summer, for her multimillion-selling disco-rocker "Hot Stuff."

Bonnie would later explain, "I like [*The Glow* album] but a lot of people have told me that it seemed colder than it should have been." As she suspected she might, Raitt received some reviews that complained that the record was her least raw sounding album, and that she had lost some of her edge. On the other hand, some people felt that it showed her off at her best.

Bonnie admitted, "It's a drag to work on something for a year—selecting material, rehearsing, recording, mixing, all that—and then to have it not sell. It does hurt. And it hurts to read certain reviews,"

In the whirlwind of all of this activity, Bonnie celebrated her thirtieth birthday on November 8, 1979. "I'm not Miss Party anymore. I still like to have a good time, but my responsibility to the [socially conscious political] movement has taken over," she claimed.

She added, "I'm pleased to be getting older. Everybody's settling down with mates, things aren't so crazy anymore. I've cleaned up my act. I started running. You hit thirty and you become aware that the things you do really can kill you. And, if you're involved in politics, you have to be really careful. Linda [Ronstadt] and I were talking about that last week. You have to be super clean all the time. One drug bust could undermine this whole [rock and roll political] movement."

Suddenly she was granting more press interviews, because she now had something more relevant than her career to discuss. She said, "I'm going to be doing a lot more interviews when I tour, because I have a lot more to talk about than just my new album. Of course, I'll answer questions about the music, but then I can talk about more important things—like nuclear power and the American Indian movement. *The Glow* is like the bait!"

Bonnie had a feeling that she was in the music business to

produce something more significant than just a Top Forty hit, or a Platinum album, and her way of thinking about her career and her degree of fame began to change. She said during this era, "I don't think I've done anything historically significant yet. But I think the way I live my life is gonna be more historically relevant than my particular music. The kind of things you do with your power are a lot more important."

When *The Glow* failed to live up to the sales expectations Warner Brothers had pinned on Bonnie, some changes clearly had to be made. While the album climbed the charts, Bonnie continued to tour the country playing to enthusiastic audiences. As far as she was concerned, she was doing exactly what she wanted with her life, and her mainstream political awareness was now fueling her on to new creative and personal heights.

7

Green Light

By the age of thirty-one, Bonnie Raitt had been a recording artist for nine years, and had produced seven finely crafted albums with distinctively different musical accents. From the jam-session country-blues-folk looseness of her debut album, through the big-city slickness of *Streetlights*, to the polished and rocking sound of *The Glow*, she had maintained her musical integrity and perfected her expressive singing and guitar playing. Yet mainstream success continued to elude her.

When the *No Nukes* album was certified Gold in 1980, it brought attention to her music and an awareness to her career that her own albums had not yet attracted. Appearing on the album with million-selling rockers like Bruce Springsteen and the Doobie Brothers made Bonnie Raitt a more high-profile star. While somewhat apprehensive about finding a huge breakthrough hit, she had begun to realize the value that commercial success carried, especially in light of her political aspirations.

She expressed her ambivalence, "I don't want a hit, but I

sort of want a hit. You see, before there wasn't any reason for me to need more money. But now there's a political reason. Like Jane Fonda, for example. She does a lot more movies than she has to, because she wants to raise money for the movement."

In 1980 Bonnie recorded two country and western songs that were included on the soundtrack album for the movie *Urban Cowboy.* The film, which starred John Travolta and Debra Winger, was a huge box-office success, and its music spurred a renewed interest in country music in general. The resulting album zoomed up the charts, and hit number 3 in *Billboard.* It was certified Platinum with over a million copies sold, and became the biggest selling and most successful album in which Bonnie had ever been involved.

The *Urban Cowboy* album stitched together the work of the rock world's most country-sounding stars with several of Nashville's top performers, circa 1980. In addition to Bonnie, the other rockers included on this album were Joe Walsh, the Eagles, Dan Fogelberg, Jimmy Buffett, Bob Seger and the Silver Bullet Band, Boz Scaggs, and the vocal duo of Linda Ronstadt and J. D. Souther. The country acts were Kenny Rogers, Mickey Gilley, Anne Murray, Johnny Lee, and the Charlie Daniels Band. Not only did the movie make mechanical-bull riding the year's hottest new fad, but its soundtrack introduced country fans to several of these rockers, and rock fans had their horizons broadened in a Texas-sized fashion as well.

The better of the two songs that Bonnie recorded for *Urban Cowboy* is "Don't It Make Ya Wanna Dance?" an uptempo number that finds her accompanied by a lively country swing band. Pedal-steel guitar, fiddles, and eighties Nashville sounding arrangements make this a natural transition for Bonnie. The stylistic closeness of country music and folk music presented a fitting segue into country for Raitt. The slower, country-blues Texas two-step beat of "Darlin' " also worked well with her expressive voice. These two successful songs suggested that a full country-western album could prove a viable possibility for Bonnie's next effort.

With two rockers on the *No Nukes* album, two country songs on *Urban Cowboy*, and *The Glow* on the charts, Bonnie was on three Top Forty albums in 1980. It was her most high-profile year yet.

In 1980 Bonnie's six-year relationship with Garry George ended. Their affair had basically run its course, and it was time to move on. She thanked him in the liner notes of *The Glow* "for standin' by the same old love." However, now that the new decade had begun, for Bonnie, it seemed like it was time for major changes in her life—politically, musically, and personally.

Bonnie had long been troubled by the dichotomy inherent in show business. When the curtain goes up at a concert and a performer appears on stage, a bad mood or a disaster in the singer's personal life suddenly has to take a backseat to entertaining the audience. "Sometimes I feel like a whore," she said, "No matter how depressed I am, I go out [on stage] and I'm okay. It's kinda like being . . . phony."

To be more true to herself she decided to focus on her favorite political causes. "I've always been political," Bonnie said. "I was raised in a Quaker family, and my parents were pacifists. But recently, the political part of my life has become much more important. I would say the music is about 40 percent of my life now, and the politics 60 percent."

She said, "I can imagine walking into a party now and having everybody walk away from me, 'cause they think I'm gonna ask them to do benefits. Don't get me wrong: I still like to have a good time, but changing the world is a lot more important to me."

In 1980 the film version of the *MUSE Concerts* was released under the title *No Nukes.* It was directed for film by Julian

Schlossberg and Danny Goldberg. Originally, the *No Nukes* documentary was expected to be the kind of hit the *Woodstock* film and album had been in the seventies. However that was not to be. In fact, the *No Nukes* documentary made no impression at all. Like the other participants in the film and the concerts, Bonnie was disappointed. "It's true that MUSE was not as successful as we had hoped because the film was promoted so badly. But in the long run it's going to make money. And I never feel frustrated about giving my time to causes I believe in. I *do* feel frustrated at the stupidity and ignorance and greed responsible for things like Three Mile Island [nuclear plant near-meltdown scare]."

Bonnie was at the height of her benefit-concert cycle in 1981. "I did six months of benefits for the Pacific Alliance and for Water for Life, which is a project to make people aware of the problems of radioactive waste, toxic wastes, and acid rain. The benefits are all tremendously successful in terms of raising consciousness and money. But I would like to see a really big group that can fill a giant arena for a week running donate one night to this, because I'm just making chicken feed, playing three-thousand-seat halls."

She also realized she had to somehow find a good balance between making music and being a political activist. "The political stuff often takes precedence," she said. "But it's not just the music on one side and the politics on the other. It's the whole thing: When the music's not happening then the politics suffer too. They feed off of each other. When I'm productive in one area it usually rubs off on the other."

Having made so many strong political statements lately, it was again time for Bonnie to return her concentration to her recording career. She had been exposing herself to some of the new stripped-down back to basics rock music that appeared at the time. Groups like Blondie and the Stray Cats were making a huge impression, and Bonnie intended to become part of that scene. "What I wanted this time out was a combination of the music I've been listening to recently: Billy Burnette, the Blasters, Rockpile, and the rock-a-billy New Wave scene," she said. "I knew I had to get away from the slick sound I had with the Peter Asher record."

Before starting her next album, Bonnie took off on a sabbatical, mainly since the past year had been such a busy one for her. "I needed a break," she claimed. "I went to visit friends in Tulsa, Oklahoma, and got involved in the music scene there, off and on over the past two years [1980–1982]. I was around people who were looking at music in a much more direct way. Tulsa is not big bucks. It's a little quiet town that has a lot of musical history. It's funkier, there's less traffic, less pressure, less *everything*. I really enjoyed getting away emotionally and musically—jamming, going to clubs, playing blues. I had my own little town, which you can't do in L.A. without everyone knowing that you're there. I became friends and played with a great band named Rockin' Jimmy Byfield and the Brothers of the Night, and a girl named Debbie Campbell, and got the spirit back that I had when I was first starting out in Boston, with a bunch of underdogs that weren't famous and couldn't get a [record] deal, but were playing stuff so much better than anything I was hearing on the radio."

Aligning herself with a new musical producer was another important element in Bonnie's rocking recipe for success. "I was looking around for a producer," she explained, "thinking I would either record in Tulsa or Muscle Shoals [Alabama]. And as usual, I started looking for material and came out to L.A. I met Rob [Fraboni] through some friends of mine who had worked with some of these Tulsa people. He was out at Shangri-La Studios in Malibu, where they did *The Last Waltz* [The Band's farewell documentary and album]."

She went to see Rob in action, and was impressed with what she discovered. "Rob was producing Ian McLagan's second solo album, which he was recording with The Bump Band. And, I loved the way Ian's record sounded. Plus, the band members all loved each other and were having a great time, and I thought, 'Gee, I wish I could make a record where everybody *chose* to work with each other,' as opposed to being chosen by me or a producer saying, 'You bring those three and I'll bring these three, and we'll see if they get along.' It was like a family situation." *Baby Come Back* (1963)

She was also impressed with the low-tech look and feeling in the studio. "There was the sound of the studio, which is why *Green Light* sounds a bit like the [Rolling] Stones. They use that same miking technique: for example, using one big room mike from far away, instead of millions of mikes on the drums. It's a real funky studio with hippie bedspreads on the wall, a 1969 board, I think—no digital this or that. There's not even any Dolby. They spent all their money on great old microphones. It was just the kind of situation I needed to feel more comfortable."

It was a complete musical change for Bonnie when she went into the recording studio in the summer of 1981. When she emerged from Shangri-la Studios in Malibu, California, she had produced her first album devoted entirely to rock and roll. Her *Green Light* album made it clear from the very start that Bonnie was onto something hot and fresh.

Explaining her transition into full-fledged rock star, Bonnie declared, "I was a little stung by the lack of response to *The Glow*. And I was disappointed by not being able to make a record that sounded the way I wanted it to sound. Moving to Shangri-la, I wanted to get back to the roots and to the funkiness I had on earlier records, even though I'm not crazy about how they sound. They sound like I was having a lot more fun than I really was. *Green Light* is the first album I actually had fun doing."

When the 1970s ended, the American and British music

scenes were drastically changing. The salsa-like disco music that defined much of the decade was suddenly "out," and a funkier rock-edged hybrid that called itself "dance music" took its place. Extravagant synthesizer-driven rock and roll, like the Electric Light Orchestra (ELO) and Yes, was being replaced with New Wave and punk rock. In the female singer arena, pop-folk-rockers like Cher, Bette Midler, Linda Ronstadt, and Carly Simon were now singing with stripped-down garage bands. The most successful recording was Ronstadt's Platinum smash, *Mad Love* (1980)—produced by Peter Asher.

Bonnie's musical transition occurred at the same time as the ending of her personal relationship with Garry George, and of her professional life with Freebo, her long-time bass and tuba player. Freebo performed his last concert date with Bonnie in early 1981. She then began utilizing the Malibu garage group, known as the Bump Band. The new four-piece rock band consisted of Ricky Fataar on drums, bass player Ray Ohara, Johnny Lee Schell handling drums and vocals, and ex-Faces member Ian McLagan on keyboards. She not only chose rocker Rob Fraboni to produce the album, he became romantically involved with her as well.

Bonnie claimed that her new band was partially responsible for allowing her to be freer while recording. She said, "I tend to worry too much, to analyze and anguish over everything. It's the businesswoman side of me. I manage my own affairs along with a team of people, but I pretty much make the decisions. That tends to make you look at things in a more serious framework. But then there's the side of me that likes to let go and party all the time. It's difficult to reconcile the two. Rob and the guys in the band helped to bring out the rebellious, crazy side of me."

The back-to-basics rock approach is evident from the first number, "Keep This Heart in Mind." Bonnie, presenting her rockingest vocal approach, attacks each song like a buzz saw—

sharp and ragged. Featuring Jackson Browne on background vocals, and Fleetwood Mac's Rick Vito on additional guitar, Raitt sets the tone of her most cohesive album on this great rocker.

Even Eric Kaz's "River of Tears" has wailing electric guitars. When Bonnie had done his tunes "Love Has No Pride" and "I'm Blowin' Away" on albums in the past, they were pensive ballads. Here, Bonnie and the Bump Band make this a slow rhythmic rock number. Her signature slide guitar completes the mournful blues feeling of the song.

"Willya Wontcha" is presented as a duet between Schell and Raitt. With McLagan's fifties/Jerry-Lee-Lewis-style piano, the ensemble jams on this one. According to Bonnie, "This song is one of the highlights of the album and our live shows. Written by Johnny Lee Schell, the other guitarist in my live band since '82, it's got that loose double-guitar-vocal raunch that's what I love about rock and roll."

She then takes Bob Dylan's "Let's Keep It Between Us" and turns it into a steamy blues/rock romp, with William "Smitty" Smith setting the mood on the organ. The Dylan song features Bonnie warning her lover not to treat her like "a slut," making it the perfect rock and roll "tough girl" vehicle for her.

"Me and the Boys," on which Bonnie sings about being on the highway for a joyride, is the album's high point. Extolling the merits of cruising around town with the night air in her hair, this rocker sounds like Bonnie is truly getting off on the music. Written by NRBQ member Terry Adams, "Me and the Boys" could have easily been the title cut to this light, message-free rock album.

Writing with Schell, Fataar, and Ohara, Bonnie again picked up her pen for the rollicking "I Can't Help Myself." Another jamming profession of love, Bonnie gets background singing support from 1990s country-rock star to-be, Vince Gill. Telling a lyrical tale of the men in her life, and the life in her

men, Raitt again sings of being a tough woman of self deter-
mination.

"Baby Come Back," from the songbook of reggae star
Eddy Grant, sounds like it was recorded during a party in the
studio. This was the kind of feeling that Bonnie wanted to cap-
ture on this album, and it takes the song to a celebratory height.
Since the album was recorded in a hippie-beach-house of a studio in Malibu, "Baby Come Back" reflects the fun-loving atmosphere of a raucous garage band on a roll.

The album ends with the title cut, "Green Lights," which
finds Bonnie in another rock and roll car song, this time with
her pedal to the metal. Again she sounds like she is in total command on this rock-a-billy showcase.

When the album was released in early 1982, Bonnie immediately drew great reviews for *Green Light*. *Stereo Review* her-
alded the album as "an all-out, aggressive, rollicking affair;
buoyant, emphatic, and charged with a Stones-like energy."
Rolling Stone wrote, "It's one of her best and cagiest records
ever; backed by a raucous, witty group of musicians." And,
People declared it "a scorcher LP."

No one was more pleased at the results of the album than
Bonnie. "I love it!" she said. "Johnny Lee Schell, the guitar
player, has obviously been influenced a lot by Keith Richards.
But it really hasn't been that sudden. There were inklings of the
direction I was going in all along: when I started standing up
in my shows about five years ago [1977] instead of sitting in a
chair; when I began to play the Gibson instead of the acoustic,
and then a Strat instead of the Gibson; when I moved my up-
tempo songs from the encore to the beginning of the set. . . . I've
been waiting my entire career to make this record, and I finally
got the right band with the right producer in the right studio.
It's the most productive experience I've ever had in the studio.
I had a ball.

"The last six months have been the best in my life—less

worrying and less pain. And to have a bunch of musicians that know each other and who would choose to play with each other over anybody else—it's been a pleasure!"

It amazed her that she had actually produced such a smash rock and roll album since she never really considered herself a rock singer. "I never thought I was a strong enough vocalist to sing over this kind of rock music without my voice being washed out by the band."

According to Bonnie, "The album shocked a few people. Well, a lot of my friends thought I had moved to the beach and turned into Gidget. But it's not like I suddenly became an airhead. I needed to lighten up a little bit, that's all. I was laughing all the time, having a lot of fun, hanging out at this funky old studio that had hippie blankets hanging from the ceiling. Now I'm getting some feedback from people who feel the same way that I do about rock and roll. Then there are other, more conservative friends whom I've known for years who still wish I was sitting in a chair playing acoustic guitar."

Again poised for superstar fame, Bonnie insisted, "I don't have any great aspirations to be Joni Mitchell or Jackson Browne and make a great artistic statement. I just want to have a good time—a great time. I'm not stupid. I'm not making records to be heard by three people. I'd like to have a hit, and so would Warner Brothers. Everybody in the business always says, 'Any minute now, Bonnie's gonna happen'—I've got the biggest 'any minute now' quotient of anybody in the business."

Bonnie claimed to be happy just to have a career. "I'm amazed that 200,000 or 300,000 people want to buy my record. I'm grateful that we draw as well as we do. All the people that come to see me year after year after year—I feel I have a pact with them!"

She was able to keep her success in perspective. She said, "In terms of fame, that brings you more influence and I would like to have more influence. I believe in the kind of music I do, and I'd like to be able to get more people to appreciate Howlin' Wolf and Sippie Wallace, and to listen to Little Feat and Jackson Browne. I hope this new record, for example, shows people that they should have more of a sense of humor about music. That it's funny to really rock out. I mean, this stuff gets me off!"

She also put her whole heart into lending her talent toward promoting Sippie Wallace's first new album in years, *Sippie.* Singing vocal accompaniments and adding slide guitar to three songs ("Woman Be Wise," "Suitcase Blues," and "Mama's Gone, Goodbye"), Bonnie enjoyed participating in this new LP by her blues idol. It was recorded in February of 1982—at Solid Sound Studios in Ann Arbor, Michigan.

Discussing Sippie's wise-woman-style blues, Bonnie said, "Sippie has always seen the struggle of the sexes with a sense of humor and compassion. She knows that freedom is the name of the game even though women have always had to answer to men."

According to Sippie, "There isn't anything I sing about that hasn't happened to me."

March 2, 1982, was officially proclaimed Sippie Wallace Day in Detroit. According to the mayor's proclamation, "[Her] life has been a moving drama of success and failure, heartbreak and pain, love and joy woven into the lyrics of her songs and expressed through her powerful, resonant voice."

In concert programs, Sippie's biography pointed out that she was a true pioneer, who "originally recorded in October 1923, and less than a year later a little-known cornet player by the name of Louis Armstrong was working in her studio band." It concluded with, "Sippie currently lives in Detroit and occasionally makes concert appearances as her health permits." It was Bonnie Raitt who gave eighty-three-year-old Sippie Wallace the impetus to continue to perform, and it was a labor of love for Raitt.

Recorded with Jim Dapogny's Chicago Jazz Band, the *Sippie* album has a Dixieland tone to it. Adding to the ragtime quality, pianist Jim Dapogny is heard playing on an authentic 1905 Baldwin concert grand. "Women Be Wise" finds Bonnie and Sippie trading off verses in a great studio version of this legendary classic. Bonnie's seductive slide adds nice accents to the two other cuts she appears on, and she sings a couple of solo lines, plus vocal accompaniment, on "Mama's Gone, Goodbye." While Sippie's enunciation could be sharper, this historic blues album (now available on CD) captures her classic 1920s blues singing approach. In addition to new versions of her own compositions like "Up the Country Blues" and "You Got to Know How," Sippie also sings Irving Berlin's "Say It Isn't So," and Palmer and Williams's "Everybody Loves My Baby," delivering them with sassy phrasing and a lot of intuitive pizzaz.

This was to be Sippie's big resurgence, and Bonnie was determined to do what she could to lend her time and energy to exposing Wallace's blues to a new generation of blues fans. In addition, Bonnie helped raise $45,000 to film a documentary about Sippie's life.

Helping Sippie out, Bonnie felt like a grateful pupil who was turning the spotlight on the woman who had inspired her and taught her the most about singing the blues. She derived a great deal of satisfaction from having a hand in this project.

She also learned many life lessons. One of the major lessons was on the subject of not self-destructing. Although Bonnie was still a few years away from dragging herself to an Alcoholics Anonymous meeting, she was seeing how Sippie could still have a satisfying musical career after the age of eighty. It would take a while for the lesson to sink in, but it was eventually to have a profound effect on her. According to Bonnie,

"Sippie constantly teaches me. She makes me want to not burn myself out."

Chicago Jazz Band leader Jim Depogny still teaches music theory at the University of Michigan in Ann Arbor. In a 1995 telephone interview, he recalled the evolution that led up to Sippie's Atlantic album. "When Sippie Wallace had a recovery after her stroke, her manager was asking around for some musicians who might back her up for some future performances. A couple of people gave him my name. We put together a group and toured a bit with Sippie. Fairly often we were the opening act for Bonnie, because she was nice enough to bring Sippie on these shows. So over a period of 1979 to 1986, I was basically Sippie's accompanist and arranger and band leader, at almost all of her performances—except when I had troubles because of a car accident—I did with her."

According to Peter Ferran, another member of the ensemble, "The band is James Dapogny's Chicago Jazz Band, and I'm playing clarinet and alto sax; Paul Klinger, another guy from [University of] Michigan is on trumpet; Rod McDonald is the guitar player, and Jim Dapogny is the piano player and the musical director. He did all of the arrangements, and he knows Bonnie a lot better than any of us because he spent more time with her. Actually, I think, including trying to talk her into recording an album of older jazz-based standards. The kind of album that Linda Ronstadt did a year or so later [*Lush Life* 1983] and sort of made it impossible for anyone else to do it."

In that way, does Ferran feel that Bonnie's career was eclipsed by Ronstadt at the time? "That was one of the impressions I had at the time," he replied in a 1995 interview.

Regarding his band's interaction with Bonnie Raitt from 1979 to 1982, Depogny explained, "We often did shows with Sippie, without Bonnie, but Bonnie would also find it possible to take us along as well."

Peter Ferran, who at the time taught theater and drama at

At twenty-five,
Bonnie's youthful
enthusiasm endeared
her to blues fans and
rock and roll fans
alike. According to
Bonnie, she was a
social drinker in
the seventies and
mid-eighties.
(*David Gahr
for Warner
Brothers
Records/MJB
Archives*)

Bonnie recorded her 1974 album *Streetlights* in New York City. She posed on Broadway with this trio while she steeped in the Manhattan ambiance. (*David Gahr for Warner Brothers/MJB Archives*)

While Bonnie headlined at Lincoln Center, her father, John Raitt, was one of the stars of *American Musical* (also known as *American Jubilee*) at the St. James Theatre.

At one time, Bonnie headlined in New York City at the prestigious Lincoln Center. (*Lincoln Center/MJB Archives*)

It cost only $6.50 to see Bonnie at Avery Fisher Hall in 1975. She was responsible for keeping her ticket prices at a range that was affordable to her fans.

When Bonnie's 1977 album *Sweet Forgiveness* came out, her record label gave her a huge promotional push. Her remake of the Del Shannon song "Runaway" from this album, became her first hit single. (*New York Times/MJB Archives*)

One of Bonnie's main trademarks throughout her career has been her ability to masterfully play the slide guitar. She is known for her guitar playing musicianship as well as for her emotion-packed singing. (*Chuck Pulin/Star File*)

Throughout her first decade as a recording star, Bonnie was always accompanied by her trusty bass and tuba player, Freebo. This 1978 photo captures them at the height of their musical interaction. (*Chuck Pulin/Star File*)

Bonnie's involvement in the 1979 MUSE concerts really galvanized her political activism and put her on the same stage at Madison Square Garden as the Doobie Brothers, Carly Simon, and James Taylor. (*Joel Bernstein for Asylum Records/MJB Archives*)

Her rousing version of "Runaway" was one of the biggest hits of the *No Nukes* album and movie that was made from the MUSE concerts. (*Lynn Goldsmith for Asylum Records/MJB Archives*)

In the mid-eighties when Bonnie was in her late thirties, she was overweight, depressed, and without a record label. It signified her career's lowpoint. (*Chuck Pulin/Star File*)

In 1992, Bonnie, forty-two years old, was again in the Grammy winner's circle. She won this time for her album *Luck of the Draw*, which went on to sell over five million copies! (*Chuck Pulin/Star File*)

Charles Brown and Bonnie Raitt share the stage together at the sixth annual Rhythm and Blues Foundation's Pioneer Awards in Los Angeles. (*Mark Bego*)

Charles Brown, Mary Wilson, Wanda Young of the Marvelettes, Bonnie, and Little Richard share a laugh at the press conference for the Pioneer Awards. (*Mark Bego*)

Bonnie Raitt and Martha Reeves at the Rhythm and Blues Foundation press conference, March 2, 1995. (*Mark Bego*)

An all-star line-up was on hand to bring attention to the Pioneer Awards: Mary Wilson, Charlie Brown (behind), Inez Foxx, Bonnie, Fats Domino, Little Richard, Lloyd Price, Martha Reeves, Charles Foxx, and Katherine Anderson Shiffer of the Marvelettes. (*Mark Bego*) the University of Michigan, explains, "I can remember when we were first working in the band that was in the process of being put together to back Sippie Wallace. It was because both Bonnie and this guy from Detroit—Ron Harwood—had sort of rediscovered Sippie. And, Ronny Harwood had decided that he was going to be her manager, so he got himself all ingratiated with Bonnie Raitt, and the whole organization, too. But he's a real jerk. In fact, the album that we made for Atlantic, he produced it—not Atlantic—and he never paid us. Jim Dapogny is the guy who lost the most on it."

Ferran continued, "When we were first doing this, we thought we would try out the band with Sippie at the Royal Oak Theater in Detroit—Royal Oak. We did a couple of other gigs in the area, one of which was at Hill Auditorium, and another one was in Lansing. That would have been in the summer of '80. Anyway, that was enough to make Bonnie decide to take Sippie and the band on two different legs of her tour of 1981, in the summer—July and August or September. We did four or five things on the East Coast—including someplace outside Washington—and a last-minute David Letterman appearance, when he was on [TV] in the morning, and Lennox, Massachusetts—Tanglewood—with broken down vans. Central Park, too, that was another place that we worked. And later that summer—in September—we did the West Coast thing, which was two things in Berkeley, with John Raitt coming up onstage at the conclusion, with everyone coming up onstage and singing 'Oklahoma.' "

According to Ferran, "From my point of view we [the Chicago Jazz Band] were the old guys here—we were the old moldy musicians. Bonnie's band had all of these hip, cocaine-taking guys, who were playing rock and pop and stuff like that, and they didn't know 'Oklahoma.' We knew 'Oklahoma,' and they didn't, so we were out there jamming behind John and Bonnie as they were singing 'Oklahoma,' in the Greek theater in Berkeley—outdoors. From there we flew to Los Angeles and played two nights at Universal Amphitheater. That was very very hip—big stuff. But the night before that we played in a guitar shop in Santa Monica—a jazz joint whose name now escapes me. And we went up to Santa Barbara, at the county stadium that they had up there. Those were the brief and separated acquaintances we all had with Bonnie Raitt.

"I remember her as being very very pleasant, and very very nice, a naturally very sweet person. Not at all condescending or patronizing toward us. In fact, we were all in love with her, because she was very very pretty, very very talented, and thirty-years-old, and we were not. I was forty-three at the time, and she just looked terribly enticing and witty, smart, could talk about things, not just entertainment. She could think, and that's what appealed to us. And she just handled this thing very nicely. It was very pleasant to be on tour with her. And it was the source of a lot of subsequent points with everyone else: 'Oh, yeah, the summer I was on tour with Bonnie Raitt.' We were properly ironic and self-conscious about that. We were not professional musicians. We were not doing this for a living, this was all avocational for all of us, except for Jim Depogny."

Like so many of Bonnie's musician friends, Peter Ferran claims that Raitt is one of the most ego-free music stars he has ever encountered. Often, he says, she turned the concert into an onstage party, adding, "One of the things that Bonnie did with the musicians in Sippie's band, was invite us to come onstage late in her act and join the band in a jam session on the tune called 'Give It Up,' which was a big, long, extended blues, and had this nice rocking tubey feel to it. We played a lot of jazz choruses on that, all three of us—trombone, trumpet, and me—I was playing soprano sax. I remember that very nicely."

"Several nights we were sitting up 'til all hours in somebody's motel room, gassin'—drinking. We drank, but she didn't seem like she was blown by it there. She was very congenial. It didn't seem like a problem at all. She looked real healthy. She didn't look like she was strung out at all. She was partying a lot, but she was thirty-years-old. She was energetic and had a lot of stuff. I suppose she was also still young enough to think that she was indestructible."

Peter Ferran recalls Bonnie's band in the early eighties, right before she started using the Bump Band. "Freebo was the bass-tuba player who didn't belong on this Earth, because he is not of this Earth. Her boyfriend at the time was the piano player, a very good piano player." According Ferran, Bonnie's manager, Dick Waterman was still directing her career. "I remember Dick Waterman, he was one of the people who I think talked her out of doing that jazz-standards album with Jim Dapogny. He didn't think that was going to help her much at the time. I never really liked him, I thought he was a calculating bastard, but that was just my opinion. Just that he was all business, and smooth and oily and all that."

Describing the evolution of the *Sippie* album, Depogny explains, "Ron Harwood, Sippie's manager got this contract with Atlantic, and he asked Bonnie if she would help by appearing on it. And Bonnie, who was a big fan of Sippie's—and also a nice person to boot—said she would. So, basically, we used my touring band, which toured with Sippie, to make that album and Bonnie came in and was added to those three tracks. The one track, 'Woman Be Wise,' was just Bonnie and Sippie, and that was nothing but Bonnie playing a guitar. What she did was absolutely perfect. And the other two tunes, we just added Bonnie to. These were things we had performed, and performed subsequent to that too, on the road with Bonnie and Sippie. So, Bonnie came in and just sort of dropped in her part. My recollection of it was that it was extraordinarily easy."

According to the liner notes on the back of the *Sippie* album, the entire LP was recorded on Valentine's Day 1982. Depogny denies this, explaining, "No, that's not true, it was actually done over two days. It was done quickly, and the album doesn't contain everything we recorded. Ron and I thought a couple of things weren't quite perfect, and so they weren't on there. But, my recollection of it was that it went quite easily, and certainly, what Bonnie had to do went easily, because she just absolutely nailed everything, because she was perfect." By record industry standards, to record an entire studio album in just two days is incomparably impressive!

Was Bonnie's participation in the album used as bait for Atlantic Records to sign Sippie to a recording contract? "I would imagine," was Ferran's observation.

When I commented on Raitt's obvious respect for Sippie, Peter Ferran responded, "Oh, yeah, and learned a lot from her, too. She sang her songs and learned about certain kinds of blues feeling. She had a lot of respect for us, too, as musicians. That's another thing that impressed me. She was willing to take us on our own merits, although we didn't play or appreciate the kind of stuff she did necessarily."

Both Depogny and Ferran still speak glowingly of Bonnie's professionalism on stage and in the studio. According to Depogny, "One of the things that has occurred to me is how Bonnie is about her music the way that I am. At the same time that she has a great deal of fun, she's serious about getting it right. That combination is what for me pays off. In listening to her, it's perfectly clear that it is these two things, which I think are necessary to make anything work. That it has to be peculiarly schizophrentic in that regard."

Depogny added, "I'm a traditional jazz pianist, and I play minority-within-a-minority music, and it's sort of tangential to what Bonnie herself is interested in. Bonnie, I think, is an awfully nice friend to have. As a musician, I think, maybe, some people don't realize how good she really is. She's certainly a wonderful singer, but she's a good player too, and I often wonder if people realize how well she plays. But she's also very professional. She's very fast about learning things, and very quick to sense what needs to be done. She's just a joy to work with because of that."

In another impressive musical display, Bonnie recorded the duet "Ladies' Nite" on jazz vocalist Michael Franks's 1982 *Objects of Desire* album. Her lush jazz singing with Franks exposed her to still another audience as she stretched her wings musically. Her vocalizing on this cut is slinky and playful, and makes one hypothesize about her some day doing an all-jazz album.

Like *The Glow* before it, *Green Light* could have been another sales breakthrough album for Bonnie. She was proficiently performing the kind of straight-forward rock and roll that was selling at the time. Peaking at number 38 on the charts, *Green Light* did become her third largest selling album while at Warner Brothers.

In January 1983 Bonnie was honored with a Grammy Award nomination for the album *Green Light.* Again, she was nominated in the category Best Rock Vocal Performance, Female. However, it was Pat Benatar's *Shadows of the Night* that ultimately took the award.

Now, at the age of thirty-three, Bonnie was thrilled by the in-concert reception that her new rock and roll album had received. The Grammy nomination was encouraging, too. However, she was receiving mixed signals from her record company. Although she was excelling musically, they seemed to be unable to break her albums through to a wider audience, or to garner airplay for her singles.

It was almost as if Warners released the album and let it flounder on its own. There were no videos filmed, minimal TV exposure, and just a very slight promotional push. With so many new acts on the charts, like Joan Jett and the Blackhearts, Culture Club, and the Go-Go's, Bonnie seemed to be getting lost in the shuffle.

However, Bonnie was excited with, and encouraged by, her new rock and roll sound and with her new band. It would probably take one more album to really maximize her new eighties rock audience. With that, rocking Raitt and her Bump Band began to make plans for her projected next album, *Tongue in Groove.*

8

Too Long at the Fair

$\mathcal{A}$ ccording to myth, it is possible to live your life in seven-year cycles. Seven years of good luck can be followed by seven years of bad luck. The years between 1982 and 1989 were among the rockiest ones for Bonnie Raitt. It was during this period that she experienced serious problems as a result of her heavy social drinking and her hard-partying lifestyle. She gained weight, eventually adding over thirty pounds to her once-svelte frame. She got out of shape, battled with her record label, and cruised through the bulk of her savings account to keep her career afloat. In addition to being an emotionally trying period, however, it was also the era of some of her most adventurous career moves. This artful dodging included performing on a rap record, planning an album with Prince, recording on a Disney album, singing in the Soviet Union, and joining an all-star backup band for rock legend Roy Orbison.

Bonnie was so happy with her new rock band, and the sound that they had come up with on *Green Light*, that she was eager to return to the recording studio to do a follow-up LP. Originally entitled *Tongue in Groove*, this recording resulted

in numerous problems. She again used Rob Fraboni as the producer, with her Bump Band playing behind her. They again
recorded the album at Shangri-la Studios in Malibu. Several
guest musicians also participated, including Sippie Wallace, and
Christine McVie of Fleetwood Mac. However, when Bonnie
played the resulting tapes for Warner Brothers Records, they
did not like her approach on many of the songs. Trying to keep
in step with the changing music scene, Bonnie had stretched out
stylistically. She had blended elements of reggae and ska into
her rock and roll blues numbers.

Although she did not agree entirely with Warner's complaints, she rerecorded and remixed some of the tracks to comply with the record company's critique. The day after Bonnie
finished the second version of the album, the record label announced that they had dropped her from their roster. She was
in shock.

Along with Bonnie, Warners also dropped several other
big-name artists who weren't creating big hits at the time. They
included Van Morrison and Arlo Guthrie. In each of their contracts, Warner Brothers had retained the option to drop the
artists if their albums didn't sell a certain amount of copies.
Bonnie fell into this category. Raitt explained in 1990, "There
was a corporate sweep, coming from upstairs, and they needed
to trim the fat. I had just completed an album called *Tongue in
Groove*, which was produced by Rob Fraboni, who had also
done *Green Light*. And I don't think they maliciously said,
'Let's let her finish her album and get the tour all lined up and
print the covers and hire the people to do the video and then
drop her.' You know, ha, ha, ha. But that's what they did. It
was literally the day after I had finished mastering it. I had already finished the album once, and [Warner's claimed] the
Jerry Williams tune would be more commercial if it didn't have
quite as reggae a beat. Or something like that. So I went in and
redid it. I thought if I cooperated a little more, maybe they'd

promote the album more. But instead they dropped me and pulled the rug out from under my tour. I thought the way they did it was real crummy. They sent a letter. I think I suffered from not having a relationship with the A&R department there, because I had an independent production deal."

Besides being hurt by this move, she was also furious with herself for having signed with Warner Brothers and not having moved to Columbia Records when she had the chance. Since she had recorded and released "Runaway" in 1977, Bonnie had failed to produce another hit single. At the time, all of the record companies were reporting losses—even usually successful Columbia. In fact, if it hadn't been for the Columbia Record Club—the company's mail-order record and tape division—Columbia Records would have had to report huge losses for 1981 and 1982. Bonnie was a victim of the economic climate in the record business, as well as of her own creative frustration. When *The Glow* and *Green Light* had not become huge hit albums as expected, she found herself without a label, and with very little bargaining leverage.

"They barely promoted *Green Light.* I thought they should have been more supportive if I re-signed with them. But who knows? I guess if they don't like where you are going, they have the right to terminate you. They told me I can take the tapes and shop them around. But they wanted about $500,000 for them, and nobody wanted to pay that much."

Hurt, mad, and frustrated over technically being "fired" by her record label for not selling enough product, she was stunned by the rejection of being dumped by Warners after eight albums and ten critically acclaimed years in the record business. It made her take a good look at her career, and where she wanted it to go in the future.

"Nobody wants to be disliked," she admitted, "and I have a big streak of that, as do most performers. I had to look at the question of what happened with Warner Brothers, and why I wasn't breaking through. I don't care about Madonna-level superstardom. I don't pretend to be deserving of great accolades and be the major spokesperson of my generation or the best white-girl blues singer. I reach people that I reach, and I don't reach people that I don't reach."

During this traumatic time in the early eighties, along with Bonnie's new rock and roll sound came even more rock and roll partying. She continued with her drinking and recreational drugging, which helped dissipate some of the pressure she felt she was now under. Looking back, Bonnie said, "It wasn't until about 1983 when I really messed up."

For a while it seemed like everything for which she had worked so relentlessly was falling apart. She said, "When *Green Light* wasn't promoted, it was kind of heartbreaking for me and Rob and the band, who had worked so hard on it. And then to make the next record and then be dropped. . . . We spent a lot of time on that record, and then we had no album. I just went out on the road anyway and went through my savings because I felt responsible to my career and to them. But it can really eat into a relationship when you are involved with someone you work with and the world is not reinforcing your work together."

Bonnie and the Bump Band continued to tour through 1983 and 1984. Finally, the pressure of Bonnie's career disappointments capsized her affair with Rob Fraboni in 1985. He had received an offer from Chris Blackwell of Island Records, which meant moving to New York. Bonnie wanted to stay in California. Their relationship officially ended. Then Bonnie was really depressed. She felt she was experiencing rejection from all sides. "It was a love affair that just ran its course," she said. "But it was a real hurtful breakup, and I felt like a failure. I couldn't stand myself."

Bonnie also had to dissolve the band, since she could no longer afford to pay them. She continued to perform, with only

Johnny Lee Schell playing behind her. "To put it mildly," she recalled, "there were a couple of painful aspects of the splitup that—coupled with the fact that I was not in the best state emotionally and physically—and it just broke me down. I mean, I stayed on the road, playing acoustic sets."

Bonnie was in a downward spiral and couldn't seem to stop her descent. "I was heartbroken," she says. "The political thing didn't work out—I didn't save the world. I did the best job I could for Warners and they didn't seem to appreciate it. I had problems in my personal life. I lost a sense of myself and let partying take over and numb the pain I was feeling."

On January 23, 1985, Bonnie appeared at Arie Crown Theatre in Chicago as part of an all-star musical memorial for folk performer Steve Goodman. Among other songs, she sang a stirring version of John Prine's "Angel From Montgomery," as a duet with Prine. It was included on the album *Tribute to Steve Goodman*, which was released on Red Pajama Records later that year.

She said, "Over the years, John and I have sung this song so many times—but to sing it together that night for Stevie, surrounded by so many other musicians and friends who got together to celebrate not just his life, but the power and timelessness of a good song sung with just an acoustic guitar. It makes me so proud and grateful to be a part of that tradition."

The following year, the album *Tribute to Steve Goodman* won a Grammy Award in the category Best Contemporary Folk Recording. In 1990 this version of "Angel From Montgomery" was included on the album *The Bonnie Raitt Collection*.

In late 1985 Bonnie joined the stars participating in a fundraising recording called "Sun City." To date, this is the only time she has ever recorded a rap record. Recorded and released to raise funds and political consciousness about apartheid in South Africa, Bonnie performed with several of the world's top rock stars under the umbrella name Artists United Against Apartheid. Bonnie's one solo line of rap verse declares the time has now come for everyone to accept their responsibility in ending apartheid—to a blasting rap beat. Among the other music stars on this nine-and-a-half-minute twelve-inch vinyl single are Pat Benatar, Jackson Browne, Jimmy Cliff, Bob Dylan, Peter Gabriel, Daryl Hall, Herbie Hancock, Nona Hendryx, Eddie Kendricks, Darlene Love, John Oates, Lou Reed, David Ruffin, Bruce Springsteen, Ringo Starr, Pete Townsend, Bobby Womack—and over two dozen more top acts. It was produced by Little Steven Van Zandt (of Bruce Springsteen's E Street Band) and mix master Arthur Baker.

At the time, Bonnie explained, "One of the projects that I've been involved in lately, that is kind of a good melding of music and politics is the 'Sun City' project [which entailed recording artists refusing concert bookings in racist South Africa]. Little Steven and Jackson Browne called me up to participate. I really enjoyed doing that project. The day that we taped it, Miles Davis came in the same time as me, which is definitely one of the more interesting pairings that I've ever had in the studio. As a matter of fact, when we shot the video, some of it was done in New York, and some of it was done [in Los Angeles]. The day that they were taping us, they had to get the people in California, I was in the studio and couldn't get back East, so I got to tape my part with George Clinton and Clarence Clemmons, and I think it's terrific that the music and artistic communities rallied behind some of these causes, because they've been lazy in the past."

"Sun City" became a very important record when it was released in late 1985. It peaked on the U.S. charts at number 38, and on the U.K. charts at number 21. As one of the many singing stars seen on the accompanying video, it helped keep alive Bonnie Raitt's public presence, and marked her first music-video appearance on MTV.

Unhappy about not having a record label or a boyfriend, Bonnie was depressed and continued to eat and drink excessively. Explaining her drinking problem, she later said, "I only got loaded after the gigs with a close circle of friends. I didn't want to get loaded in public. I cared about my career. I have too much pride to let people see me like that in public. But I did look bad. I had put on about forty pounds. And it actually got to the point that someone once asked me when the baby was due. And another time, a guy in Louisiana passed a really sweet little note up to the stage, saying, 'What happened? You got fat. Maybe you should work out or something.' "

She began wallowing in her own unhappiness. At the age of thirty-six, she felt like life was passing her by, and that she had no control over any of the variables. "I didn't care," she recalls, "I didn't care because I must have felt I deserved how unhappy I was. The thing about the addictive personality is that you have some kind of weird combination of cockiness and insecurity. In my case, I'm singing as well as these other people who are on the radio. You know, I would listen to me sing these beautiful Eric Kaz songs and go, 'God, that's as moving as Emmylou's record.' And the other side of it was that 'maybe they all know something that I don't know, that I'm not very talented or I'm superficial or shallow.' But I was just in too much pain or too angry to care whether I was going to die. I think that being addicted makes you not care. What interests me is that I think most people either get busted, have a drunk accident, run out of money and lose everything, or make fools of themselves. I didn't do any of that. I just got fat."

Just when she was feeling herself at a career low-point, Warner Brothers Records announced that they were preparing to release Bonnie's *Tongue in Groove* album, which had been produced two years earlier. When Bonnie heard the news, she became quite upset. She recalls, "Warners said they were going to put the record out. I said it wasn't really fair. I think at this point they felt kind of bad. I mean, I was out there touring on my savings to keep my name up, and my ability to draw was less and less. So they agreed to let me go in and recut half of it."

Released in August 1986, *Nine Lives,* as the album came to be titled, was a very different album for Bonnie. First of all, it was her only Warner Brothers album that did not have her photo on the cover. She had been gaining weight, and judging by some of the low-self-esteem statements that Bonnie has made about this era of her life, she must have preferred the cartoon of her on the cover to a photograph. Lindsey Loch's woodcut-looking artwork on *Nine Lives* is cute and colorful, depicting orange-haired Bonnie and her green guitar jumping into the azure blue sky in front of a music saloon. A cartoon version of her tour bus was on the back of the album. Inside of the original vinyl release are two photographs of Bonnie by Jim Shea, both shot in slimming silhouette.

More significantly, the music contained on Bonnie's ninth and last new album for Warner Brothers is clearly the product of three totally different production teams. The first five cuts on the album were newly recorded in 1986, with Bonnie's Little Feat pal Bill Payne and George Massenburg producing and with master session drummer Russ Kunkel assisting on one of the songs. Steve Terrell produced the sixth song, which was recorded for use in the film *Extremities,* and the final four cuts were left over from the *Tongue in Groove* sessions, produced by Rob Fraboni. Each session carries its own distinctive sound. The first five songs are contemporary rock, number six is synthesizer rock, and the final four are similar to back-to-basics rock à la *Green Light.*

Bonnie said at the time, "In the past, I've used really pretty much garage-band-sounding records—which I like—so half the record is kind of that sound, and the other half has got some of the more modern sounds, but it also has the great Tower of Power Horns on a couple of songs. Like I feel about all of my records, I'm really proud of this one, and I hope everybody likes it!"

"No Way to Treat a Lady" kicks off the album, and it's a sharply performed progressive rocker. Written by Bryan Adams and Jim Vallance, the lyrics carry that kind of "I'm-not-gonna-take-it-anymore" stance that Bonnie is so good at portraying. As eighties contemporary as the concurrent releases by Pat Benatar, Cyndi Lauper, and Heart, this crisp-sounding rocker was an obvious bid for a commercial hit.

"As a Bryan Adams fan, I was really glad when I got ahold of this song," Bonnie said. "I sing a lot of songs for women who've 'had it,' and this is a powerful dose of that feeling. Michael Landau's guitar playing has been the secret punch to a lot of great records and he really makes this one for me."

"Runnin' Back to Me" also has a high voltage rock edge to it—nicely accented by the Tower of Power Horn Section. Bonnie is one of the four guitar players on this cut, which features Bill Payne's exciting keyboards. A brilliantly hard rocker with Richard Elliot's blasting sax solo, this is one of the album's finest cuts.

According to Bonnie, " 'Runnin' Back to Me' is one of my favorite rockers on the record. It was written by a friend, Karla Bonoff, and Ira Ingbar, and we got to use the Tower of Power Horns on that one, and it's one of my favorite tunes on the whole record. I think it really kicks."

Bonnie slows down the pace for the R&B number "Who But a Fool (Thief Into Paradise)." A jazzy, medium tempo ballad, she adds her slide-guitar touches, and joins in on the background chorus, which also features Ivan Neville, whose father, Aaron, is one of the Neville Brothers.

Bonnie says, "When people ask me what my favorite album is out of the nine, or what my favorite song is on this one, I feel like a mother that's not supposed to say that I like one kid over the other, but I'm partial to 'Who But a Fool.' This is a song that I first heard a few years ago. It's got that kind of slinky feel, that R&B-rock kind of feel. It's a song that could appeal to a lot of different tastes, and that's how we came up with 'Who But a Fool.' "

A slow rocking beat characterizes "Crime of Passion," while "All Day, All Night" bounces along to a bopping reggae beat. This was to be her last album for Warners, and she wanted to cover all of the bases. Says Bonnie, "People like myself, who fall into the cracks between rhythm and blues and rock and roll, a lot of times radio stations had a rough time trying to figure out where to play us. There's a lot of competition out there, but there's still room for R&B to make a great comeback. There's an awful lot of great musicians that haven't gotten their due yet. I wouldn't only want to do ballads, or only do blues, or only do R&B, or only do rock and roll. It's just kind of a nice blend when you mix them all together."

"Stand Up to the Night" was a unique song for Bonnie. It has sort of an "urban contemporary" feeling to it. The number is dominated by synthizers. The song was originally recorded for the soundtrack of the movie *Extremities,* which is about a woman who is attacked by an intruder and then physically gains control and extracts revenge. The strong-woman stance of the lyrics appealed to Bonnie. Of its evolution, Raitt elaborated, "I was first approached by Steve Terrell, who works with Barry Mann, a great songwriter, to try to get some music together for this Farrah Fawcett film called *Extremities,* and I heard the song, and I really liked the synthesizer sounds, and I liked the lyrics, I liked the message. It was a very powerful song to sing. I think the message of 'Stand Up to the Night,' definitely goes with the female movie."

The last four songs were rockers from the unreleased *Tongue in Groove* project, and carry the early eighties stripped-down rock approach. Jerry Williams's composition "Excited" has an energetic hard rocking feel to it, and "Freezin' (For a Little Human Love)" is also a fun rock song about traveling around town looking for a new love. Along the way, Bonnie weighs her odds, including flirting with her auto mechanic.

"True Love Is Hard to Find" is pure calypso-reggae, complete with Sippie Wallace's sassy repartee in the background. Bonnie explained, "I've always loved Toots and the Maytals, and this song is a particular gem. The acoustic guitar added a nice touch over Ian Wallace's killer drumming. My favorite part, though, is Sippie's improvising at the end. Just imagine this eighty-one-year-old blues singer in a pair of headphones, nodding her head to a modern reggae beat, and you get the picture."

The album ends with a beautiful emotionally somber ballad called "Angel." It was written by Eric Kaz, who had given Bonnie such gems in the past as "Love Has No Pride" and "Cry Like a Rainstorm." Mainly carried by Bonnie's plaintive voice, and Kaz's piano, Stevie Nicks would probably have loved to have recorded this song first. Stevie's Fleetwood Mac partner Christine McVie is heard on the etherial background tracks. It's a Bonnie trademark to end the album with a slow, sad song, and this is one of her best.

Bonnie did her best to promote the album when it was released and appeared on several radio shows. She said at the time, "I think that this album—although it's got different production styles—basically covers the things that I wanted to say, and a lot of the music that I want to sing. I think that when I hear a song that says something that I have to sing, and you work with good people, it can't help but be a good record.

"This is my ninth album, and, you know, you can kill a cat eight times, and still have it come back. It's basically a little 'wink' to surviving. I called it *Nine Lives,* and being my ninth album, and having the myth attached to it, I thought that was an appropriate title. On all nine albums, there's usually a blend of covers of R&B songs, there's some rock and roll, there's some songs by some of the best songwriters around today.

Everything basically has kind of an R&B feel to it. We picked four cuts—put the soundtrack song on, which Warners likes, and everyone likes too—and then we did five new songs. Nothing makes a record sound less like something I would want to do than if it's overdubbed to death."

She continued, "I believe in live recording as much as possible, and sometimes you can get a real live sound in the studios with some of these effects that they're using. I think you should have the right sound, the right singer, the right musicians, and then just kill it!"

The album was released in September 1986 without much fanfare. Since the 1982 release of Bonnie's *Green Light* album, the contemporary music scene had entirely changed. MTV began broadcasting on August 1, 1981, and was viewed as an interesting curiosity at first. However, by 1983 most American cable TV services carried it, and the channel became a huge hit by programming music videos twenty-four hours a day, every day of the year. It wasn't long afterward that the era of the million-dollar music video had arrived, and suddenly, if you weren't on MTV, you weren't anywhere on the music charts. Madonna became the first new artist who broke into the Top Ten on the strength of her videos.

In 1986 the same Warner Brothers Records promotion and publicity departments that were responsible for promoting Bonnie Raitt's *Nine Lives* album were busy working on Madonna's number-1 album, *True Blue,* and Prince's Platinum-selling *Parade—Music From Under the Cherry Moon.*

Bonnie never made a video to support any of the songs on *Nine Lives.* Unknown to MTV, except for her brief "Sun City" appearance, she consequently received almost no publicity for the album's release. As a result, the album peaked on the charts at number 115, which was quite a comedown from her three-in-a-row Top Forty albums (*Green Light*—number 38, *The Glow*—number 30, and *Sweet Forgiveness*—number 25). Only the music critics seemed to know Bonnie Raitt had a new album out. It was a disappointing way to end her fifteen-year association with Warner Brothers Records, but now it was truly over, and Bonnie went back to being a performer without a record contract, floating in space like the illustration of her on the cover of *Nine Lives.*

On November 1, 1986, her eighty-eighth birthday, Sippie Wallace died. She had once said, "If I was in the middle of dying, and someone said, 'Sippie, sing me a song,' I'd stop dying to sing that song." Her last recorded appearance came on Bonnie's "True Love Is Hard to Find."

Sippie's passing signified the end of Bonnie's hopes to finish her planned documentary about Wallace's remarkable life. It was Raitt's intention that the film should be released while Sippie was still alive. This was not to be.

"We just couldn't get any money to finish it," Bonnie said in 1988. "It's a very sad situation the way blues is treated in this country, I could go on for an hour on that. We started filming it ten years ago and ran out of money. And now Sippie's gone, so it's a little bit late. The lack of appreciation for the great traditional blues people, while they're still alive, is a very depressing state of affairs. It's a sociological dilemma that we have in this country: Nobody teaches about blues or black musical history in schools, so black people don't appreciate their own roots."

Right after *Nine Lives* was released, Bonnie again went on a concert tour. In December 1986 she headlined at the Beverly Theater in Los Angeles. She had just turned thirty-seven a month before. Long considered a "musicians' musician," Bonnie's shows drew a "who's who" of the music business. Prince, one of her biggest fans, attended her Los Angeles booking. He was so taken by her music that he offered her a record deal with his own label, Paisley Park.

As Raitt would explain, "What happened was, he had seen

my show at the Beverly Theater in L.A., in December of '86, and he called me up and said he was interested in working with me. He was renting a place in L.A., and he sent his private limo over to pick me up. I don't ride around in limos much, and this car had all kinds of neat stuff—all kinds of purple stuff and neat lighting and little porcelain masks. I didn't realize I'd be whisked away in a fairy tale. We got to know each other a little bit, and he told me he was starting a new record label and was interested in having me on it. I told him I was interested if it was a true collaboration and not just me singing his music— if we could meet somewhere in the middle."

Bonnie agreed to get together with Prince in Minneapolis after the first of the year. However, in January 1987 she went snow skiing, had an accident on the slopes, and had to recuperate for two months. During this sabbatical she took a hard look at her life and her career.

Looking back on this pivotal era in her life, she says, "It's true that I wasn't a mainstream Top Twenty artist, but I don't consider success that, and never really did, or else I would have gone after making more commercial records. I just think that the years in the eighties, my kind of music was off the radio. My old record company couldn't get me played, that in conjunction with the fact that my lifestyle in my mid-thirties— staying up and partying a lot—was showing up as a weight gain, and was showing up as getting sick and not being able to get better fast like you could when you were in your twenties— where you could bounce back from an all-nighter. You end up spending a lot of time wondering if you could be more productive, and being angry at other people for things that weren't happening in your life that were happening to them, that were caused by you. Making some lame choices in who to hang out with, and how many hours to hang out with them, and what hours of the day you would make those." In other words, her partying-till-the-sun-came-up days were about to end.

"I started looking around when I was thirty-five-years-old and going, 'You know, there seems to be a line here. Some people are moving toward getting married and having kids, and being healthy and writing songs. And these other people are doing the same thing, but their lives don't seem to be working. They look terrible, and they're not successful; they don't seem to be happy. They're kind of in a rut. It seemed that some changes needed to be made. I looked at myself and just felt that I wasn't being the best version of me as I could. I wasn't going to blame anyone other than myself."

Also in January 1987, while Bonnie was contemplating her past, present, and future, she was again nominated for a Grammy Award. She received the nomination in the category of Best Rock Vocal Performance, Female, for the song "No Way to Treat a Lady" from her *Nine Lives* album. Ultimately, red hot Tina Turner—still in her mid-eighties comeback sweep—took the award for her song "Back Where You Started."

"For a long time I had this rock and roll mama persona. But as I got older, drugs and alcohol weren't working—they beat you up too much," Bonnie says. "I had a skiing accident and I was sidelined for two months. I look back on it now, and I realize that it was really me asking to have an excuse to get off the road. I knew that I was not feeling great and not looking great."

Although she was overweight, depressed, and her self-esteem at its nadir, "I wasn't rolling around vomiting," she says. "I wasn't kicking and screaming into dementia, but I did have a complete emotional, physical, and spiritual breakdown."

Bonnie also faced a wave of pending financial problems. "There are people I know who party too much and don't get fat and don't stop, because they are still rich. But I was going to run out of money!"

Ultimately, her upcoming project with Prince pushed her

over the line. "I knew that if it were a successful collaboration, I would probably do a video with him, and frankly that was the thing that made me have enough self-respect to slap me into wanting to do something about it. And I knew there was a relationship between drinking too much and being heavy," she admitted. "It's one thing to go onstage if you're a little chunky, it's another to make a video with a guy who's known for looking foxy. I decided to lose weight, which you can't do if you're drinking all the time."

Feeling older than her thirty-seven years, she finally decided to attend an Alcoholics Anonymous meeting. "A couple of friends who were really close to me told me about a meeting, and they took me with them. And then I got a bicycle and went on a diet. And I've been sober ever since!" she exclaims. "Within about two weeks of starting AA, I felt like a different person. I used to just cry several times a day because I knew how lucky I felt." Although it was not a forced intervention, she had essentially been saved from the depths of depression.

Looking back on her newfound sobriety, Bonnie admits, "I just couldn't come up with any more excuses why I feel like this, and they feel like that. I thought, Maybe I should give this a try. I was one of the lucky ones, because I had some help. But at the time I started out, I don't think it was as 'in' to be straight, and now it's totally not 'in' to be messed up."

Her skiing injury and her two decades of drinking behind her, in April 1987 she flew to Prince's recording studio in Minneapolis for two days of work. It had been sixteen years since she had gone to Minneapolis to record her first album at the old abandoned summer camp. Since that time, Prince and his Paisley Park recording complex had redefined "the Minneapolis sound."

According to Bonnie, "The basic tracks were all done when I got there, and one day we worked together on a song. The next day I pretty much sang and played on my own with his engineer. He wrote some songs that were in the vein of what I would do, although not knowing what key I sing in, some of them were kind of low. It was really a preliminary collaboration, and he said, 'Let's get together in July when I get back from Europe.' But I was touring then, and his tour went on longer than he expected, and we ended up not doing anymore work together. And, in the meantime, I realized that I didn't want to be working for the Warner Brothers promotion staff, which was handling his label."

Looking at the whole situation with clear eyes, Bonnie began to have her doubts about the collaboration. None of the material she worked on with Prince was ever released. It wasn't that Bonnie and Prince purposely disbanded the project, it just sort of fizzled.

In the summer of 1987 Bonnie was indeed busy touring. On Saturday, June 20, I attended a Bonnie Raitt concert at a campsite in Croton-On-Hudson, in upstate New York. It was situated alongside the Hudson River, just north of Tarrytown. Although I was never much of a camping trip fan, when my friend Sue McDonald announced to me, "Bonnie Raitt's going to be there, she is the main act on Saturday afternoon," I began searching for a sleeping bag.

Victoria Green and I took a train from Grand Central Station on Friday night, and were met by Sue and her husband, Tom. The scene at the campground was a yuppie version of a sixties hippie event—lots of tie-dyed shirts and long-haired music fans in shorts and sandals—with designer camping gear.

There were several different makeshift wooden stages constructed in clearings in the trees in the park, with different acts performing simultaneously all day long. An hour before Bonnie was scheduled to perform, my three friends and I staked out a spot in the clearing, about twenty feet from the stage. We sat there on our newly-purchased camp chairs, reeking of Off mosquito repellent and caked in forest dust. There we awaited Ms. Raitt.

That afternoon she performed a great acoustic set, seated on the stage before us. She was accompanied by her bass player, Johnny Lee Schell, and she wove a mesmerizing spell. It was an intriguing and different setting in which to see her, especially since the only other concerts of hers I had attended were in Lincoln Center and Madison Square Garden. She looked relaxed, and was in good voice that day, performing her more folk-oriented songs like "Angel From Montgomery." Surrounding her, sitting in new camp chairs or cross-legged on towels, blankets, and sheets spread on the forest floor, were no more than two hundred people. For this particular clearing in the woods, it was a capacity crowd.

Later that year, Bonnie told a reporter from *Frets* magazine about her 1980s phase of performing all-acoustic shows. According to her, "I've been doing a lot of it the last couple of years. I started out doing ten- or fifteen-minute acoustic sets, at benefits where I'd be on the bill with seventeen other people. Then sometimes it would go longer—to a half-hour. I've really enjoyed playing acoustic music again and as that's become more popular, I've decided to go back to playing an hour-and-a-half show. So now I have a dual career: I play acoustic concerts, which brings me a lot more in touch with my older blues stuff. I have a bass player, Johnny Lee Schell, who played on *Green Light* and *Nine Lives*. He backs me up on bass and guitar. We've been doing that all over the country for a couple of years, as well as touring with the band."

Only weeks after I had seen Bonnie in the woods at Croton-On-Hudson, she was performing in the Soviet Union. On July 4, 1987, along with the Doobie Brothers, Santana, James Taylor, and several Russian groups, Bonnie performed in what was billed as The July Fourth Disarmament Festival. With Gorbachev in power and cultural exchanges between the United States and the Soviet Union increasing, Russia was welcoming several foreign performers to their country. Raitt said, "We just did one show, and I only did two songs. It was a peace concert, it wasn't a 'tour.' It was a fantastic experience. One of the reasons I went was because I'd like to return and do a longer tour; to get to know the situation over there musically and expose them to some women musicians. In Europe and Japan they do know your stuff and a lot of the people do speak English. In Russia, I don't think it's as easy. You'd have to make sure there were translations of your stuff before you went over. I'm looking forward to going back again."

On September 30, 1987, Bonnie was one of the celebrity performers who backed legendary rock and roll star Roy Orbison—who was amid a sudden revival of his career. Recorded live on stage at the Coconut Grove nightclub in Los Angeles, the video footage of the performance was first broadcast on the Cinemax cable TV network on January 3, 1988, as "Roy Orbison and Friends: A Black and White Night."

It was the 1985 David Lynch film *Blue Velvet* that had been responsible for bringing Orbison back into the mainstream. His classic song "In Dreams" had played an integral part in the bizarre flick. Roy was suddenly "in" in a big way. The "Black and White" session had the most amazing backup band assembled for any one recording in the eighties. It included Bruce Springsteen, Tom Waits, Elvis Costello, T-Bone Burnett, and John David Souther in the band, and the background singing group included Bonnie Raitt, k.d. lang, Jennifer Warnes, and Jackson Browne. The TV special proved to be a huge hit, and was later released on video cassette.

On January 23, 1988, Bonnie was one of the star performers in Oakland, California, at a benefit for refugees who were displaced by political unrest in El Salvador. Billed as "Blues for Salvador," the five-hour concert event included Boz Scaggs,

NRBQ, the Tower of Power Horn Section, Carlos Santana, Jerry Garcia and Bob Weir of the Grateful Dead, and jazz sax star Wayne Shorter. "This is a night about survival," Bonnie announced from the stage that evening. "We're brothers and sisters in cause!" The event was organized by Bay Area rock promoter Bill Graham. It raised $100,000.

Speaking of her support for several political causes during this time, Bonnie said, "Politics is just how you treat your fellow man or your fellow woman, or your fellow dog, or whatever it is that you're treating. Basically, my involvement with the No Nukes concerts, Amnesty [International], and our involvement in Central America, those kinds of things have to do with a lot of fund-raising and consciousness-raising type of events, and obviously I'm interested in environmental causes and getting us out of Central America. The Sanctuary Movement is something that ranks high on my priorities. . . . Of course, the No Nukes thing is still something that's pretty strong. I was part of this concert series at Madison Square Garden back in 1979, I was one of the founders of the MUSE organization. There are an awful lot of issues out there: the farmers, the famine in Africa . . . There are things that, just as people, we should wake up and look around and educate ourselves and help out people who aren't doing as well."

At the time—circa 1988—Bonnie was sort of free-falling. She still had no record label. *Nine Lives* had failed to revive her recording career. Not even her third Grammy nomination jump-started the sales of the album. Looking back from a nineties perspective, Bonnie would later say, "There wasn't room on the radio for you unless you were a classic oldies artist. And I didn't have hits. At the same time, I kind of lost touch with myself and my hope. I was probably just dispirited from making so many albums nobody listened to. But I never let it get in the way of my music. I never worried about whether I'd have a career or not, even if it was gonna be on some little label in Sweden. 'Cause I could always play acoustic guitar. There's a great deal of security in that."

Although she did not have to start shopping for obscure record labels in Scandinavia, 1988 was a hard year for her. "At that point I couldn't afford to take the band on the road, so I was doing acoustic gigs, just me and Johnny Lee Schell. Don [Was] came to see me and he said, 'You should make a record really simple like that.' I said, 'The way my career is going, I have to make a record that simple, 'cause I'm broke.' "

As she put it, "The [music] industry just kept slapping me around!"

It was Don Was—of the avant garde rock group called Was (Not Was)—who would help Bonnie find the winning sound that would break her through with her milestone *Nick of Time* album in 1989. When they first met in 1988, Don's group, Was (Not Was) had just scored a big hit with the song "Walk the Dinosaur." It was a catchy R&B tune that put the group on the map, and established Don as a talented producer.

Don and Bonnie's first opportunity to work together came on single tracks from two different childrens' albums. The first album was *"Stay Awake" Various Interpretations of Music From Vintage Disney Films* for A&M Records in 1988. Hal Willner was the producer of Bonnie's cut, and Don Was served as the arranger. The second song that Bonnie and Don worked on together appeared on Marlo Thomas's *Free To Be . . . A Family* album. On that recording, Don was elevated to the job of producer.

The Disney album featured several other artists, including James Taylor and Ringo Starr, singing classic songs from Disney films. The number that Bonnie performed was the lullaby "Baby Mine" from *Dumbo*. Using the group Was (Not Was) as her band, and Sweet Pea Atkinson and Sir Harry Bowens as her doo-wopping background singers, the song receives a very simple, sophisticated treatment. Bonnie's smoky vocals give this touching and comforting lullaby a beautiful and jazzy rendition.

On the album *Free To Be . . . A Family* by Marlo Thomas and Friends, Bonnie performs the raucous "I'm Never Afraid (To Say What's on My Mind)." This song, written by Christopher Cerf and Sarah Durkee, is a perfect fit for Bonnie's tomboy childhood background and her musical bluegrass-polka mode. In fact, the song sounds very much like "Let Me In" from her 1973 *Takin' My Time* album, which was such a delight. With everything from a tuba to a slide whistle providing a lively New Orleans feeling to the swinging upbeat song, the outcome is sheer fun. This "oom-pa-pa"-Dixieland song became the perfect vehicle for Bonnie to get back in contact with her old friend Freebo, who keeps this tune alive and bouncing with his distinctive tuba playing. In this song's lyrics, a playful Bonnie sings about being afraid of the monsters in her closet, the neighborhood bully, and some of the stuff she sees on TV. And, while her friends are frightened of snakes and of heights, she's never afraid to open up her mouth and say exactly what she is thinking.

The *Free To Be . . . A Family* album is a pleasant mixture of such actors as Robin Williams and Whoopie Goldberg reciting little vignettes of stories, and of singers like Bonnie Raitt, Pat Benatar, and Carly Simon singing songs to children about belonging in the world. Bonnie's song is one of the most memorable segments of this thoroughly entertaining twenty-cut album.

With the recording of both of these children's songs, a magical union was created. Don Was and Bonnie loved working together, and at long last she had found the perfect person to produce her music. All she needed now was a record label!

Since Bonnie had stopped drinking and partying all night long, her musical taste had changed. Raitt said at the time, "It's time to make a change. My taste tends to swing back and forth.

I did a real hard-rock LP a few years ago: *Green Light.* Lately I've been getting back into my roots of folk music and blues. I like to keep it fresh. When you play music for a living, you have to be really careful it doesn't get stale."

In mid-1988, Bonnie finally landed a new record deal. Since 1986 she had been managed by Danny Goldberg of Gold Mountain Entertainment. He was instrumental in her signing with Capitol Records.

"Someone once asked me what women's music was, and I told them, 'rhythm and grief,' " Bonnie had said. In the mid-eighties she had learned a lot about both rhythm and grief. Now it was time for the reward. Her new recording deal with Capitol would rescue her—just in the nick of time!

9

Nick of Time

In 1988, after three years without a recording contract, Bonnie started on the trail to what has come to be known as her big career comeback. At the age of thirty-eight, with her new sobriety, and a renewed sense of self-worth, she had even written several new ballads about personal issues that reflected the way she now felt about life and the world around her. Bonnie was amused by journalists and critics using the term "comeback" to describe this phase of her career. "I never had a hit record so how can I *come back?*" she said, "I didn't go away, I've been on the road for twenty years!"

"I have my own solid base of an audience that has been very loyal, and I'm really appreciative," she told *Frets* magazine in 1988. "I want to make sure I'm on a [record] label that knows how to target that audience and will appreciate me and let me do the music that I should be doing and not try to encourage me to do something I *shouldn't* be doing. Because I'm not going to do it anyway. I'm in a period of transition, and happily so. I've made a lot of changes in my life, and I'm just taking it nice and slow to make sure I don't make any mistakes."

Finding the right record company had been an important element. "It's like picking a college. I want to take my time. I've narrowed it down to two labels. The music business is completely different now than it was when I started. For somebody like me who plays music that's not mainstream, I have to make sure it's a label that doesn't have too many people from my era on it already. A lot of labels are signing new singer-songwriters."

The company she was most strongly considering was Capitol Records. Once the home of such 1950s giants as Peggy Lee and Frank Sinatra, Capitol had recently taken Tina Turner's career from washed-up to triumphant.

Another key ingredient was the material she chose to sing on her forthcoming *Nick of Time* album. She said at that time, "I have to find something besides 'If you don't get it together or I'm leaving' or 'I'm sick of your bull.' I do a lot of those songs and I do them well, but I'd like to sing about something other than love, other than pain. As someone that's used to singing about both, it's gonna take me a minute to come up with something. In terms of a record, I'm switching labels and haven't settled on a producer yet. I have four or five really great songs."

From the moment she signed with Capitol Records in 1988, things seemed right. Meeting producer Don Was had been another important ingredient. Describing his recipe for record producing, Was explained, "You have to feel out what these people want and help them get there. It's a delicate thing. You're not invisible, but if you enter with preconceived notions that don't fit the artist's plan, you're going to clash. If you're doing it right, you get so deep into these people that you see through their eyes."

Despite the well-produced albums for his group Was (Not Was), and the two single cuts he had made with Bonnie, Don Was had yet to do any major superstar producing. And, work-

ing with Bonnie circa 1988–1989, he was certainly not working with an established superstar either. Through her nine
Warner Brothers albums she had become a respected blues-
rock musician who had experienced the peak of her career from
1977 to 1980. The new MTV generation that had grown up
since then had no idea who she was. That would all soon change
for both Raitt and Was.

Describing her intention with *Nick of Time*, Bonnie said,
"I wanted to make a record that was more like *Give It Up*. It's
a return to roots, as it were. It's been really refreshing for me
to play a lot of guitar and just go back to stripped-down production."

Nick of Time represented a change of pace for Bonnie. Unlike her past releases, there were no "you done me wrong"
songs or tearful laments about love lost. The songs were much
more personal. She was neither trying to appeal to twenty-
year-old rockers, nor to fans of 1920s blues. She didn't cover
any fun Motown tunes or classic rock material. Instead, she
chose to aim directly at "baby boomers" like herself, who were
looking middle age straight in the eye. The title *Nick of Time*
was itself highly prophetic. This new album had come about at
just exactly the *nick of time* in her career, and if it wasn't more
successful than *Nine Lives* had been, it could have been her last
chance at a high-profile mainstream musical career. This time,
it was now or never. Fittingly, she gave every song on this
album her all!

Nick of Time, Bonnie's tenth album, was released in April
1989, and it instantly caused a stir in the record business. Raitt
was proud of the album she and Was had created. "There's less
production, less slickness. Basically it's a return to my roots,"
she said.

With trade ads and press interviews scheduled, Capitol
Records was fulfilling the publicity and promotion campaign
it had promised. Having just made Tina Turner's resurgence the

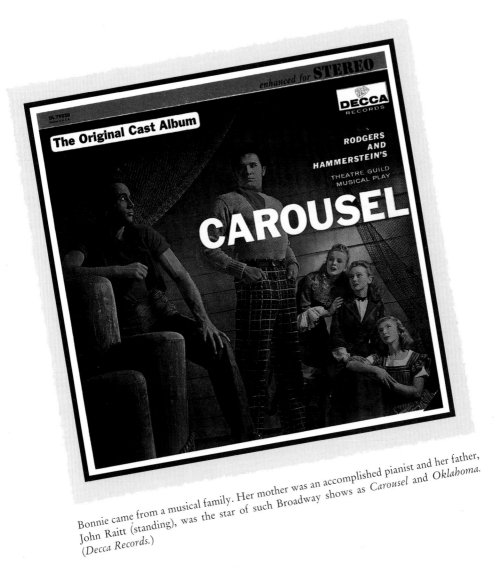

Bonnie came from a musical family. Her mother was an accomplished pianist and her father, John Raitt (standing), was the star of such Broadway shows as *Carousel* and *Oklahoma*. (*Decca Records.*)

While recording her
debut album *Bonnie
Raitt,* the twenty-one
year old singer culti-
vated the image of a
hard-drinking blues
balladeer. (*Warner
Brothers Records*)

A fresh-
faced singer
with an
expressive
voice, Bonnie
recorded her
second album,
Give It Up, in
the Woodstock,
New York area
with a close circle
of friends as her
back-up band.
(*Warner Brothers
Records*)

Home Plate,
Bonnie's 1975
album, repre-
sented a rock
and roll break-
through for her,
and the album
cover played
upon her child-
hood image of a
tomboy. (*Warner
Brothers Records*)

Bonnie's
1979 album,
The Glow,
recorded when
she was twen-
ty-nine years
old, was mar-
keted to make
her into as huge a
recording star as
her friend/rival
Linda Ronstadt.
This cover photo
by David Alexander
shows off the glam-
orous new image she
was projecting.
(*Warner Brothers
Records*)

Bonnie's phenomenal 1989 album, *Nick of Time*, shows a new Bonnie at thirty-nine years old. This album totally resurrected her singing career and became a huge number-one smash! (*Capitol Records*)

It gave Bonnie great pleasure to contribute to Sippie Wallace's 1982 album. The pair dueted on Sippie's 1920s classic *Woman Be Wise*. (*Atlantic Records*)

Bonnie Raitt and John Lee Hooker filming a video for their Grammy-winning blues smash "I'm in the Mood." (*Richard E. Aaron/Star File*)

Bonnie with her longtime idol and friend Joni Mitchell. Not only do they share their creative musicianship, but career longevity as well. (*Vinnie Zuffante/ Star File*)

Bonnie and her mother, Marjorie, share a night on the town in Los Angeles. (*Vinnie Zuffante/Star File*)

John Raitt (Bonnie's father), Natalie Cole, Bonnie and her husband Michael O'Keefe, cut a stunning profile in Los Angeles. (*Vinnie Zuffante/Star File*)

March 1, 1995, Producer Don Was, Bonnie and her sound engineer Ed Cherney, show off their Grammy awards for their work on Raitt's *Longing in Their Hearts*. (*Jeffrey Mayer/Star File*)

rock and roll metamorphosis of the decade, they were poised
to repeat that feat with Bonnie.

According to Don Was, he and Bonnie kept their expectations in focus. He said, "We figured it would sell 150,000 copies,
enough to break even and enable her to make another album."

A crucial aspect in Bonnie's Capitol Records debut in 1989
was the all-important video. She had to star in videos to launch
the first two singles from the album. It was mandatory that
Bonnie reach MTV-watching record buyers.

"Thing Called Love" became the first single to be released
from *Nick of Time*. For the video presentation, Bonnie was de-
picted as a singer in a sunlight-streaked bar. Decorated with
beer bottles and cattle skulls, illuminated by bare-bulbed hanging lamps, it looked like the interior of a funky roadside dive.
Wearing skin-tight jeans and a blue silk shirt, Bonnie looked
sexy as she sang this come-on of a rock ballad. Movie star hunk
Dennis Quaid, wearing fifties-style two-toned shoes and a
sleeveless Sun Records tee shirt, sat at the bar looking on with
a seductive grin on his face, encouraging Raitt's impassioned
performance. As Dennis moved from the bar to a table close to
ringside, Bonnie blushed and grinned with sexually charged excitement. According to Bonnie, Quaid's appearance was a natural event. "We live near each other. We hang out. We like the
same kind of music. I think he's got a lot of charisma. He looks
great, he has a great stage presence, and he sings great. I enjoy
watching him!" she explained.

Comprised of womanly-wise songs about confronting middle age and pursuing your dreams with rock and roll gusto,
Nick of Time was consistently lively and expressive. For Bonnie, it was a career milestone of an album.

From the first twenty seconds of nonverbal intro to the
song *Nick of Time*, the listener can feel the excitement building, musical layer by musical layer. Floating on the ethereal
background chorus of Arnold McCuller and Sir Harry Bowens,

Bonnie's voice is clear, direct, and charged with emotion. The opening title song was Bonnie's smartly targeted composition, dealing with members of the Peter Pan-like baby-boomer generation realizing that the sand in the hourglass is fleeting past them. The lyric line about being scared of running out of time is a chilling call to arms. She sings about a friend who is listening to her biological clock ticking, wondering if she'll ever have a child. The song's emotional theme sets the scene for the entire album. It is about taking charge of one's life, and doing something constructive with it, while there is still time, which is a topic Bonnie knew a lot about by this phase of her life.

John Hiatt's composition "Thing Called Love," while musically lighter and funkier, also asks how long one should wait in one's life for love. With her Bump Band players Johnny Lee Schell and Ricky Fataar behind her on guitar and drums, Bonnie uses this hook-laden rock ballad as a stunning slide-guitar showcase for herself. Bonnie sings it with sassy confidence and verve. A stone-cold smash, "Thing Called Love" is one of the most exciting cuts of her entire career.

Slowing the pace for Bonnie Hayes's slinky composition "Love Letter," Raitt rips into the song with increased vocal confidence, illuminating the longing she felt in her own life. Sexy as a hot summer night, "Love Letter" is a seductive rock ballad.

Mining sentimental gold with Michael Ruff's "Cry on My Shoulder," Bonnie declares that real men not only eat quiche, but are strong enough to cry. Backed by David Crosby and Graham Nash, Raitt's singing and slide-guitar playing are poignantly restrained. This is a perfect example of the simple layers of sound that producer Don Was was able to balance behind her. Stripped down but multifaceted in sound, this pensive song gives Bonnie a chance to show off her sad ballad singing.

Similar in theme to "Love Me Like a Man" from the *Give It Up* album, Bonnie spells out what she wants in a romantic partner with "Real Man." This time around around she wants a man who is looking for a woman—not a little girl. This Jerry L. Williams composition reflected exactly what Bonnie was thinking at the time, having spent the last couple of years with no romance in her life.

Stripping the instrumental tracks down to just acoustic guitar and Chuck Domanico's acoustic bass, Bonnie sings "Nobody's Girl" straight from the heartstrings. It's about that feeling of loneliness, even while in a crowd.

The last three numbers are trademark Bonnie Raitt strong-girl songs that match the warrior-woman look of the photo on the front cover of the album. "I Will Not Be Denied" has a demanding urgency to it, set to a slamming and jamming beat. "I Ain't Gonna Let You Break My Heart Again" snaps with heartbreaking "I'm outta here!" pathos. And "The Road's My Middle Name" is a page from a true rock and roll road warrior's diary.

"I Ain't Gonna Let You Break My Heart Again," which noted background session singer David Lasley wrote, was one that Bonnie had had in her possession for quite some time. She was just waiting for the right moment to record it. "I really don't think I could have sung it before this—vocally or emotionally," she said. It is a song that is meant to be sung by someone who was confident enough to walk away from a dysfunctional relationship. Only now—with her newfound sobriety—could she do it justice. With heartbreaking fervor, Bonnie's voice is mesmerizing and cracks with pain.

"The Road's My Middle Name" was written by Bonnie, and celebrates the acceptance of her traveling lifestyle. Instead of closing the album with a somber classic like she usually did, she chose something more strongly autobiographical and self-affirming. Her whole "sorry babe, I've got a six-month concert tour to do" stance perfectly summed up her unconventional lifestyle.

Nick of Time is a watershed of rock-solid songs, each punching another emotional button. From the first cut to the last, Bonnie is jazzed to the max. Every path she takes on this LP displays another shading of her many musical strengths and personas—from guitar-toting rocker to world-weary survivor.

After completing *Nick of Time*, Don Was said, "More than anyone I've ever worked with, Bonnie has a complete artistic vision. She really knows herself. The cool thing about her is that she's not portraying a character. She'll only sing a song that pertains directly to her life."

Nick of Time received critical praise from the moment it was released. In *Stereo Review* Alanna Nash called it "Raitt's best since the early-seventies classics *Give It Up* and *Home Plate*. . . . *Nick of Time* is held together by three strong, unifying elements: her emotional and tangy slide guitar playing, her uncommonly expressive, husky soprano—soaring here with thrilling gospel and R & B leaps—and her selection of sassy, knowing songs about the ups and downs of romance. The album is remarkable!"

In *Newsweek*, Ron Givens wrote, "*Nick of Time* is her best work since the late seventies. . . . Her voice rides high and sassy over the rockers and dips low and plaintive under the ballads, always taking us for a tour of her heart . . . a new beginning for a recording career that was in tatters six years ago."

Bonnie Raitt was suddenly the media's darling. In *People* magazine she talked about the fact that she began psychotherapy in 1986, AA the next year, and was feeling better than ever before. She also admitted that there was no love affair in her life, "for the first time since I was about six. Although I'm not *celibate* or anything."

However, Bonnie's big "comeback" was far from an instant

success. In fact, *Rolling Stone,* the one magazine that one would expect to be the most excited about this album, seemed blasé. Giving *Nick of Time* only three and a half stars (out of five), Fred Goodman wrote in his review, "For almost any other pop singer, *Nick of Time* would be a solid victory. For Raitt, who is clearly capable of being great, it is another near miss."

Bonnie said, "In many ways this is like a first album. It's for a new label and getting all of this attention and critical acclaim. And it's my first sober album. My first single and sober album. Being this age and being straight—it's been the greatest time."

With *Nick of Time,* Bonnie successfully made succinct musical statements that voiced the feelings, emotions, and frustrations of the baby boomer generation. Her songs about standing at the crossroads between youth and middle age, struck the perfect chord for her age and her position in life. She was the first to admit, "If I had put this record out a few years ago, no one would have played it."

She also noted that *Nick of Time* was an adult-oriented album. "Every song on there is about somebody who had to have lived this long. 'I Ain't Gonna Let You Break My Heart Again'—I had that song for eleven years, and until this album I couldn't really mean it. But there are some great records being made by people in my generation: Don Henley, Tom Petty."

As she had done in the past, Bonnie immediately went on a concert tour after the release of her new album. With her folksinger/songwriter buddy Richard Thompson as her opening act, Raitt took her music to her legion of devoted fans. Reviewing her May 12, 1989, show in Chicago in *Rolling Stone,* Moira McCormick said of Bonnie, "Raitt is at the height of her powers!" And she was, as a songwriter, guitarist, and seasoned performer.

Referring to the latest folk-oriented females on the record charts—Toni Childs, Tracy Chapman, and Melissa Etheridge—

that night, Bonnie thanked "the new crop of women who have helped me and Phoebe Snow get some more attention. Now maybe Joni Mitchell will have another hit!"

Reviewing her standing-room-only Manhattan performance in June, Jon Parales of the *New York Times* wrote:

> Bonnie Raitt has suddenly found new acclaim for her long-established virtues: her clear voice, her bluesy phrasing, and songs carefully chosen to treat love as a complex but equal partnership. . . . Her sold-out concert Thursday at the Ritz was a confident reaffirmation that during her years in rock's commercial middle ground between obscurity and mass popularity, she was on the right track. All she needed was a set of consistently excellent songs. She has those songs on *Nick of Time.*

Nick of Time became the bestselling album of Bonnie's eighteen-year recording career. However, by the week of July 22, 1989, after three months on the charts, it was already sinking from the Top Twenty to number 31 in *Billboard* magazine. Bonnie's career had always been album oriented, and this continued with *Nick of Time.* Although the songs "Thing Called Love" and "Love Letter" received a lot of radio airplay, and significant rotation on the MTV and VH1 video networks, she still did not score a breakthrough hit single.

However, sales on the album remained consistent throughout the year. Bonnie's touring schedule continued to expose her and her finely crafted music to increasingly larger audiences. By the end of the year the album was still on the charts and had sold the requisite 500,000 copies to become Raitt's second Gold LP.

Meanwhile, in September 1989, Bonnie again appeared on a charity record, the homelessness awareness single, "Wake Up

America." She had volunteered her time to help others, and came away from it with a new love interest. No one was more surprised than she.

It had been only months since she had publicly lamented the lack of romance in her life by stating that she would like to find "a soulmate to share it with . . . It's exciting to know there's somebody living on the planet now that I'm probably going to end up spending a lot of time with." He turned out to be a thirty-four-year-old actor named Michael O'Keefe.

Michael O'Keefe's acting career had really gotten off the ground when he appeared in the 1979 film *The Great Santini*. He played one of Robert Duvall's rebellious sons. In the early nineties, he was one of the stars of the Fox TV network show *Against the Law*. Bonnie met him while she was filming the video for the song "Wake Up America." Tall, with curly hair and a slight build, Michael immediately appealed to Bonnie. He had a warm smile and a great sense of humor. She found him instantly attractive, so attractive, in fact, that *she* made the first move.

"I was single for three years," she would later explain. "That doesn't mean I wasn't dating people. I was enjoying dating them. I just meant that I was enjoying not belonging to someone. And I still am enjoying it. But this relationship kind of snuck up on me. I was in Los Angeles for a while in the fall, and I made a video about the homeless called 'Wake Up America.' It didn't get on MTV, because it was only me and Bonnie Bramlett and Rita Coolidge and a few other celebrities, none of whom was famous enough for MTV. But it was a kind of 'We Are the World' thing, filmed in MacArthur Park, and Michael sang on the record and was directing us. And I gave somebody my number to give him, and I went back out on the road. He called, and when I got back, we went out and have been hanging out ever since."

Bonnie's relationship with Michael O'Keefe was perfect

for her new and hectic lifestyle. Garry George and Rob Fraboni had been great running mates for her partying days, but now she was ready for a different kind of affair. The fact that Michael was as focused on his career as she was on hers was very appealing. Since she spent several months at a time on the road, she needed someone who would understand that kind of a show business existence. In their first few months together, Bonnie's emotions would run both hot and cold. She would be in love with him one minute, uncertain the next, and then in love with him again. It wasn't long, however, before she decided that she preferred having him around.

Also in the fall of 1989, Bonnie participated in a pair of new top-rated albums. The first one was her old blues singing pal John Lee Hooker's album *The Healer*. On it, Bonnie sang a funky blues duet with Hooker called "I'm in the Mood." In this blues thump and grind version of his 1951 hit, Hooker and Raitt really meshed musically. Wrote *Rolling Stone*, "As John Lee states his need, Raitt, at her seductive best, sidles up to and curls around each phrase in a sassy moan and response."

Bonnie was also heard on Roy Orbison's posthumously released album *A Black and White Night Live*. Roy had been solidly enjoying his career comeback in 1988, both as a solo act, and with the all-star band the Traveling Wilburys, which included George Harrison, Bob Dylan, Tom Petty, and Jeff Lynne. He died suddenly in December 1988. Bonnie was one of the celebrity performers at a memorial tribute to Roy that same month, along with Tom Petty, Graham Nash, and Don Henley. The 1989 release of Orbison's album, an excellent recording of the 1988 Cinemax TV special, was a fitting way to celebrate Orbison's music and his life.

By the beginning of 1990, Bonnie was on top of the world. She had a new record label, a hit album, a new boyfriend, and enough laudatory press clippings to make her many years of struggling in the music business seem worthwhile. Several days later, the nominations for the upcoming Grammy Awards were announced. Bonnie was up for awards in four different categories: *Nick of Time* was nominated as Album of the Year, Best Rock Vocal Performance, Female, and Best Pop Vocal Performance, Female. In addition, Bonnie and John Lee Hooker were nominated for Best Traditional Blues Recording for the cut "I'm in the Mood."

Overwhelmed by her good fortune, Bonnie fled to Northern California for a creative retreat. She needed to be alone to mine her thoughts and feelings, to see if she could come up with some new and relevant songs for her next album. She didn't want any outside influences, phones ringing, or distractions. She felt that if she won any of the Grammy Awards she was nominated for, she would find herself under the weight of a whole new set of expectations. If she didn't win any of the Grammys, she didn't want to be crushed by the feeling of rejection and end up with a creative songwriters' block.

She went to the little town of Mendocino, which was where she had written the song "Nick of Time." She didn't venture outdoors for several days, and sat with pen in hand, just thinking about the emotions she wanted to write about. "I did it on purpose to see if I could come up with anything," she explained. "In case I won, I wanted to make sure that I had done some writing and didn't feel that *Nick of Time* was a fluke. I didn't want to win just 'cause I quit drinking and spent twenty years not making any money, you know? There wasn't enough. So I basically forced myself to go to songwriting boot camp. There were three or four days when it didn't happen—but because I didn't have alcohol or unhappiness or anything to get in the way, it started to open up and I started three of the four songs of mine that are on this album [*Luck of the Draw*]. And then it didn't matter if I won or not, because I had proved to myself that it was okay."

The Thirty-Second Annual Grammy Awards ceremony

was held at the Shrine Auditorium in Los Angeles on February 21, 1990. It was to be one of the most unforgettable evenings of Bonnie Raitt's life. She won all four of the Grammys she was nominated for.

Bonnie became the undisputed star of that evening's awards telecast. "I was as out of my body as I've ever been," she recalls. "I honestly could not tell whether I was dreaming. Everything moved in slow motion, and the sound of it—your ears get kind of numb, like there's a crowd roaring or something. I remember saying to myself that 'if this isn't a dream, you'd better do something, because you're on TV and you're wasting all these people's time!' "

Her father, John Raitt, shared the excitement with her. "My dad was also overwhelmed. When I came down after I made my thank-you speech for the 'Rock-Female' one, he gave me a hug, and I saw him start to go. You know, here is this big, stoical leading man, and the whole building saw him lose it. And I started crying, and we held each other for a good minute and a half until they told us to sit down. To have that kind of response in public—there is just no way of avoiding it. And for that alone, it was worth the evening."

By the time the awards ceremony reached the three biggest awards of the evening (Album of the Year, Song of the Year, and Record of the Year), Bonnie was in a state of disbelief. Was it possible that *Nick of Time* could actually win *Album of the Year*? When her name was read as the winner of that award, she was in shock. When she took the podium to accept her fourth Grammy of the night, she exclaimed, "Wake me up when it's over!"

"That was just so unexpected!" she said later. "I figured I might win the 'Rock-Female' award, that the record did well enough and people were gonna give me sort of a career nod: 'Alright Bonnie, you got your shit together. Got a new label, you wrote a song *straight*—hallelujah—let's give you a prize.' Kind of a pat on the back. But the others were beyond belief. I wasn't even there the rest of the night, after the album won. Ella Fitzgerald was reading my name! I mean, I'll never get over it as long as I live. And if I do, you can shoot me!"

Bonnie became a heroine to other women in the music business; to finally receive such honor and recognition at the age of forty, and not at twenty-five. "What are there, six thousand people in NARAS [the National Academy of Recording Arts and Sciences]?" Bonnie said. "And I happened to beat out a tie between Don Henley and Tom Petty and the [Traveling] Wilburys—just sneaked through there. But whatever the circumstances, it ended up having a deep effect among people my age in the music business who are now not so discouraged. And, man, I thought my life was going great *before* that happened!"

She went on, "Like I said at the Grammys, I'm glad God brought me to this now, meaning that I got pulled out of the fire. Some people don't get out. They die. You know, the Richard Manuels, the Paul Butterfields. There's a whole bunch of musicians who had their drug and alcohol problems encouraged by the lack of validation for their music."

Three days later, Bonnie was on stage performing at another benefit—the Roy Orbison Concert Tribute to Benefit the Homeless. Whoopie Goldberg served as hostess. The event also starred Dwight Yoakam, Bob Dylan, B. B. King, k. d. lang, David Crosby, and Chris Hillman, and Roger McGuinn of the Byrds.

Catapulted back up the charts by her televised Grammy sweep, the album *Nick of Time* hit number 1 the week of April 7, 1990. At that time, Bonnie was on a concert tour across the Atlantic: "I was in Europe promoting an unknown person— which was me! 'Cause I'd never done well enough in America before to warrant going there. It was like, 'Who is this person who just won all these awards? We've never heard of her!' "

While in London, on April 14, Bonnie was one of the star performers to headline a concert to celebrate Nelson Mandela's release from prison in South Africa after twenty-seven years. Also on the bill were such international stars as Neil Young, Soul II Soul, Simple Minds, Tracy Chapman, and Anita Baker. Performing in front of a sell-out crowd of seventy-two thousand people in Wembley Stadium, Bonnie and her singing again became a bridge between popular music and politically correct social issues.

Before the cheering crowd, Nelson Mandela said, "I think artists can play a very decisive role in the fight for human rights. Artists can reach quarters not necessarily interested in politics through music, which interests everybody, so that the message can go further than we politicians can push it."

Of his political intentions, Mandela predicted, "Dear friends, it will not be long now before we see the end of the apartheid system. The dreams of millions of people to see our country free and at peace will be realized sooner rather than later. We are determined to ensure that our country is transformed from being the skunk of the world into an exemplary oasis of unrivaled race relations, democracy for all, a just peace and freedom from poverty and human degradation." His comments paralleled so many of Bonnie's thoughts and feelings on racial equality for all and she was proud to be a part of the celebrity event.

Nick of Time went on to sell four million copies, making it not only Bonnie's first quadruple-Platinum album, but the first million-selling album in her entire career! Everywhere she went, she was hailed on stage like a conquering heroine.

"This is the first time in my career that I've ever had this kind of response," she said. "You don't get an opportunity like this too many times."

Her Grammy victories provided her with renewed creative drive and conviction. "It was so great to get recognition and validation, because it made it easier to stay true to my instincts. Now I feel like I stand for something: I have a mission to keep [roots] music alive. I learned I'm going to be all right. That's an incredible gift to be given at this age—at any age." As she had always done, Bonnie continued to use her position in the music business to help others.

As the summer of 1990 concert tour season approached, Bonnie was in demand to headline bigger and bigger arenas across America. In characteristic fashion, when it came time to select opening acts for her tour she relied on her friends—some old and some new. The old friends were embodied by the group NRBQ. And the new friend was R&B legend Charles Brown. As a piano player and a singer, Brown was best known on the pop charts for his 1960 hit, "Please Come Home for Christmas." However, he was first recognized for the R&B hits "Get Yourself Another Fool" (1949), "Trouble Blues" (1949), "I'll Always Be in Love With You" (1951), "Seven Long Days" (1951), and "Hard Times" (1952).

Bonnie came to hear Brown when he headlined at a small nightclub called the Vine Street Grill in Hollywood. Charles Brown recalls, "Bonnie Raitt came in with Arsenio Hall's music director. I didn't know Bonnie. I just knew about what she had done. When I would sing, she would carry on and say, 'Oh Charles! Ohh, Charles!!' You know, everything like that. So I didn't pay no attention.

"Intermission came. They say, 'Don't you know who that is sittin' out there?' I said, 'No.' They said, 'That's Bonnie Raitt and look like she loves all the things you do.' I said, 'Really?' But she never came back [after the show] 'cause there was too many people tryin' to get back to the little dressin' room."

Brown continued, "So, a few months later, I got the Lifetime Achievement Award from the Rhythm and Blues Foundation. They had a big affair for us. And Bonnie Raitt was there, again. So after we got our plaques and big envelope with all the money—$15,000 in it, you know—then everybody had a word to say. They came to me and they said, 'Who do you think would be great singers for them young men comin' up in the blues, and the ladies?' So I had heard Bonnie Raitt sing, I said, 'Well, Bonnie Raitt would be wonderful 'cause she can sing everything. Robert Cray would be very good, too.' When I got through, Bonnie Raitt came over. She said, 'Thank you, Charles!' And she hugged me. I didn't pay much attention."

Brown went on, "Then Joan Myers, who had Bonnie's publicity [account], she said, 'We want to have dinner this evening, all of us, in Howell Begle's house in D.C.' He's a big attorney who established the Rhythm and Blues Foundation, givin' people back their royalties who didn't never get nothin'. We went over there, wasn't but a few of us, just Bonnie Raitt and Joan Myers, myself, I think Carla Thomas, [and] Howell Begle's wife. So we sat at the table. They had nice food and everything. We're all talkin'. So Bonnie Raitt said, 'You know what? I want to hear you. *Nobody* can sing and play like you. You're really Mr. R&B.' She said, 'You know what? I could marry you musically!' I said, 'Bonnie Raitt, you don't want to marry an old man like me. Why, you'd be smellin' liniment all night long!" And she just fell out laughing.

"From then on," says Brown, "we began to talk. She had never got a Grammy then and the Grammys were comin' up very soon. When the Grammys did come, she won four of 'em. Then her management started wantin' to set up a tour. Somehow, they had asked if she wanted Charles Brown to be on this tour with her. They inquirin' about, 'Does he need a doctor?' So this one fella told 'em, said, 'Listen, the way I saw Charles Brown goin' up and down them steps at the racetrack, I don't think he needs a doctor!"

Plans for Charles Brown to be Bonnie's opening act began to unfold. It was an offer Brown could not refuse. For years he had played in small jazz clubs in front of a couple hundred people. Now, as part of Bonnie's 1990 concert tour of stadiums and concert halls, he would reach a huge audience. Having just won all of her Grammy Awards, Raitt was one of the hottest draws of the year, and with her newfound fame and notoriety she would help a true musical legend.

"I agreed to go and it was A-plus. Everything was A-plus," says Brown of his first tour with Raitt. "We were on the bus with Bonnie. We went over so great in New York. At a rehearsal, Bonnie Raitt wanted me to play for her, a song, you know. We were playin' and everybody said, 'Bonnie Raitt sound better with you playin' than with anybody else we ever heard!' I said, 'We'll do a finale together.' We did that. I played solo and she and I sang. And it went over *everywhere* we went, a standing ovation at the finale. . . . It went around like that, all because Bonnie Raitt came along and brought me to the front after I was dormant for so many years. She's the most wonderful person. She's beautiful and she's real."

In July 1990 Bonnie began her concert tour in Poughkeepsie, New York, near the place where she had attended summer camp, and had launched her musical career.

Reviewing Bonnie's stage act in late September, *Down Beat* magazine's Dan Ouellette found, "On stage, as always, she was her outspoken, vulnerable, vivacious, and generous self. . . . Raitt commanded center stage by the sheer power of her exceptional slide-guitar playing and her exquisite voice—gutsy and assertive on the rousing rockers, feisty R&B numbers, and pungent blues tunes; vulnerable and almost delicate on the soulful ballads. She got soft and tender on '(Goin') Wild for You Baby' and 'Louise.' "

Just like in the song, "The Road's My Middle Name," Bonnie was used to life on the road. "I'm on the road touring five or six months a year," she said. "I've played every place twice a year for the last twenty years,"

Though she no longer drinks, she still parties. "I still stay up and jam," she says, "It's just that I can remember everything I did the next day and I don't have to feel sick."

While she was on the road, Warner Brothers Records released a CD compilation of twenty of her best songs from her first nine albums. Bonnie was asked to participate in the package, and she selected the numbers that would be included on *The Bonnie Raitt Collection.* Two of her trademark songs, "Angel From Montgomery" and "Woman Be Wise" were presented in rare "live" duet performances. Bonnie and Sippie Wallace are heard on "Woman Be Wise," taken from a 1976 San Francisco radio broadcast. And, "Angel From Montgomery" is represented by a John Prine–Bonnie Raitt duet version from the 1985 Grammy-winning *Tribute to Steve Goodman* album. Earlier that year, *Nine Lives* and *Green Light* had been released on CD for the first time.

Meanwhile, Bonnie's relationship with Michael O'Keefe was continuing to develop. However, she kept vacillating. "One minute I'd act like I really liked him, the next like I couldn't stand him," she said in mid-1991. One of the issues that she was weighing was their age difference. She had just turned forty, and he was thirty-five.

Besides that, there was the matter of their different lifestyles. Bonnie was used to recording her albums, and then taking off on concert tours for several months at a time. Michael was more of a homebody, used to early morning calls on movie sets, while Bonnie was more of a night owl. Could they mesh in spite of their differences?

Bonnie said, "We were close to a year into the relationship, and the thing in the way of moving forward was uncovering these rocks of really scary stuff. Like: What is the scariest thing about you that scares me? What if I can't handle the age difference? What if I can't stand the lifestyle difference? You gotta work on those issues or they'll come back a year into the next relationship. If you can't accept what you look like in the daytime with no clothes on, it's not got any better if you switch guys, you know what I mean? You have to make peace with who you are, and let the person you're loving be themselves. It becomes a leap of faith."

In the fall of 1990, Bonnie capitalized on her newfound fame by performing benefit concerts for her favorite causes. As she so often stressed, "The music's great, but what's important is doing something meaningful with your life."

On August 31, 1990, Bonnie sang "Amazing Grace" along with Jackson Browne and Stevie Wonder, at the funeral for blues singer Stevie Ray Vaughan, in Dallas, Texas. Like Bonnie, Stevie Ray had just gone through rehab for drug and drinking problems, and was enjoying his revitalized career with newly-sober enthusiasm. It seemed like Vaughan had just pulled his life together when he was killed in a tragic helicopter accident.

On October 4, along with Rickie Lee Jones, Melissa Etheridge, and Dianne Reeves, Bonnie performed at a Vote Choice concert for the Hollywood Woman's Political Committee at the Wadsworth Theater in Los Angeles. On November 16 and 17, at L.A.'s Shrine Auditorium, Bonnie appeared with Bruce Springsteen and Jackson Browne in two all-acoustic concerts for the Christic Institute, to finance a lawsuit against the United States government for its part in the Iran-Contra arms deal. And, on December 16, Bonnie and Jackson gave a concert in Sioux Falls, South Dakota, to commemorate the one hundredth anniversary of the massacre of Sitting Bull and his warriors at Wounded Knee.

It had been an absolutely incredible year for Bonnie Raitt, and she was overwhelmed by all of the attention she had received, and by the millions of albums she had just sold. Thrilled by it all, she said, "I really feel like some angels have been carrying me around. I just have more focus and more discipline, and consequently more self-respect. And that really feels great.

I'm not worried about anything anymore. I don't sweat the small stuff."

Her increased income didn't alter her lifestyle. "I'm not into clothes or cars or houses," she said. "I'd like to buy more time, but you can't do that."

She added, "I don't think I'm a major artist. I mean, I think I'm a respected survivor in a business that usually eats its young and that I'm a bona fide blueswoman and a political activist, and respected as such. And I think that after twenty years I became significant because I stuck around and not that many people do what I do, whereas at twenty-five I wasn't cutting edge enough and I didn't have the drive or the manager or the inclination or the face or the boobs or whatever it takes to be a star."

Her career finally in order, she began to evolve in her personal life as well. Stubborn in nature, and ambivalent about change, Bonnie was finally willing to make some major alterations.

On Christmas Day—December 25, 1990—Bonnie Raitt and Michael O'Keefe announced their engagement. Now she could really give her friends, fans, and followers something to talk about!

10

Let's Give Them Something to Talk About

On the evening of January 16, 199CS-co shrt1, at the elegant Waldorf Astoria Hotel, Bonnie Raitt appeared at the Fifth Annual Rock and Roll Hall of Fame ceremony, to present and induct one of that night's honorees, her blues buddy John Lee Hooker.

Wearing a spangled short black cocktail dress, nylons, and heels—Bonnie looked beautiful. Her cascading red hair—with its trademark shock of silver above her left eyebrow—flowed into the glittering design on the front of her dress.

As the ceremony began, the lights of the Grand Ballroom were dimmed, and David Crosby solemnly announced that the Middle Eastern military conflict known as Operation Desert Storm was underway, and that the bombing of Baghdad was taking place. Bonnie was later to comment about the war with dismay, "I don't think people should jump up and down like it's a Super Bowl victory, when 100,000 people got bulldozed

into trenches. No amount of misery should be applauded."
After Crosby's announcement, the ceremony continued as
planned.

Preceding Hooker on stage that night, a radiant Bonnie
Raitt spoke glowing of the accomplished bluesman. "When I
first met John Lee Hooker all I wanted to do was eat, sleep,
make love, and play the blues—I *still* do!"

The other inductees that winter night included the Byrds
(David Crosby, Roger McGuinn, Gene Clark, Mike Clark, and
Chris Hillman), LaVerne Baker, the Impressions (Jerry Butler,
Curtis Mayfield, Arthur Brooks, Richard Brooks, Sam
Gooden, and Fred Cash), Wilson Pickett, Ike and Tina Turner,
and Howlin' Wolf. The evening ended with the traditional all-
star jam that included both inductors and inductees. Bonnie,
Tracy Chapman, Chaka Khan, Phoebe Snow, Patty Smythe,
and LaVerne ("Tweedle-Dee") Baker were the rock women on
stage with Bruce Springsteen, John Fogerty, Jackson Browne,
the Byrds, the Impressions, Don Henley, David Sanborn, ZZ
Top, Wilson Pickett, and band leader Paul Shaffer.

If it weren't for the all-star jam session every year, The
Rock and Roll Hall of Fame presentations would be quite a
staid and boring event. Attended by record company executives
who pay $1,000 per ticket, rock stars, and press members, the
event begins with a sit-down dinner, and progresses to the
awards and acceptance speeches. After hours of sitting still, the
crowd is ready for some excitement.

The jam session that year began with the rare reunion of the
Byrds, doing a three-song medley of their hits—augmented by
Jackson Browne and Don Henley. Next, John Lee and Bonnie
funked and rolled on their Grammy-winning "I'm in the
Mood," and then they were joined by Robert Cray for still an-
other blues excursion. Fogerty and Khan dueted on "Proud
Mary," Patty Smythe and Laverne Baker on "Tweedle-Dee,"
and Springsteen and Browne joined the Impressions (sans May-

field—who was unable to attend) on their hit "People Get Ready."

Raitt, along with Fogerty, Springsteen, and Khan did a soul quartet version of "the wicked, wicked Pickett's" ferocious "Mustang Sally." Then Phoebe Snow added her voice to the quartet for a true all-star rendition of Wilson's "In the Midnight Hour" along with Pickett. It was truly a memorable evening of music.

On the topic of Bonnie's generosity—especially in light of her elevated celebrity status—John Lee Hooker was later to praise her by proclaiming, "I knew Bonnie when she was . . . playing the blues around Boston and places like that. I knew then that she was gonna really be a big star one day. She's got no ego, she's down to earth, she loves the blues, and she loves to hear old blues singers. With her clout, she puts them on her back, and brings them up the hill."

That spring, Bonnie's mind was preoccupied with thoughts of her upcoming April wedding. She said only weeks prior to the nuptials, "I was never really the marrying type. I always preferred to be Kitty on *Gunsmoke*—love the sheriff but not give up my independence. But I think there's certain things that you can only get by having this kind of commitment. You have to be monogamous and you have to be into each other. And if in a few years we're not, it's not like we got chained at the neck. But I am really serious or I wouldn't be doing it. And the seriousness of it really floors me. But boy, the responses I've gotten from different people I've gone out with. You can hear them just shake their head over the phone: 'First she quits drinking, then she gets married!' Like, 'It's really the end of an era.' "

On April 28, 1991, Bonnie Raitt, forty-one, and Michael O'Keefe, thirty-six, were married at the small non-denominational Union Church of Pocantico Hills, New York, near Tarrytown. It is especially known for its impressive and beautiful stained glass windows designed by Henri Matisse and Marc Chagall. The intimate ceremony had a Celtic theme, due to Bonnie's Scottish background and O'Keefe's Irish roots. Bonnie's father, John Raitt, walked his red-haired daughter down the aisle wearing a traditional tartan kilt, and gave her away.

Bonnie's mother, Marge Goddard, who had since remarried, was Bonnie's maid of honor. At the altar, Bonnie announced to her betrothed, "I stand before you Michael, to take this step I've waited all my life to take."

After they were married, Michael proclaimed, "Bonnie embodies everything I have always wanted in a woman, love, honesty, passion—and a great way with the blues!"

At the reception, held at Tarrytown House, Irish music was played, and Bonnie's father sang songs including "The Girl That I Marry" and "My Little Girl," while Bonnie and Michael danced their first dance as man and wife. A star-studded event, it was attended by Jackson Browne and his then-girlfriend, Daryl Hannah, and country star Wynonna Judd.

Aside from her wedding, one of Bonnie's main concerns that year was following up her big breakthrough album, *Nick of Time*. She explained at the time, "Well, you woulda *thought* it woulda made me nervous, but it didn't. I don't know whether it's because I went through all that rough time and came out of it, and now I don't worry about anything—which isn't true, but I don't worry about the big stuff—or what it was. But I just had a lotta faith that it was gonna work out. That can be a gullible thing, but it can also be a healthy thing for someone who's over-analytical and neurotic like I am."

Bonnie's next album, *Luck of the Draw*, was to become another high-water mark in her career. One of the most significant aspects of the new album was the fact that it contained the greatest number of Bonnie Raitt compositions of any of her albums to date. In spite of the overwhelming acceptance she had received from *Nick of Time*, she was still slightly tentative about revealing some of her inner thoughts in song. On *Luck of the Draw*, she dug deeper to expose some more personal emotions, and the results were frank and refreshingly honest.

"I wish I had more 'chops' sometimes to play what I hear in my head," she said, "but I really am not as much a student of the guitar as I am of the song itself. I do it instinctively. Sometimes I sing and play lines together, but it's kind of arbitrary, I don't really think it out."

Previewing some of the songs on *Luck of the Draw*, Bonnie explained, "I've got a couple I'm working on that are similar to 'Nick of Time' in the sense that they are about women at my age. I'm looking at people like John Prine and K. T. Oslin for inspiration. It's like a whole new world has opened up. I think of myself as a songwriter now. Then I've got a reggae song that's pretty sexual. And there's a political one called 'Hell to Pay' that's like something Henley or Randy Newman might write. You've really got to be careful with message songs because if they are too earnest they look really schmaltzy."

Released in June 1991, the *Luck of the Draw* album crystalized the appealing sound, emotive feeling, sharp uncluttered instrumentation, and confident singing that made *Nick of Time* so brilliant. Of the twelve songs on the album, one third of them were written or cowritten by Bonnie herself. Each of them peeled back further layers of emotion to reveal some very personal thoughts and feelings. Additionally, this became the first of her albums on which Bonnie was credited as coproducing the entire disc alongside Don Was.

The frisky opening track, "Something to Talk About" shows off Bonnie at her most playful. Shirley Eikhard's song was the perfect choice to lead off the album. It carried the sense of joy that was now permeating Raitt's personal life. With her zinging slide-guitar licks, this is an excellent cut, and has become a nineties signature song for her.

One of the things that Bonnie does on this—her twelfth

album—is to tell stories with her song selections. Some of them—especially the four she wrote—are deeply personal. Some describe characters who do not exist, in others the protagonist is clearly Bonnie herself. This storyteller's stance suits her well, and she uses her expressive voice to take her listeners to some dark and sad places. Always one to weave a mesmerizing spell with her voice, she is at her vocal height on this album.

Cecil and Linda Womack's "Good Man, Good Woman" is a festive blues-rock romp about looking for a new love, presented as a duet between Bonnie and her buddy Delbert McClinton. A bluegrass-like rocker, "Good Man, Good Woman" gives Raitt and McClinton a chance to show off their singing and instrumental expertise: Bonnie on her slide guitar, Delbert on harmonica.

"I Can't Make You Love Me," a sad, solemn heartbreaker, written by M. Reid and A. Shamblin is a new zenith for Bonnie. This song, about begging to be loved, delivers one of the most somber and involving performances of her twenty-year recording career. Including the brilliant piano playing of Bruce Hornsby, this number became one of the year's most frequently played radio hits.

Raitt said, "I couldn't even get through that song. I kept crying at the line 'I'll close my eyes/So I don't see/The love you don't feel/When you're holding me'—that's the saddest line I've ever heard. Though I'm not one for melodrama. I mean, if you lose it, you use another take."

Bonnie's composition "Tangled and Dark," was about her relationship with Michael. A pounding rocker, the song delves into the depths of a love affair—to the point where one takes extreme chances with one's heart. This was one of the songs that she wrote while she was pondering her love for O'Keefe. The mix of Bonnie's slide-guitar wizardry and the jazzy addition of the Tower of Power Horn Section makes this an excellent and insightful rock number.

"I had terrible dreams the night after I wrote it," she says. "There's a point, especially at my age, where you don't want to keep starting over. It was time to do something really dangerous, like get married—the great leap of faith. Without that spiritual commitment, you're just keeping an eye open for something better. I never expected to get married. I don't take those vows lightly. Michael's the first man I've trusted enough to even think about marrying. At this point in my life, I certainly wasn't going to marry someone who didn't mean it when he said, 'I forsake all others.' He knows I mean it."

Bonnie, on acoustic guitar, takes the lighter paced musical approach on her composition "Come to Me," but the subject matter in the verse is obviously also about O'Keefe. She has already mulled over the scary part of the relationship with Michael, and beckons him to "Come to Me." Lyrically, she speaks of being tired of being beaten up by love—she's now ready for a true committed relationship. On this cut, she features three members of her 1980's Bump Band—Schell, Fataar, and McLagan—as well as a guest appearance by Kris Kristofferson singing in the background.

"One Part Be My Lover" features lyrics written by Michael O'Keefe and music by Bonnie. "He wrote this poem when he was mad at me and put it on the bed when I woke up. He said, 'Here.' Later, when he wasn't looking, I wrote music for it," she explained. "It's about the point in a relationship where you're both so beat up from before that you're just terrified. Trying to figure out whether it was really happening or whether we just weren't meant for each other, because I was scared." The result is a poignant classic.

Paul Brady wrote two of the songs on the album: the beautiful medium-tempo "Not the Only One," and the story song

"Luck of the Draw." "Not the Only One" is about finally
finding true love, and "Luck of the Draw" is an ode to a bartender who writes movie screenplays on the side, hoping that
the next envelope in the mailbox is the big acceptance letter that
will spell success. Bonnie turns both into touching vocal vignettes. Billy Vera's "Papa Come Quick (Jody and Chico)," an
amusing tale about two lovers on the run in East L.A., gets a
more humorous soap-opera treatment.

"All at Once" is one of the most fascinating of Bonnie's
compositions. It is her obvious effort toward creating the kind
of fictional female character that has filled some of her most
chilling sad songs, along the lines of "Louise." It is about a
woman looking back at a life in shambles: the daughter who ran
away, the husband who left her, and the time that has escaped
her. It ends with one of her most stinging lyric lines, which finds
her comtemplating why the guardian angels protect some and
ignore others. The cut ends with the mournful sound of the
Great Highland Bagpipe.

With regard to "All at Once," Bonnie explained, "It was a
really sad song to write. The idea came from an 'Angel From
Montgomery' type of person. But then the chorus of the song—
'all at once I hear your voice and time just slips away'—came
from a completely different place. It felt like someone was
singing or playing through me. Like, there had been times when
I've held a note on guitar and felt like Lowell George or Fred
McDowell was with me. Times during the summer when Stevie Ray was around. So I would just sit there and play this chorus like a mantra or something. And the two parts came together—a woman who's very dejected and yet very hopeful."

How was it that Bonnie Raitt could still come up with such
succinctly deft sad songs now that her life was so full of joy?
"Just because you're going through a good period doesn't mean
you don't remember how it feels to be bereft of inspiration or
love," Bonnie explained. "I remember what it was like to be

with someone who no longer loved me, but I asked him to stay just one more night."

According to Don Was, "Bonnie only chooses songs that directly pertain to her life. Her music is very personal. She's not acting. She doesn't need enhancing. People are moved by what she sings, and I just try to get that across. It's not my job to paint the picture, but to protect it."

Bonnie explains how she constructs an album: "I don't think there's a formula. There's as wide a range of songs on those records as you can hear. *Nick of Time* has a country song, a blues song, R&B songs, contemporary ballads. . . . I am probably the least categorizable artist that you can find!"

When *Luck of the Draw* originally entered the marketplace in America, all compact disks were packaged in exterior "long boxes." The "long boxes" came about so that retail stores could display CDs in racks previously designed to sell conventional twelve-inch-vinyl LPs. Before 1993, when cardboard-wasting long boxes ceased to be used, singers including the group Deee-Lite, and country star Roy Rogers looked into alternatives to packaging CDs in configurations that could be displayed in the same size format (5 3/4" by 12 1/4"). Since the long boxes were usually thrown away upon purchase, different environmental groups began to protest the waste of paper and favored the European way of packaging CDs, simply sealed in cellophane.

This became another of Bonnie's causes. When *Luck of the Draw* was still in the planning stages, she chose to pay a portion of her potential royalties toward the more expensive (but ecologically correct) four-paneled recycled-cardboard package. Held together with recyclable plastic side bars in an eleven-by-five-inch open configuration, the original version of *Luck of the Draw* resembled a cardboard package for a deck of cards, when it was purchased, unwrapped, and folded together. The first three million copies came out in this configuration, with record clubs producing their own plastic jewel-box version of the CD. Now that long boxes are no longer used, *Luck of the Draw* is only available in the conventional jewel-box version, with the original cardboard versions of the package destined to become a collector's item. Bonnie was later honored by several environmental groups for her ecology-minded efforts.

When *Luck of the Draw* was released, Don Was said, "The basic theory that I have about Bonnie, which permeated *Nick of Time* and hopefully this record as well, is that people like her and want to get intimate with her. And if you provide them with forty-five intimate minutes—not of saxophone solos or great drum sounds, but of intimacy—then they are going to be happy. Whatever the decision that needs making in the studio, I ask the question, 'Is this making me, as a fan, feel closer to her?' If you follow that program, people are going to like it."

Comparing *Luck of the Draw* to *Nick of Time*, Bonnie explained, "I was afraid I wasn't gonna be able to come up with something deep enough for people to compare with the song 'Nick of Time.' But I knew that set a standard, and I didn't want to wimp out. Other people can't always say what you want to say, and as an artist you want to express something that's from your heart. So I thought, 'What's the issue in my life right now?'"

The issues she dealt with on *Nick of Time* concerned coming to grips with middle age. The ideas and ideals that were important to her when she recorded *Luck of the Draw* had to do with reassessing the relationships in her life.

Luck of the Draw was an immediate smash. *Nick of Time* had brilliantly paved the way for another successful release. The album quickly hit number 1 on the music charts and went on to sell an astonishing five million copies.

The press reviews were equally glowing. *Down Beat* magazine wrote, "Bonnie Raitt superbly delivers once again here on *Luck of the Draw*. But that's no surprise. . . . While Raitt is a tad more reflective on this album than her earlier, rowdier

LPs, *Luck of the Draw* is merely a variation on the theme of the styles of music she as consistently recorded over her amazing but rocky twenty-year career."

Stereo Review declared,

> Raitt continues to do what she's always done—play marvelously expressive, earthy music that manages to stir the loins and the soul at the same time. The album is loose and playful, and yet seductive in a serious, subtle way. . . . Raitt also draws on a handful of songwriters who have helped shape some of her best work. These include John Hiatt, Mike Reid, and Raitt herself, who wrote or co-wrote four of the album's most emotionally intense tunes—and the ones that set its tone and theme; that adult romantic love cannot thrive without commitment and emotional honesty . . . a travelogue of emotions. . . . Such eloquence does not come from the 'luck of the draw,' of course, but belongs to survivors.

And *Rolling Stone,* bestowing her with four stars, commented,

> Raitt has recorded *Luck of the Draw,* a collection of pensive and often bittersweet new songs that, like it's predecessor, draws on the pop savvy of producer Don Was (who coproduces with Raitt this time)—and the support of an impressive array of guest musicians and songwriters. . . . Her voice, a little less sweet than it was in the seventies, but handsomely seasoned and agile, has been most emotive in recent years; age and experience have endowed Raitt with a subtlety and an effortless emotional authority reminiscent of the great soul singers, as well as the blues legends she emulated in her youth.

During Bonnie's Warner Brothers career there were no music videos. A novelty before 1983, they became a necessity after that. According to Bonnie, "I really like the creative process of making these little minimovies about your song. 'Thing Called Love' is probably my favorite one. I've never had as much fun making a video as I did [on that one]. It was my idea to ask Dennis [Quaid] to do it, 'cause I knew that I did need somebody to help me loosen up on camera, and have that kind of sexual play while showing people that you don't have to take your clothes off, to have that kind of heat going on."

When she filmed the video for her single "Not the Only One," near Carmel, California, she kept much of the casting in the family. Not only does her husband, Michael O'Keefe, appear in bed reading her love letters to him, but her father also makes a cameo appearance, looking on from the sidelines while Bonnie sings the song.

Naturally, several parallels were drawn between *Nick of Time* and *Luck of the Draw*. Don Was explained, "To say Bonnie had been dismissed by the industry for twenty years was an understatement. She was a pariah, and so there was something to prove with *Nick of Time*. That hunger wasn't there for *Luck of the Draw*. It was scary. I had to put blinders on."

Right after the album was released, Bonnie again went out on tour, this time with San Francisco-based folk-rock singer Chris Isaak as her opening act. "I've never stopped enjoying it," she said, "and I think that my dad has never stopped enjoying it, so that's where I get my encouragement to 'only improve with age.' The nice part about not being a kind of a dance-sex-bomb is that I'll be able to be seventy-five and get away with it, and they won't!"

She went on, "I've got an enthusiasm for everything again, and this is an opportunity I can't pass up. People say, 'Gee, are you gonna settle down and get off the road?' But you can't really have your first hit record at forty-one, and then take a break. You have to go out and open that market up while the opportunity's there!"

However, she did ponder the future. "I don't want to tour the rest of my life. I might want to produce some other people, and I might want to live in Marin and Mendocino counties and just grow some vegetables and have a dog and have a kid. I can't tend this career eleven months out of the year. And, [her manager] Danny [Goldberg] said that the great thing about this windfall is that if I play my cards right, I could have a career like James Taylor's, where he tours in the sheds [outdoor arenas] in the summertime, and he can take time off to write. Which is what I'd have to do to learn how to be a better writer, *or* a wife. I mean, he's a more significant artist than I am, and he's had a long career and built up his following, where I'm still having to win over the rest of the world."

No one was more amazed by her success than Bonnie. "It really is the luck of the draw," she said. "I have no idea why things happen—'why the angels turn their backs on some.' People with young children who get stricken with diseases. Here, I'll take half your disease and you can have two of my Grammys, you know? I'll be glad to share this good fortune. You really do have to give it away. It's the only way you can handle it."

Don Was was especially impressed with the career path that Bonnie Raitt had chosen. Instead of kicking back, or trying to repeat past formulas, she was forging ahead with her singing and songwriting. After the struggles that she had been through, she was not content to rest upon her laurels, but was looking for new musical and political challenges.

Was claimed, "The pattern you see in most artists is that the first three or four years they really galvanize their strengths and have this rapid development. Then they spend the next twenty-five years playing their Greatest Hits. In Bonnie's case, though I certainly love her early records, there's no question that she's gone through artistic growth over the last five years. After eleven albums and twenty years playing gigs, that's pretty unique. And, there's a growing vision. People think of her as this 'blues girl'—that's so wrong! She has that authenticity, but she's also taken pop songs to some really new places."

Bonnie no longer felt the need to break through to the record-buying audience and prove herself musically. The acceptance that she sought was validated by *Nick of Time* and *Luck of the Draw*. Now came the time to more deeply plumb her songwriting and her performing.

"I've spent the last couple of years going inside and healing," she says. "Back to pleasures like reading a book on the lawn, cutting flowers—reinventing my life in a more childlike and simple way. Michael's a serious Zen student, and I'm opening up to that world, getting in touch with the internal life I've always avoided. And letting music become inspirational to me, where it really hadn't been for a while. I wouldn't say I have complete serenity. This process isn't without effort. But once you commit yourself to the relationship you sort of surrender to the current. And once you commit to the songs you want to do, the execution of it is not so much of a problem. Five years ago, I don't think any of these things could have happened. Now it's a question of whether I can get out of my own way enough to let the creativity to come. And the ability to love and accept love. I'm just trying to take advantage of every minute I have, 'cause I've wasted so much time."

She could now afford to provide even more support to her friends in the business. "I don't have to worry about my bills. I don't have to worry about being loved. I don't have to worry about which producer's gonna be right or which record label's gonna mess me over. I feel confident and I feel grateful and I feel relieved. It's absolutely the best time in my life!"

One of her main concerns became helping out the rhythm and blues stars of the past, many of whom continued to get ripped off by unfair recording deals that they had made in the forties, fifties, and sixties. Without proper legal and contractual advice, many singers signed contracts that gave them money up-front, but did not pay royalties. With the advent of compact disks, much of the music of these by-gone eras was being rereleased and repackaged, while the singers received nothing. Whenever an old record is played on the radio, it is the songwriter who gets paid a royalty, not the performer. However, when the recording sells on the retail level, the performer should share in the profits. The injustice started to anger Bonnie, and she decided she would try to do something to rectify the injustice.

Championing their cause, Bonnie claimed, "I make money based on their music, and it's not clean money if I don't share it with them. It's not guilt. It's just what's right."

Part of the solution came with the organization of the Rhythm and Blues Foundation. Bonnie explained, "The Rhythm and Blues Foundation, which was started about five years ago to attempt to get the music industry—and other artists like myself—to donate money to rectify something that none of us knew was a really big injustice, which is, that most of the artists who started out playing our kind of music, that was the roots of rock and roll and soul music as we know it, never received any royalties. People in the forties and the fifties and sixties, that I grew up adoring, only got paid for the afternoon they recorded! That's like: 'Thanks for painting the walls in my house.' Now, of course, CD reissues are bringing in incredible amounts of revenue, because that music has never gone out of style, and people buy it all the time. And, I don't think that the public knows that these artists never got paid. This is another form of slavery, in my opinion.

"There wouldn't be any rock and roll and none of us would be here, without this music. To be able to take Charles Brown, the great rhythm and blues songwriter and pianist out on the road with me—because now I have the clout to be able to tell the promoter who I want to have open [my concerts]—that's a really great sideline to being successful."

One of the catalysts for the Rhythm and Blues Foundation occurred in 1990 when Motown singing star Mary Wells ("My Guy") was diagnosed with throat cancer. She found herself with a life-threatening illness, no medical insurance, and no income. Several musician peers came to her rescue, including Bruce Springsteen and Rod Stewart. It was the Rhythm and Blues Foundation—which had been established in 1988—that oversaw the assistance she received.

"We always considered Mary Wells to be the first lady of Motown," former Supreme Mary Wilson said, "Everyone in the business is calling to offer their help,"

Mary Wells's hits "You Beat Me to the Punch" and "The One Who Really Loves You" helped define the Motown era. When the Rhythm and Blues Foundation came to the rescue, Wells said, "I'm overwhelmed and so relieved. I didn't know what was going to happen—I was ready to panic. This has been a tremendous rescue and relief to me. It's also been embarrassing to me, because I've always been self-sufficient and independent, but I'm also grateful."

Mary Wells's composition "Bye Bye Baby" had been an important song on Bonnie Raitt's album *The Glow.* She took Wells's plight to heart, and it had a profound effect on her. Since then, Raitt has been increasingly more active in volunteering her time and her energy toward raising money for the Rhythm and Blues Foundation. (On a sad note, in 1992 Mary Wells lost her valiant battle against cancer.)

To help the revival of Charles Brown's career, Bonnie recorded two different vocal duets with him during 1992. On Brown's *Someone to Love* album, she sang the title cut with him, and lent her slide-guitar mastery to the Brenda Holloway song "Every Little Bit Hurts." As a contribution to the Special Olympics' charity album, *A Very Special Christmas, 2*, Raitt and Brown sang "Merry Christmas Baby."

In February 1992 Bonnie won three additional Grammy Awards: the *Luck of the Draw* album won the trophy as Best Rock Vocal Performance, Female, the single "Something to Talk About" won as the Best Pop Vocal Performance, Female, and "Good Man, Good Woman," by Bonnie and Delbert Mc-Clinton, took the Best Rock Performance, Duo or Group trophy.

With her name now a household word, Bonnie began to receive offers to perform on several television programs. In July 1992, Bonnie and her father, John Raitt, appeared with the Boston Pops Orchestra on PBS. Not long after Natalie Cole had released her version of her father's "Unforgettable," in which they sang a posthumous duet, Bonnie repeated the same feat—but with her father alive and in person. During the show, Bonnie performed some of her folk-rock hits, John did his Broadway hits, and the show ended with a duet version of the show-stopping "Oklahoma."

Bonnie said at the time, "When I was younger, I loved the songs my father sang, yet I never saw myself singing anything but the more comical songs." With her father at her side, she found that she could project herself into the heartbreaking songs of Broadway as well. The concert was taped before an audience of eighteen hundred in May. In the context of the show, John Raitt sang the ballad "Soliloquy" from *Carousel,* which is a song from a father to his little girl. Suddenly, out from the wings came Bonnie. Singing with her father made for a touching musical finale to the show.

"I anticipated it being incredibly moving and it was," Bonnie said after the show. Not only did she perform some of her father's best-known tunes with him, but he performed her music with her as well, on "I'm Blowin' Away." According to John, "We spent almost three hours the first time we got together, with her telling me how to sing her music, and me telling her how to sing mine."

In May 1993 Bonnie was among the legendary rock, pop, and soul worlds' finest singers to perform with the Queen of Soul, Aretha Franklin, on her "Duets" TV special. Also on hand to pay musical tribute to Sister Ree were Rod Stewart, Elton John, Gloria Estafan, and Smokey Robinson. Originally staged in April as a four-hour benefit to raise money for the AIDS charity, the Gay Men's Health Crisis, the resulting television program chose forty-five minutes of that evening's strongest numbers for the Fox Network TV special.

Awed by the presence of Franklin, during the rehearsal for the concert, Bonnie repeated over and over, "I just can't believe I'm here!"

All of the singing stars performed with Aretha. Gloria Estafan sang a duet version of her hit "Coming Out of the Dark," and Bonnie and Franklin did one of Aretha's hits, "Since You've Been Gone." *USA Today* referred to "Bonnie's whiskey-soaked vocals on 'Since You've Been Gone' " as the evening's biggest hit.

According to the TV review in *Daily Variety*, "Highlights include Franklin and Elton at twin pianos battling choruses on 'Border Song,' Franklin and Stewart's 'People Get Ready,' and a version of '(You Make Me Feel Like a) Natural Woman,' featuring Franklin, a particularly strong perf by Bonnie Raitt, and Gloria Estefan."

Introducing that trio version of the song, Rod Stewart said of Aretha, "I've just got to tell you, this is the highlight of my life, to be standing on the stage with this wonderful woman, who's surely got the best voice of the twentieth century, in my opinion."

Bonnie added, "You know, it doesn't get any better than Aretha Franklin! I grew up wearing out 45's of 'Respect,' 'Chain of Fools,' "I Never Loved a Man,'—and although the music was always incredible, somehow I knew that she had to always get into the lyrics before she could sing them. If it didn't mean a whole lot, it wouldn't get cut."

With that, Aretha, Bonnie, and Gloria launched into "(You Make Me Feel Like a) Natural Woman." When they came to Bonnie's solo lyrics, Aretha chimed in "sing the song, girl!" It was a special television moment, which was later captured on the album *Aretha Franklin's Greatest Hits 1980–1994*.

Later that same year, Bonnie was one of the singing stars to appear on Elton John's own *Duets* album. She and Elton were heard performing Ketty Lester's 1962 hit, "Love Letters," (Elvis Presley also made it a Top Twenty hit in 1966). The dramatic torch ballad received a stellar performance by Elton and Bonnie, with Raitt sounding crystal clear and thrillingly intense. Her slide-guitar solo in the middle of the song, followed by his piano solo, adds a beautiful point-counterpoint from this ultimate superstar pairing. The result was a wonderful performance from both singer-musicians.

Less than a decade before, Bonnie Raitt was a sad, lonely woman helplessly watching her once-brilliant career disintegrate. Now, ever since the decade of the nineties began, all of the projects she became involved in were turning out to be successful.

According to Bonnie, part of the magic was due to the fact that the bad karma that once bedeviled her had disappeared when she turned her back on self-destructive substances. Since Bonnie gave up recreational drugs and liquor, she stays away from places where any temptations might exist. She said, "I don't see it anymore because the people I hang out with have cooled it. When I'm around somebody who's polluted, I just move away. It's not entertaining to me. I'm really sorry that there's this lure of the dark side—heroin and more dangerous drugs—that has a hold on kids. It's the same hold that was on Keith Richards. It's always been in the art community and has been an ongoing problem in Hollywood since the twenties. It's too much money, too much time. I hope that people will come to realize you can be funky, hip, smart, and creative without being loaded. In our generation, we didn't believe that. It's so much cooler now to be sober. In my own family, the nieces and nephews have chosen to not be messed up because they've got a petri dish—they watched what it did to me!"

Bonnie adds that her newfound celebrity status has not changed her. "For anyone who's wondering, I really appreciate it! But I have good friends who are without a job, friends who are lonely, friends with terminal illnesses. I'm not some sort of Moonie that got swept away by all this. I have good days and bad days and irritability and fears. When you're in the middle of the good stuff, you remember the bad. And I sing the songs that I sing to remind myself, too."

She laughingly explains, "I have my cranky days. I did last Friday. I got home and I couldn't even get horny, which is a *low* point for me. I was just so tired I was drained, you know? Because you have to be really careful that you don't burn yourself out with enthusiasm and health."

In 1993—in between the Aretha TV special and the *Elton John: Duets* album—Bonnie continued to make guest appearances on several other people's albums, running the gamut in musical style from country to pop to blues to jazz. When Don Was produced Willie Nelson's *Across the Borderline* album, he enlisted Bonnie to record the song "Getting Over You" with Willie. Bonnie provided a smooth counterpoint to Nelson's rough-edged singing, and the cut is one of the highlights of the excellent country-folk LP. She is also heard on Bruce Hornsby's jazz-influenced *Harbor Lights* album, singing background vocals on "Rainbow's Cadillac" and "The Tide Will Rise." She also took Hornsby on the concert road that year as her opening act. And Bonnie appeared on blues star Buddy Guy's 1993 *Feels Like Rain,* dueting on the title track, plus adding slide guitar to it. Suddenly, Bonnie Raitt was everywhere—and, she was just beginning to hit her stride.

11

Love Sneakin' Up on You

I t had been three years since *Luck of the Draw* was released, and had subsequently become the biggest-selling album
of Bonnie Raitt's career. Capitol Records released her third
album for them, *Longing in Their Hearts*, in March 1994. With
Don Was coproducing with Raitt again, Bonnie had surrounded herself with several of her devoted music industry
friends, including David Lasley, Levon Helm of the Band,
Ricky Fataar, David Crosby, Richard Thompson, and Charlie
Musselwhite.

Recorded in six different studios in the Los Angeles area,
from August to October 1993, *Longing in Their Hearts* would
become one of Bonnie Raitt's most successful, most personally
revealing, and most musically satisfying albums. Her musical
integrity and newfound personal confidence really went into
this album, and it is evident in each well-crafted song. Bonnie's
instrumental playing is tight, her lyrics are insightful, and her
phrasing is self-assured and filled with emotion.

She again turned to several of her composing comrades, and
then wrote a record number of five songs herself—more than

appear on any of her other albums. This quintet of new Bonnie Raitt compositions reflect another part of her complex personality—from childhood pain to political awareness to adult frustrations.

The tried and true songwriters who she turned to on this, her thirteenth album, included Tom Snow, who had written "(Goin') Wild for Your Baby" for *The Glow,* and "Who But a Fool (Thief in Paradise)" for *Nine Lives;* Paul Brady, who had penned "Luck of the Draw" and "Not the Only One;" *and* her husband, Michael O'Keefe, who had composed the lyrics to "One Part Be My Lover." She also turned to her close friend Richard Thompson for a song as well, and received another from Terry Britten, who had written "What's Love Got to Do With It" for Tina Turner.

Bonnie loved to help out her fellow musicians, especially the ones who rarely get their songs cut in the highly competitive music world. Bonnie says, "I'm supporting a lot of really great musicians who don't get enough support—I mean the songwriters. The style of music that I'm championing is rhythm and blues. I'm celebrating roots music that's basically American roots music, that's basically African, Celtic, Spanish, Mexican—all that stuff's mixed up together. There's a little bit of something for everything, I think."

As always, the task of finding just the right songs to appear on her next album belonged to Bonnie. Don Was tried to assist her, but confesses, "We start pretty early looking for them. I try to find songs for her, but it's such a personal thing. It's like trying to pick out her clothes."

With reference to the five songs she wrote herself, Raitt explains, "These songs are definitely a product of this period in my life, that yearning. The theme of this record, if there is a thread, is that there's something more out there we want. You'd think that being married and having all this success would make you complacent or content. My life's going pretty well, but there's still a tremendous drive to go deeper. It's a spiritual longing, an existential question and very, very personal. It's not something you can put easily in a pop song."

The yearning that she referred to was for creative fulfillment, personal happiness, and the sense that she had some control over her destiny. The commercial acceptance of her last two albums, the Grammy Awards, her sobriety, and her marriage to Michael O'Keefe had changed all of the hollowness that had come before.

One of the most brilliantly planned and executed albums of Bonnie's three-decade recording career, *Longing in Their Hearts* is a stunning vocal statement by an artist at the peak of her musical expression. The first time I heard the album, I was flying home from an Anchorage, Alaska, skiing holiday. Every time I hear the lively first notes of this disk, I think of the sun coming up over the snow-covered Alaskan mountains, and Bonnie Raitt's voice singing of "Love Sneaking Up on You."

Pulsing, swampy, and raunchy, Bonnie's rhythmic singing, in front of the jangling tambourine and drum beat of "Love Sneakin' Up on You," is instantly appealing. Throbbing and exotic in sound, this song is about finding love when you least expect it. Singing it with a sassy stance of someone who has known pain, Bonnie tells of cold rainy nights waiting for the phone to ring, and then—from out of nowhere—*like* turns into *love.* Written by Tom Snow and Jimmy Scott, the cut went on to become the first hit single from the album.

According to Bonnie, " 'Love Sneaking Up on You' is just your out-and-out funk tune, you know? That's perfect, and the kind of thing I like to do. It just has a real infectious beat, and it makes you want to 'do the wild thing!' That's what I do, break peoples' hearts, and *do the wild thing!"*

"Longing in Their Hearts" is another of Michael O'Keefe's poems set to music. In addition to being about Michael and

Bonnie, he also assumes the role of story teller, and illuminates the tale of a short-order cook, and his wife—owner of the tiny diner they work in—then compares their relationship to his with Raitt. He speaks of the longing the other couple feels for something more, and compares it to "you and me." The song is a beautiful medium-tempo ballad with Bonnie on acoustic guitar and Levon Helm of the Band on harmony vocal.

Talking about Michael O'Keefe as a lyric writer, Bonnie explained, "He's a poet, anyway, so he writes poems and lyrics, and then I sort of read what he's writing. The song he wrote on the last record ["One Part Be My Lover"], he wrote specifically for me, and then I sort of snuck around and put music to it without telling him." Again, Bonnie set her husband's poem to music, and then recorded it.

"Both times it was solitary work on both of our parts," she said, "I've never really tried to write with somebody in the same room. You'd have to have so much courage to take someone else's criticism, especially about your creative work. Don Was told me a story about how he and [former songwriting partner] David Was used to wear masks when they were writing songs together. One of them wore a Colonel Saunders mask and the other put on a President Kennedy mask. That way, they wouldn't take it personally when one criticized the other. That's what I might have to try!"

"You," written by Bob Thiele Jr., Tonio K, and John Shanks; and Bonnie's own "Cool, Clear Water" are both pretty ballads with layers of acoustic musical touches. "You" is lilting and etherial, while the equally effective "Cool, Clear Water" has more musical kick to it.

In her autobiographical "Circle Dance," Bonnie sings about life in show business, traveling from town to town doing one-night stands. She recalls that it is a family show business tradition handed down from her father. In the fourth stanza, Bonnie chides her father for the heartbreak she felt as a little girl when she said goodbye to him at the front door, knowing that he would be on tour for months at a time. It is shattering to hear her bury her unhealed hurt in the statement "you did the best you could." With David Crosby harmonizing behind her, Bonnie's voice is wonderfully expressive on this deeply personal ballad.

Breaking up the somber and poignant mood that "Circle Dance" sets, Bonnie next offers the funky "I Sho Do," a raunchy and pumping R&B number with the Memphis Horns behind her, and her Bump Band buddy Ricky Fataar on drums. Richard Thompson's pensive and intricate "Dimming of the Day" is a seductive ballad with cleverly phrased lyrics and a heartfelt performance by Bonnie. A confession of love, featuring a nineteenth-century-sounding harmonium on it, the song conjures up images of Bonnie as a woman standing on a windy beach, waiting for her love to return.

The song "Feeling of Falling" is Bonnie's admission that—although newly sober—she misses the nothing-to-lose chances she used to take with her life. She said, "I wrote that song so I could relive it every night. Doing that song, I feel the danger of what I'm singing about—going too fast, staying up too late, losing my mind, being out of control. It has to do with abandoning yourself to that feeling—the lure of the dark side. Or just sheer rapture. It's human nature to want to push yourself too far. Jumping off a bridge with a bungee cord on your ankle is probably right up there with a rock and roll lifestyle. And I miss the wild times. I miss the danger of it."

From atop her own political soapbox, on "Hell to Pay," Bonnie shakes her clenched fist at sleazy politicians who have placid smiles on their faces while they rape and plunder the land with their crooked deals. Her parable of "what goes around comes around," speaks of lawmakers who stack up the bad karma against themselves, and eventually have to watch their house of cards crumble. At the end of the song, she promises that they won't have to wait to go to Hell to pay—it'll happen right here on Earth.

The album finishes off with an exquisite blues number, "Shadow of Doubt." With blues master Charlie Musselwhite on harmonica, Bonnie plays the acoustic guitar, taps her foot, and sings earnestly about wanting a sign that she is on the right path in life. She begs God not to make her path easy, just to let her know if she is on the right one.

This great, downhearted blues number was written by Nashville songwriter Gary Nicholson. He had aligned himself with some of Bonnie's songwriting buddies, wanting to come to her attention. Says Nicholson, "I had tried to get on Bonnie's records every way in the world. I cowrote with Mike Reid because he was on her last couple of records. I wrote songs with guys in her band—Gene Clark, who's an old friend of mine, and Ricky Fataar, who played on a record project I did."

He had hoped that somehow—through his contacts—one of his songs would end up in Bonnie's studio, and that she would be impressed. He was so convinced that this particular song was perfect for Bonnie that he finally decided to give fate a little shove.

"I guess you could call it a gospel-blues thing," Nicholson says of his song. A secretary at the Nashville-based music publishing company, Sony Tree, asked him why he didn't just send it directly to Bonnie. He looked at her with one of those "Why didn't I think of that?" kind of stares. Gary explains, "I just put it in the mail to her, to the address that's on the back of her album. Bonnie heard it and said she was going to cut it."

The chances of a songwriter dropping an unsolicited demo tape into the mail, and actually ending up with the song being recorded, are somewhere between slim and none. "It was the coolest thing that's ever happened to me," Nicholson said. "It's one of those things that'll never be a single or get on the radio, but I'm tickled to death."

Comparing the *Longing in Their Hearts* album with her 1971 *Bonnie Raitt* album, Bonnie says, "I don't see any difference between the styles of my first album in 1971 and the last one, that we just finished.... I like to play a wide range of stuff, because I'm going to be out there touring with it. I pick songs that I know I won't get tired of."

The critics immediately praised her new album. *Time* magazine wrote, *Longing in Their Hearts* is "as bluesy and beautiful as they come.... In Raitt's poignant voice you can hear the ache of angels as they gaze down on a dark and tangled earth."

Entertainment Weekly said of Bonnie's performance, "She's continuing to push herself and grow as an artist.... How many of her peers can make that kind of claim?"

Again, Bonnie Raitt was in the winner's circle. The album shot up to number 1 almost instantly, giving her three consecutive million-selling chart-topping new (nongreatest-hits) albums in a row. It went on to sell over two million copies in the United States alone.

Right after the *Longing in Their Hearts* album was released, Bonnie made a brief concert tour through Europe and then returned to the States. A week before the American leg of her summer 1994 concert tour began in Milwaukee, Bonnie, along with Stevie Wonder, Melissa Etheridge, Al Green, Kenny G, Michael Bolton, (formerly) Prince, and Garth Brooks were honored on the VH1 video network in a concert special simulcast from the Shrine Auditorium in Los Angeles.

Each of the recipients of the first annual VH1 Honors awards was saluted for his or her individual participation in different charity events, and for charitable causes. Bonnie's award was specifically for her work with the Rhythm and Blues Foundation.

The show that evening began with Stevie Wonder at a grand piano, playing "Heaven Help Us All." He was then joined in song by Al Green, Bonnie Raitt, and Melissa Etheridge.

From the stage that night, Bonnie said, "To be able to raise money for the Rhythm and Blues Foundation and to be able to take Charles Brown, the great blues songwriter and pianist on the road with me, that's a real great sideline to being successful. This, among all nights of the year, means more to me to be able to honor the people who made the music that is our livelihood, and to be able to turn things around so that there's medical insurance and financial and career assistance to people—without whom there would be no music industry."

Handing over the trophy that evening, Mavis Staples of the gospel-rock Staples Singers proudly called out, "Ladies and gentlemen, my baby sister: Bonnie Raitt!" When the crowd's cheering and applause subsided, Mavis continued, "Now, Bonnie, I hope you find a special place for this award, because it honors you for something that goes beyond your music. It reads in part: 'To Bonnie Raitt for your dedication to the Rhythm and Blues Foundation and your appreciation and understanding of the real contribution of those artists who created the best music of our lives.' Bonnie, I love you—everybody loves you."

As the crowd again began applauding and cheering, Bonnie said, "Thank you—and coming from Mavis Staples, one of my all-time heroes—this means so much to me. Mavis, thank you for introducing me. This is fantastic! So much has happened to me that has been unbelievable in the last few years and I . . . One of the greatest things that's been able to happen in my life, is that because of my being in this building a few years ago [referring to the Shrine Auditorium, and the Grammy Awards], I was able to draw more attention to the artists who ended up not getting paid royalties when they first got signed [to recording contracts] back in the forties and fifties and sixties, and I never knew—and I don't think many of the artists out here know that those people who built rock and roll and rhythm and blues, never got any royalties for it. And, the Rhythm and Blues Foundation is something that's very close to my heart, and a lot of people who helped found it. I really appreciate you giving me this honor, VH1, and all the rest of you guys [more cheers from the crowd]. Let's keep supporting the music, and remembering where it came from! Thank you! I may have gotten something to put on my mantelpiece, but I'll tell you what my reward is, it's being on the same stage as Mavis, and the Reverend Al Green!"

After that, Bonnie launched into song with Al and Mavis. The evening was a triumphant one for Raitt, and it demonstrated how serious Bonnie is about her work with the Rhythm and Blues Foundation.

The next morning the *Los Angeles Times* wrote, "[Al] Green's solo spot ['Let's Stay Together'] was the evening's highlight, though his subsequent soul-a-rama teaming with Raitt and her presenter, Mavis Staples, on a medley of 'Tired of Being Alone' and [the Staples Singers'] 'I'll Take You There' was the clear crowd favorite through sheer quantity of charisma."

Bonnie's 1994 U.S. tour finally began in July, with Bruce Hornsby as her opening act again. "I've been really upset that I haven't been able to tour," she told Susan Whitall of the *Detroit News*. "It's like being assigned to summer school—you *will* finish your record and you *won't* go out on one date until you do! Although I love working in the studio, there was a long time between the record being finished and the tour starting. I happen to love touring. I'd be nuts to be in this business and not love it."

On August 3, 1994, Bonnie appeared in Radio City Music Hall in New York City, for two sold-out shows. At the conclusion of the program, John Raitt came out on stage and the father-daughter team sang a duet version of the song "They Say It's Wonderful" from *Annie Get Your Gun,* and then he sang "Oklahoma." Reviewing the show that night, the *New York Times* proclaimed, "Ms. Raitt is one of the least showy singers in rock; she makes the song seem to tell its story by itself. Her voice has a girlish sweetness deepened by a grainy sense of experience; it can cut through a full band in a rock song, but it can also make ballads float in their own world."

Her continuous touring did not seem to affect her marriage to Michael O'Keefe. He had been steadily working on his own acting career. In 1991 he had been offered the role of the love interest of Roseanne's sister (actress Laurie Metcalf), on the top-rated TV show *Roseanne.* However, he was busy with the show *Against the Law* at the time, and he passed on it. Then, in 1993 he ran into Roseanne at a benefit for President Bill Clinton, and she offered him the role again.

O'Keefe said, "Roseanne asked why I didn't want to do her show. I told her I didn't know where I fit in—but she convinced me I could be part of her team." With that, he joined the show as Fred.

Speaking of her relationship with Michael, and how they balance their careers and their marriage, Bonnie explains, "I think, 'How wonderful it is that you took this scary step!' Yet, the comfort level—having someone there for you, has a very tender and sweet side. To be in a committed relationship brings up all those issues about your parents' marriage, your preconceptions about male and female roles. It's tested me in ways I didn't expect. When things are difficult, you can't just run off or have an affair, because you made a commitment. That's an adult response. I don't think you get to any real growth until you're in a committed relationship. Some of my hardest moments have been learning how not to run away and how to resolve an argument and compromise. Only last year [1993] did we really live together rather than visit each other on the road. It's been a real challenge."

According to Bonnie, marriage hasn't tamed her, it's freed her: "You'd think that being married and having all this success would make you complacent or content. My life's going pretty well, but there's still a tremendous drive to go deeper. The urge to push the envelope didn't go away with maturity and sobriety. It's hard to be responsible all the time. I don't like these limits that adulthood put on me. Even though you're sober, you still have a desire to go too far. But it's a real part of who I am."

In addition to having her own album on the charts in 1994, she also appeared on five other albums as well. That year a series of four albums entitled *Grammy's Greatest Moments* were released by Atlantic Records. On *Volume 1* Bonnie is heard singing "Thing Called Love" from the 1990 show on which she won her first slew of Grammy Awards. *Volume 3* has her live version of the touching "I Can't Make You Love Me." She plays the slide guitar on three cuts on the album *The Tractors,* by the country music group of the same name, and on an album of Richard Thompson compositions entitled *Beat the Retreat,* she performed "When the Spell Is Broken." She also harmonized with the Queen of Soul on the *Aretha Franklin's Greatest Hits 1980–1994* album. Suddenly, Bonnie Raitt was everywhere!

In January 1995 Bonnie debuted her own line of Stratocaster guitars. At a benefit concert in Anaheim, California, she raised money for the Boys and Girls Clubs of America for a new program aimed at teaching underprivelidged girls to play the guitar. Bonnie said, "Because I'm a musician I'd like to encourage people who can't afford guitars—and girls who wouldn't even think about playing a guitar. We hope to offer access to music for people who otherwise wouldn't have access to it."

Bonnie has started appearing more frequently with her dad lately. In addition to the two shows they performed together at Radio City Music Hall in 1994, they were also seen on stage at Red Rocks outside of Denver, Colorado, and they have appeared several times at the Hollywood Bowl.

On December 17, 1994, Bonnie starred in her own ABC-TV concert special (which was rebroadcast on February 25, 1995, on the A&E cable network.) As her special guests she chose two of her all-time favorites: John Raitt and John Lee Hooker. The special was taped at one of her concert performances during the fall of 1994. "It was a dream come true," said Bonnie, adding, "When I was on stage alone, I'd laugh thinking about the two of them in the dressing room talking about their health problems. But they're really vital, an inspiration to anyone who wonders if you can still cut it in your seventies."

The elder Raitt was at work on his first new album in twenty-five years, *John Raitt: Broadway Legend.* On it, he sings three duets with Bonnie including "They Say It's Wonderful" and "Anything You Can Do" from *Annie Get Your Gun,* and "Hey There" from *The Pajama Game.* The selections on the album are taken from the classic era of Broadway, not from the productions of the 1990s. According to Bonnie's father, "There's nothing better than those melodious and tuneful numbers, the songs I belong to. I mean, what would I sing from *Sunset Boulevard?* Every musical has to be bigger than the last: the chandelier in *Phantom of the Opera,* the helicopter in *Miss Saigon,* the hugeness of *Show Boat.* I guess people want something they can't get on the little box at home."

When Bonnie had won the first of her three Grammy Awards in 1992, she came up to the microphone to accept it by saying, "Man, oh man, I've had enough already." Apparently, in 1995 the voters at the National Academy of Recording Arts and Sciences thought otherwise, as they nominated her for five different awards, including Album of the Year (for *Longing in*

Their Hearts) and Record of the Year (for "Love Sneakin' Up on You)."

Prior to the awards, she said, "Winning isn't as important as having critical and peer acclaim, and I had that *before* the nominations. There will never be anything like the lottery feeling of the first time. Having been in this rarefied air for a few years now, I'm still surprised to get nominations."

Bonnie ended up winning her eighth Grammy Award, for *Longing in Their Hearts* in the category of Best Pop Album. I was in the audience that night at the Shrine Auditorium, to see her perform a live version of the song "Love Sneakin' Up on You." She appeared calm, confident, and focused that evening as she greeted industry friends during the commercial breaks, chatting with her buddy, Ray Benson of Asleep at the Wheel, and Clive Davis, president of Arista Records.

Along with the March 1, 1995, Grammy Awards presentation, Bonnie had just released her latest hit single, her version of the Roy Orbison hit "You Got It." The lead cut from the soundtrack album from the movie *Boys on the Side,* this song became a huge Top Forty hit for Raitt, which turned the female rocker soundtrack album into a certified Gold one. *USA Today* proclaimed, "Bonnie's exquisite version of Roy Orbison's 'You Got It' is the standout on the *Boys on the Side* soundtrack, a girl's club of pop talent."

On March 16, 1995, ABC-TV presented, as part of their *Afterschool Special* series, the afternoon special "Bonnie Raitt Has Something to Talk About." Premised as a casual interview by Whoopie Goldberg, it was clearly aimed at a teenage audience. Introducing Bonnie, Whoopie exclaimed, "This is one of the all-time great women on the planet. One of the all-time great activists, and one of the all-time fabulous singers."

When Whoopie asked Bonnie, "Do you consider yourself a rocker?" Raitt said, "Rock and roll can be a lifestyle, as opposed to pop music. Pop music to me would be like Olivia

Newton-John, Gloria Estafan—although she's kind of Latin oriented, so she's Latin-pop. And, Mariah Carey does soul music, but pop music too. . . . Some of my ballads—that's not rock and roll. I feel like a rocker because of my attitude. There's the straight people, and then there's the rockers. And, I suppose that I'm a folkie and a blues fan and a political activist, but all of that falls into that big rock and roll world of people that don't go to bed on time. I think that's the bottom line: people that don't go to bed on time."

On May 11, 1995, Bonnie was one of several rock legends to gather at a Texas soundstage to pay musical tribute to Stevie Ray Vaughan. Also on hand for this superstar jam were Eric Clapton, Buddy Guy, Robert Cray, Dr. John, Art Neville, B. B. King, and Jimmy Vaughan. "Hey, old home week!" exclaimed Bonnie when she met Buddy at that afternoon's rehearsal. One of the evening's highlights was Bonnie's sizzling interpretation of Stevie Ray Vaughan's "Pride and Joy." The event was recorded for television and for CD release as well.

Not long afterward, Bonnie set out on her 1995 summer tour, taking along with her rhythm and blues legends Ruth Brown and Charles Brown. In addition to performing her 1990s hits, and several of her early career signature songs like "Louise," Bonnie also covered some of her favorite R&B classics including "Rock Steady" and "Burning Down the House." While on this tour, she recorded several of her performances, yielding the two CD live concert album *Road Tested*, which hit the stores in November 1995.

12

What Is Success?

In a way, everything had changed for Bonnie Raitt: Her marriage brought her stability, her sobriety gave her a clear vision, and her wide-spread fame added self-confidence. Yet, in many ways nothing had changed. Her lyric honesty, her musical integrity, her dedication to her ideas and her ideals, and her devotion to her musical idols, are aspects of her life that have remained unwaveringly intact.

For so many years Bonnie had shied away from mainstream success. Yet everyone who heard her passionate music in the seventies and early eighties knew that she had the potential to become a truly significant force in the music business. Eventually she recognized her own strengths and weaknesses and began to work harder at defining and eliminating self-defeating behaviors and at achieving her goals. It took her nearly twenty years before she finally become a full-fledged singing star. But when it did happen, she was prepared.

Many achieve greatness, few can sustain it. However, Bonnie Raitt is someone who is determined to continue creatively. She has many of the qualities that truly great performers like

Ella Fitzgerald, Aretha Franklin, Peggy Lee, Patsy Cline, Joan Baez, Barbra Streisand, Linda Ronstadt, and Sarah Vaughan have possessed. These performers have never gone out of fashion, and the passage of time has never diminished their appeal.

Bonnie Raitt has the same career integrity as these other great ladies of song, and her music is destined to endure. Albums like *Give It Up* and *The Glow* sound as alive and contemporary today as they did when they were released. They are every bit as enjoyable and musically varied as *Nick of Time* and *Luck of the Draw*.

Also, her music is appreciated by a wide-ranging audience. Pop and jazz singing legend Peggy Lee proclaims, "I love Bonnie Raitt—she's fantastic!"

In many ways, it is fortunate that mainstream success didn't come to Bonnie too early in life. She simply wasn't ready to handle it. Speaking about her own personal and professional postsobriety evolution, Bonnie claims, "I didn't really change, although I think I started making better records when I started having my head screwed on straight!"

In 1990, as she became the media's darling, she was able to accept and enjoy her success for what it was. However, after all of the celebratory confetti and streamers were swept up, Bonnie still knew who she was and what she was going to do with the power that her fame brought. She insisted upon giving the spotlight back to those people who had inspired and helped her along the way. They have included Ruth Brown, Charles Brown, John Lee Hooker, Buddy Guy, Richard Thompson, Bruce Hornsby, NRBQ, Billy Vera, Bill Payne, *and* John Raitt. In addition, every time she sets foot on a stage and sings "Woman Be Wise" or "You Got to Know How," she is proud to keep the memory of Sippie Wallace alive.

Bonnie's ongoing habit of teaming up with artists of past eras has continued to be a two-sided coin for Bonnie. Not only has she been able to derive great satisfaction from reviving their stalled careers, but it also tends to refuel her own thirst for new musical influences. Having showcased the undeniable talents of Sippie Wallace, Ruth Brown, Charles Brown, and John Lee Hooker has added a fascinating dimension of blues authenticity to her stage act.

Bonnie is thankful for the opportunity to do what it is that she does best. She says appreciatively, "To have a career as long, and a following as loyal as I've had is a blessing, and hardly—probably only a handful of people have in this business. So, this latest, much more exulted success is kind of unreal and fantastic. But, if it simmers down, I still can go back to the place where I came from and be really happy. That security, and that inspiration—there's incredible freedom and security in knowing that you're gonna have a job! I don't need a band or a record to make a living, so that's what keeps me going, I think. That, and the fact that everyone seems to understand what I'm doing now. So, for my next fifteen minutes of fame—I'll rule!"

For Bonnie, it's almost as if this new phase of her life is a whole different career than the one she had before. "Being successful and famous is hard," she said. "People are 'in your face' a lot. . . . I wouldn't want to be on the cover of those magazines, so consequently, I make sure that I don't do a big song, I'll just do a sort-of-big song. I get squeamish at the thought of people looking at my private life. Fame came to me pretty late in the game. I was just semifamous, and I could live with that. But people waving at me at red lights, and following me home, that makes me nervous."

Just like her song, "The Road's My Middle Name," she says that concert touring is her real joy. "To me, that's the most fun. That's sort of like camp, running away with the circus. They can't get you—you know, what it's like on vacation? Somebody's taking care of you, you've got room service, your clothes—you can send them out if you can't get them washed."

As James Brown says, "It's a Man's World," but Bonnie Raitt has made a name for herself in it, on her own merit. She holds her own ground next to male superstars like Bruce Springsteen, Eric Clapton, Elton John, Stevie Wonder, and Al Green. "There's a ton of famous women in the music business," Raitt is quick to point out. "In the generation before me, there's Grace Slick, Joni Mitchell, Joan Baez, Judy Collins, Chrissie Hynde, Tina Weymouth, Laurie Anderson. We're all still doing the same job. If you're good, you get to keep doing it. If you're not good, you won't!"

Always a trailblazer, back in the seventies, Bonnie said that if she were a gay woman, she would address those issues in her songs as well. Although she is not gay, she is quite supportive of a singer who is: Melissa Etheridge. The two have become good friends and frequently appear on the same bill at benefits and music industry awards shows. According to Etheridge, when she told Bonnie that her female fans had taken to tossing their brassieres to her during her concerts, Bonnie laughingly replied, "Girl, I never got no bras on stage!"

Since her new widespread success began, Bonnie has become quite a champion and a symbol for late-blooming baby boomers. She admits to being happy to have that distinction: "Hitting your stride in your forties has been a great thing. I'm a real happy role model for a lot of women who are all depressed about getting older: 'Come on down, it gets better!' "

According to Bonnie, touring represents "goofing off" and working on a new album "is much harder." "You have to go 'inside' and peel those onion layers back," she says, describing her deeply personal lyrics. She has been given validation by being almost universally accepted as a politically conscious voice of her generation. She claims that is especially challenging "after as personal as I've gotten as a new songwriter."

"I started writing in my forties," she said. "I wrote about eight songs on the previous nine albums before that. Lately, since I've gotten all this acclaim and good response with the songs that I've been writing, it means that I've got to knuckle down and do it. It's a scary thing to stretch out at this age, but it's necessary, because nobody else knows what I want to say. It'll be interesting to hear what there is left to sing about. Because, after twelve [new, nongreatest-hits, studio] albums, I've already covered a lot of material, and frankly, I don't think you're gonna get another 'I Can't Make You Love Me,' that Mike Reid–Allen Shamblin song."

Describing her own writing style, Bonnie claims that it is different from writing poetry, which Michael O'Keefe does. "I have a lot of admiration for people who write poetry," she says. "I write it according to whether they're gonna sing. I think if I was just going to sit down and write poetry, I think that I would think about it differently. I write on one of these little portable keyboards with the speakers built in. I take it on the road, with a little drum machine and a little bass thing."

Bonnie claims that hits just keep gettin' harder to find: "It's always been the hardest thing to find good songs—especially because a lot of songwriters are able to have record deals now. In the old days, songwriters would write tunes and people with 'better voices' would sing them. Then it opened up, and people appreciated originality in singing. It's hard now to find songs that aren't clichéd, or a deliberate attempt to copy something I've already done. That's really a surprise to me. Somebody somewhere must actually be saying, 'Let's sign somebody and make a demo that sounds exactly like "Something to Talk About," and then maybe Bonnie Raitt will do the song!' "

Advising new songwriters, Raitt says, "I'm the recipient of hundreds of [songwriters' demo] tapes—and many of them come with letters apologizing for the quality of the demos. But for me as a musician, the quality of the tape isn't as important as whether it's a heartfelt performance. What I tell people is, 'Don't worry if you don't have a big budget. Just work on the song. And if a song is good enough, you'll be able to get it heard by someone.' There are A and R people at record companies who have paid staffs to listen to these things. I'd suggest looking on the back of a record by an artist that you like, then sending your song with a note to the record label saying, 'My music is like Bonnie Raitt's,' or 'I'm a big fan of Otis Rush,' or whatever. Then again, it can work against you if the music is too similar. Also, I'd say to learn your instrument and be able to emotionally involve yourself in a song. It's not about production. It's about the immediacy of the music and how good your lyrics are. This may seem like simple advice, but it's what I say to people just breaking into the business. To everyone else, I just say, 'Good Luck!' "

Beyond her 1990s fame and her sobriety, her marriage to Michael O'Keefe represents the most significant change in her life. Speaking of their relationship, Bonnie says there have been some adjustments, like: "Having to get along, as opposed to: 'I can leave anytime I want,' doesn't calm you down, it just makes you have to pay attention more. There's more at stake. I'd had great passionate love affairs, but I knew somewhere early on whether they were going to be the one I'd be with for a long time. And I was never in the mood to settle down. I felt that this was somebody that meshed enough, that this was a good idea in my life to do this with this person at that time. But the idea of settling down, I feel that I'm always pulling at that rope all the time. Because I like those grand gestures of getting in the car and slamming the door and driving away. . . . It's not as much fun to do in your mid-forties. It's silly."

For the first time, she enjoys that sense of security that marriage has brought her. "The comfort level, having someone there for you, has a very tender and sweet side. [Marriage] tested me in ways I didn't expect. When things are difficult, you can't just run off or have an affair, because you made a commitment. Some of the hardest moments for me have been learning how not to run away and how to resolve an argument and how to compromise."

Opting for motherhood, after the age of forty-five, however, is unlikely. "I don't see it in the cards because I really want to get out and perform. I have too much respect for the institution of mothering to do it in other than a fully committed way."

Since she is married to a well-known actor, does this mean that we can look forward to seeing Bonnie in the movies anytime soon? "I've been asked," she says, "but I just don't have time. I might do it eventually."

According to O'Keefe, "Bonnie doesn't have a head for acting. You're more likely to see *me* make a hit record!"

She would much rather concentrate on the causes that she supports throughout the year. But, are there too many benefits?

Bonnie responds, "Every single year of my whole life in music, I've been asked the same question. To me, it's part of the obligation. I personally don't think there's enough benefits. If a person says, 'I'm sick of reading about benefits,' then think about where your own head's at. It probably means you're guilty because you don't give enough money away."

Throughout the years, Bonnie has tended to flit from cause to cause with no sense of direction. The Rhythm and Blues Foundation has given her a strong focus. Instead of tackling ambitious—but difficult to solve—problems like ending the use of nuclear power, she is taking on an issue that she can see tangible results with. Because of the Rhythm and Blues Hall of Fame, and Bonnie Raitt's efforts, the organization and Bonnie have witnessed several record companies changing their policies with regard to giving the great performers of bygone years their long-overdue sales royalties.

"Actually, only a few have readjusted their royalty rates and started to pay: Capitol/EMI, Warner Brothers, Atlantic, and

MCA," Raitt told the Detroit News in 1994. "The rest are shamefully remiss. And they know better, and they know they're stealing, and they're still doing it. They had a choice to do the right thing, but they decided not to. We're in the process of trying to talk them into it. There's going to be a public no-tification of who's not paying royalties. I want to know, when I buy a particular reissue album, whether the artist is going to get any money out of it. But I shouldn't say in the press that they deliberately haven't paid. Maybe it just hasn't been on their docket. So it will take a bit of prodding."

She explains that there is a course of action that consumers can take as well: "Some of the industry people have chosen not to do what is the right thing to do, and some of them have, and it's important that we, as consumers of this music, support the labels that are paying royalty rates and avoid the labels that aren't. We've got the power in our pocketbook. If you notice companies who are recycling, and promoting environmental health and protection, buy the product that's made by them. There's a 1–800–Rhythm and Blues Foundation number, call up 'information.' It's housed in the Smithsonian Institution in Washington, D.C., in donated offices, which, of course, the tax-payers get something good that's coming out of it. There wouldn't be any of my music if it weren't for Ruth Brown, and the people who started it all. It's only the right thing to do."

With all of the Bonnie Raitt songs on the market, there are still several unreleased recordings of hers that remain "in the can" like half of the *Tongue in Groove* sessions. Hopefully, one day the tracks that Bonnie recorded with Prince will be re-leased. According to Prince, they are still on tape somewhere. "Oh, those sessions were kicking!" he exclaims. "There was no particular reason it didn't come out. I was just working on a lot of things at the same time, and I didn't give myself enough time to work with her. I used to do that a lot—start five different projects and only get a couple done." Perhaps they will still come out at one point or another. It will certainly be fascinating to hear the tracks that they came up with together.

Through it all, Bonnie is her own harshest critic. "My own struggle is about not being too hard on myself," she admits. "At the moment, I'm pretty happy with myself, but there are times I feel I've become a workaholic. The public doesn't see cracks in the armor, but [in my music] I wrote about them."

She's worked so hard to accomplish what she has, that she is afraid to relax and take a vacation. "Everyone wants to go to Bali for six months, but it's not in the cards for me. Luckily, I love my job!" she exclaimed in a 1995 interview.

"There is no time off," she said another time. "That's my biggest problem, figuring out a way to wedge some reflective time into a schedule that's so packed with being in demand—demands for benefits and things I believe in. It's a self-imposed thing, but I feel an obligation because of the position I'm in and how much I vehemently care about supporting rhythm and blues musicians."

Once she is finished recording one of her albums, she doesn't go back to it for enjoyment. "I don't care for my voice much," she says. "Once I make a record I don't listen to it. If I had to think about my singing or guitar playing, I think I'd give it up."

She says she likes to listen to African and Celtic music as well as American performers. "I'll have a Muddy Waters morning, or a Randy Newman morning, or I'll go back and play Taj Mahal. Music like that is like a favorite old pair of shoes."

She categorizes her niche in the music business as a rhythm and blues artist. "I never liked fruity music. It's not a question of style, really, because I don't really count it as country or jazz or funk music or rock or blues. And, when people try to put me in a certain category, it's not going to work."

The kind of songs that Bonnie has consistently been drawn toward are songs about heartache, disappointment, introspection, and desolation. If she were going to record a Beatles' song, she would more likely choose "Lady Madonna" or "Revolution" than she would "Good Day Sunshine." There is something much more satisfying to her about shining a light into the darker corners of one's life.

As she explains it, "If you can't sing about the stuff that's rubbing you and hurting you, then there's really no point in singing music. Otherwise, you're just going to be humming some sort of ditty, going down the highway. It's nice to have light, breezy songs, but that's not really what I do. I like the places where you hurt, and there's tension, and there's problems to be worked out, as well as, you know, passion and anger and jealousy and rage and all those things, and deal with sex thrown in."

Since her career is progressing smoothly, Bonnie is looking and feeling better than ever before. Part of this has to do with the change in her diet. "When I got sober," Bonnie says, "I also changed my diet, and it's really affected my energy. I never get sick. . . . I've been healthy and less than healthy, and healthy's much better. Less than healthy's more fun, but healthy is better!"

Although the members of her family all live in different parts of the country, Bonnie remains close to all of them. She sees her parents as often as possible, and they have been consistently supportive of her career and all of her projects. Her brother David, who is two years younger than she is, now lives in Northern California, where he builds environmentally sound houses known as yurts. They are sold through the *Whole Earth Catalog*. David went the whole hippie route, even naming one of his sons Bayleaf. Her brother Steve, who is two years older than she is, lives in Minnesota, where he sells audio equipment.

As she has always done, Bonnie Raitt closely guards details about her personal life. She is more than willing to talk about music, musicians, and her career. However, she is not the type to go on television and reveal thoughts and feelings about her deepest emotions, except in her music. She remains close to nearly all of the friends she has had in the past. Even people like Freebo, who does not see Bonnie as often as he used to, remains very devoted to her. In turn, she continues to call upon her old friends time and time again. When it comes time to launch another album, tour, or Rhythm and Blues Foundation ceremony, she consistently calls upon her buddies like Jackson Browne, Ray Benson of Asleep at the Wheel, Billy Vera, and David Crosby. Whenever she needs a tuba player, she always turns to Freebo. She enthusiastically defends her friends to the death, and commands the same kind of loyalty from them.

As for the future, Bonnie Raitt says, "I don't expect to be put out to pasture and neither does anyone else. Too many trees have been cut down to write about Jurassic Rock. If you calcify and stagnate, you probably deserve to be shunted off. But look at the [Rolling] Stones—they're still doing great work. You don't go downhill if you hold onto your inspiration and your chops."

She said, "In my job I'll be able to continue singing when I'm older. But a lot of people in the music business won't be able to. The film business is worse for a woman after forty, it's hard to get a role. In rock—we'll see. Joni Mitchell is still singing, so am I, and all those other people, and we plan to be out there for a long time."

Bonnie's fashion sense has always been in the blouses, jeans, and boots spectrum. She wears a lot of browns and greens— earthy shades. She has been consistently stylish and attractive, but she has never gone the glamour-girl route. This is how she is the most comfortable. She is also not afraid of physically aging. "Nobody's famous forever," she says, "but I think my fans will follow me into our combined old age. Look at Ella Fitzgerald. She doesn't have to worry about how she looks in a bra! Real musicians and real fans stay together for a long, long time."

"I expect to be doing this until I'm eighty-five or ninety," she says. "In jazz, blues, and folk they don't put you out to pasture for getting older. They acknowledge that you're getting better. I'm in a lucky position, because I'm the musical equivalent of a character actress. [Getting older] will be harder for Madonna."

Bonnie has had great role models to follow. Especially in the blues field, singers like Sippie Wallace and John Lee Hooker kept their careers going right into their later years. "My Dad just turned seventy-three and he sings with more feeling and heart than ever," she points out. "My heroes were all playing their best stuff in their sixties and seventies. Look at B. B. King and Tony Bennett. They just got better. I feel more productive, effective, and powerful than ever. My forties are the best time of my life. I expect to be performing 'til I'm ninety-five. It's not fair that so many women in their forties and fifties don't have the job and romance security that they should. I know several women who have been dumped from jobs and relationships for younger women. Why is Sean Connery always paired with a twenty year old? It frustrates and angers me. It's important for women to find their power without the validation of work or men. Accepting yourself at every age is a valuable lesson."

Predictably, Bonnie's convictions and her devotion to supporting the charities she believes in will be constant factors in her life. "You might as well do something that's going to be artistically true to what you do," she proclaims. "I'm in for the long haul!"

From the first notes of "Bluebird" on her debut album, through her 1995 concert performances on her *Road Tested* album, Bonnie Raitt has been one of the most sincere and moving vocalists in the record business. She has gone from being a teenage blues-wannabe to a hard-drinking blues mama to a full-fledged rock and roller. She seemed to have the world on a string in the late seventies, but by the mid-eighties it had all slipped through her fingers. According to Bonnie, the angels were looking out for her, and somehow—with their help— she put her life back on track.

It was more like the angels paid her back for all of the good deeds she had done for charities, for benefits, and for friends in need. Her devotion to preserving our musical heritage and to promoting our living musical legends certainly must have amassed thousands of good karma points for her.

She's a no-nonsense troubadour of rock, country, jazz, and blues, who has won acclaim, awards, and respect in the music business. She's the tireless voice of political reason in a world of greed and injustice, and she perpetually gives of herself, her talent, and her time. She knows what it's like to be in the winner's circle, and she knows what it feels like to lose it all. With her incandescent red mane of hair, incomparably expressive voice, exciting slide-guitar licks, and boundless rock and roll energy, Bonnie Raitt is a true original.

DISCOGRAPHY

ALBUMS

(1) Bonnie Raitt
[Warner Brothers Records 1971]
Produced by Willie Murphy

   1. "Bluebird" (Stephen Stills)
   2. "Mighty Tight Woman" (Sippie Wallace)
   3. "Thank You" (Bonnie Raitt)
   4. "Finest Lovin' Man" (Bonnie Raitt)
   5. "Any Day Woman" (Paul Seibel)
   6. "Big Road" (Tommy Johnson)
   7. "Walking Blues" (Robert Johnson)
   8. "Danger Heartbreak Dead Ahead" (Ivy Hunter, Clarence Paul, and William Stevenson)
   9. "Since I Fell for You" (Bud Johnson)
  10. "I Ain't Blue" (John Koerner)
  11. "Women Be Wise" (Sippie Wallace, additional lyrics by John Beach)

(2) Give It Up
[Warner Brothers Records 1972]
Produced by Michael Cuscuna

   1. "Give It Up or Let Me Go" (Bonnie Raitt)
   2. "Nothing Seems to Matter" (Bonnie Raitt)
   3. "I Know" (Barbara George)
   4. "If You Gotta Make a Fool of Somebody" (Rudy Clarke)
   5. "Love Me Like a Man" (Chris Smither)
   6. "Too Long at the Fair" (Joel Zoss)
   7. "Under the Falling Sky" (Jackson Browne)

8. "You Got to Know How" (Sippie Wallace, additional lyrics by Jack Viertel)
9. "You Told Me Baby" (Bonnie Raitt)
10. "Love Has No Pride" (Eric Kaz and Libby Titus)

(3) Takin' My Time

[Warner Brothers Records 1973]
Produced by John Hall

1. "You've Been in Love Too Long" (Clarence Paul, William Stevenson, and Ivy Hunter)
2. "I Gave My Love a Candle" (Joel Zoss)
3. "Let Me in" (Y. Baker)
4. "Everybody's Cryin' Mercy" (Mose Allison)
5. "Cry Like a Rainstorm" (Eric Kaz)
6. "Wah She Go Do" (McCarth Lewis)
7. "I Feel the Same" (Chris Smither)
8. "I Thought I Was a Child" (Jackson Browne)
9. "Write Me a Few of Your Lines/Kokomo Blues" (Fred McDowell)
10. "Guilty" (Randy Newman)

(4) Streetlights

[Warner Brothers Records 1974]
Produced by Jerry Ragovoy

1. "That Song About the Midway" (Joni Mitchell)
2. "Rainy Day Man" (James Taylor)
3. "Angel From Montgomery" (John Prine)
4. "I Got Plenty" (Joey Levine and Jim Carroll)
5. "Streetlights" (Bill Payne)
6. "What Is Success" (Allen Toussaint)
7. "Ain't Nobody Home" (Jerry Ragovoy)
8. "Everything That Touches You" (Michael Kamen)
9. "Got You on My Mind" (Allee Willis and David Lasley)
10. "You Got to Be Ready for Love (If You Wanna Be Mine)" (Lou Courtney)

(5) *Home Plate*

[Warner Brothers Records 1975]
Produced by Paul A. Rothchild

1. "What Do You Want the Boy to Do?" (Allen Toussaint)
2. "Good Enough" (John and Johanna Hall)
3. "Run Like a Thief" (John David Souther)
4. "Fool Yourself" (Fred Tackett)
5. "My First Night Alone Without You" (Kin Vassey)
6. "Walk Out the Front Door" (Mark Jordan and Rip Stock)
7. "Sugar Mama" (Delbert McClinton and Glen Clark)
8. "Pleasin' Each Other" (Bill Payne and Fran Tate)
9. "I'm Blowin' Away" (Eric Kaz)
10. "Sweet and Shiny Eyes" (Nan O'Byrne)

(6) *Sweet Forgiveness*

[Warner Brothers Records 1977]
Produced by Paul A. Rothchild

1. "About to Make Me Leave Home" (Earl Randall)
2. "Runaway" (Del Shannon and Max Crook)
3. "Two Lives" (Mark Jordan)
4. "Louise" (Paul Siebel)
5. "Gamblin' Man" (Eric Kaz)
6. "Sweet Forgiveness" (Daniel Moore)
7. "My Opening Farewell" (Jackson Browne)
8. "Three Time Loser" (Covay and Miller)
9. "Takin' My Time" (Bill Payne)
10. "Home" (Karla Bonoff)

(7) *The Glow*

[Warner Brothers Records 1979]
Produced by Peter Asher

1. "I Thank You" (Isaac Hayes and David Porter)
2. "Your Good Thing (Is About to End)" (Isaac Hayes and David Porter)

3. "Standin' By the Same Old Love" (Bonnie Raitt)
4. "Sleep's Dark and Silent Gate" (Jackson Browne)
5. "The Glow" (Veyler Hildebrand)
6. "Bye Bye Baby" (Mary Wells)
7. "The Boy Can't Help It" (Bobby Troup)
8. "(I Could Have Been Your) Best Old Friend" (Tracy Nelson and Andy McMahan)
9. "You're Gonna Get What's Coming" (Robert Palmer)
10. "(Goin') Wild for You Baby" (Tom Snow and David Batteau)

(8) *Green Light*

[Warner Brothers Records 1982]
Produced by Rob Fraboni

1. "Keep This Heart in Mind" (Fred Marrone and Stephen Holsapple)
2. "River of Tears" (Eric Kaz)
3. "Can't Get Enough" (Walt Richmond and Bonnie Raitt)
4. "Willya Wontcha" (Johnny Lee Schell)
5. "Let's Keep It Between Us" (Bob Dylan)
6. "Me and the Boys" (Terry Adams)
7. "I Can't Help Myself" (Johnny Lee Schell, Bonnie Raitt, Ricky Fatarr, and Ray Ohara)
8. "Baby Come Back" (Eddy Grant)
9. "Talk to Me" (Jerry Williams)
10. "Green Lights" (Terry Adams and Joseph Spampinato)

(9) *Nine Lives*

[Warner Brothers Records 1986]
Produced by Bill Payne & George Massenburg *
Produced by Steve Tyrell **
Produced by Rob Fraboni ***

1. "No Way to Treat a Lady" * (Bryan Adams and Jim Vallance)

2. "Runnin' Back to Me" * (Karla Bonoff and Ira Ingber)
3. "Who But a Fool (Thief Into Paradise)" * (Nan O'Byrne and Tom Snow)
4. "Crime of Passion" * (Danny Ironstone and Mary Unobsky)
5. "All Day, All Night" * (Ivan Neville, Hutch Hutchinson, and Ronald Jones)
6. "Stand Up to the Night" ** (Will Jennings, J.A.C. Redford, and Richard Kerr)
7. "Excited" *** (Jerry Williams)
8. "Freezin' (for a Little Human Love)" *** (Michael Smotherman)
9. "True Love Is Hard to Find" *** (Toots Hibbert)
10. "Angel" *** (Eric Kaz)

(10) Nick of Time
[Capitol Records 1989]
Produced by Don Was

1. "Nick of Time" (Bonnie Raitt)
2. "Thing Called Love" (John Hiatt)
3. "Love Letter" (Bonnie Hayes)
4. "Cry on My Shoulder" (Michael Ruff)
5. "Real Man" (Jerry L. Williams)
6. "Nobody's Girl" (Larry John McNally)
7. "Have a Heart" (Bonnie Hayes)
8. "Too Soon to Tell" (M. Reid and R. M. Bourke)
9. "I Will Not Be Denied" (Jerry L. Williams)
10. "I Ain't Gonna Let You Break My Heart Again" (David Lasley and J. Lasley)
11. "The Road's My Middle Name" (Bonnie Raitt)

(11) The Bonnie Raitt Collect ɔn
[Warner Brothers Records 1990]
Produced by Willie Murphy *

Produced by Michael Cuscuna **
Produced by John Hall ***
Produced by John Prine, Dan Einstein, and Jim Rooney ****
Produced by Jerry Ragovoy *****
Produced by Paul A. Rothchild ******
Produced by Peter Asher *******
Produced by Bill Payne and George Massenburg ********
Produced by Rob Fraboni *********

1. "Finest Lovin' Man" (edit) * (Bonnie Raitt)
2. "Give It Up or Let Me Go" ** (Bonnie Raitt)
3. "Women Be Wise" [previously unreleased duet with Sippie Wallace, 1976] (Sippie Wallace, additional lyrics by John Beach)
4. "Under the Falling Sky" ** (Jackson Browne)
5. "Love Me Like a Man" ** (Chris Smither)
6. "Love Has No Pride" ** (Eric Kaz and Libby Titus)
7. "I Feel the Same" *** (Chris Smither)
8. "Guilty" *** (Randy Newman)
9. "Angel From Montgomery" **** [live duet with John Prine] (John Prine)
10. "What Is Success" ***** (Allen Toussaint)
11. "My First Night Alone Without You" ****** (Kin Vassey)
12. "Sugar Mama" ****** (Delbert McClinton and Gene Clark)
13. "Louise" ****** (Paul Siebel)
14. "About to Make Me Leave Home" ****** (Earl Randall)
15. "Runaway" ****** (Del Shannon and Max Crook)
16. "The Glow" ******* (Veyler Hilderbrand)
17. "(Goin') Wild for You Baby" ******* (Tom Snow and David Batteau)
18. "Willya Wontcha" ******** (Johnny Lee Schell)
19. "True Love Is Hard to Find" (edit) ******** (Toots Hibbert)
20. "No Way to Treat a Lady" ********* (Bryan Adams and Jim Vallance)

(12) *Luck of the Draw*

[Capitol Records 1991]
Produced by Don Was and Bonnie Raitt

1. "Something to Talk About" (Shirley Eikhard)
2. "Good Man, Good Woman" [duet with Delbert McClinton] (C. Womack and L. Womack)
3. "I Can't Make You Love Me" (M. Reid and A. Shamblin)
4. "Tangled and Dark" (Bonnie Raitt)
5. "Come to Me" (Bonnie Raitt)
6. "No Business" (John Hiatt)
7. "One Part Be My Lover" (Bonnie Raitt and Michael O'Keefe)
8. "Not the Only One" (Paul Brady)
9. "Papa Come Quick (Jody and Chico)" (Billy Vera, A. Pessis, and L. J. McNally)
10. "Slow Ride" (B. Hayes, A. Pessis, and L. J. McNally)
11. "Luck of the Draw" (Paul Brady)
12. "All at Once" (Bonnie Raitt)

(13) *Longing in Their Hearts*

[Capitol Records 1994]
Produced by Don Was and Bonnie Raitt

1. "Love Sneakin' Up on You" (Tom Snow and Jimmy Scott)
2. "Longing in Their Hearts" (Bonnie Raitt and Michael O'Keefe)
3. "You" (Bob Thiele Jr., Tonio K, and John Shanks)
4. "Cool, Clear Water" (Bonnie Raitt)
5. "Circle Dance" (Bonnie Raitt)
6. "I Sho Do" (Mabon L. "Teenie" Hodges and Billy Always)
7. "Dimming of the Day" (Richard Thompson)
8. "Feeling of Falling" (Bonnie Raitt)
9. "Steal Your Heart Away" (Paul Brady)
10. "Storm Warning" (Terry Britten and Lea Maalfrid)

11. "Hell to Pay" (Bonnie Raitt)
12. "Shadow of Doubt" (Gary Nicholson, rearranged by Bonnie Raitt)

(14) Road Tested

[Capitol Records 1995]
Produced by Don Was and Bonnie Raitt

Disc One
1. "Thing Called Love"
2. "Three Time Loser"
3. "Love Letter"
4. "Never Make Your Move Too Soon"
5. "Something to Talk About"
6. "Matters of the Heart"
7. "Shake a Little"
8. "Have a Heart"
9. "Love Me Like a Man"
10. "The Kokomo Medley"
11. "Louise"
12. "Dimming of the Day"

Disc Two
1. "Longing in Their Hearts"
2. "Come to Me"
3. "Love Sneakin' Up on You"
4. "Burning Down the House"
5. "I Can't Make You Love Me"
6. "Feeling of Falling"
7. "I Beleive I'm in Love With You"
8. "Rock Steady"
9. "My Opening Farewell"
10. "Angel From Montgomery"

ALBUM-BY-ALBUM CHART AND SALES RECORD

(14) Road Tested (1995) [Capitol Records]
  —Not released at press time

(13) Longing in Their Hearts (1994) [Capitol Records] *
  —Number 1 / Double Platinum (2 million copies sold)

(12) Luck of the Draw (1991) [Capitol Records] ***
  —Number 1 / Quintuple Platinum (5 million copies sold)

(11) The Bonnie Raitt Collection (1990) [Warner Brothers
  Records]
  —Number 61 / Gold (500,000 copies sold)

(10) Nick of Time (1989) [Capitol Records] ****
  —Number 1 / Quadruple Platinum (4 million copies sold)

(9) Nine Lives (1986) [Warner Brothers Records]
  —Number 115

(8) Green Light (1982) [Warner Brothers Records]
  —Number 38

(7) The Glow (1979) [Warner Brothers Records]
  —Number 30

(6) Sweet Forgiveness (1977) [Warner Brothers Records]
  —Number 25 / Gold (500,000 copies sold)

(5) Home Plate (1975) [Warner Brothers Records]
  —Number 43

Chart figures according to *Billboard* magazine
* indicates Grammy Awards won for that album or related cuts

(4) Streetlights (1974) [Warner Brothers Records]
—Number 80

(3) Takin' My Time (1973) [Warner Brothers Records]
—Number 87

(2) Give It Up (1972) [Warner Brothers Records]
—Number 138

(1) Bonnie Raitt (1971) [Warner Brothers Records]
—Never charted

PERFORMANCES ON OTHER ALBUMS

Ann Arbor Blues and Jazz Festival 1972
Bonnie Raitt, Sippie Wallace, Otis Rush, Luther Alison Hound
Dog Taylor, Koko Taylor, Junior Walker, Howlin' Wolf, Dr. John,
and others
>   [Atlantic Records 1973]

>   Bonnie Raitt: vocal duet with Sippie Wallace
>   —"You Got to Know How"

>   vocal solo and National steel guitar
>   —"A Tribute to Fred McDowell"
>   —"Write Me a Few of Your Lines"/"Kokomo"/"Drop
>   Down Mama"

Dixie Chicken
Little Feat
>   [Warner Brothers Records 1973]

>   Bonnie Raitt: background vocals
>   —song titles not specified in liner notes

For Every Man
Jackson Browne
>   [Asylum Records 1973]

>   Bonnie Raitt: harmony vocals
>   —"The Times You've Come"

The Pretender
Jackson Browne
>   [Asylum Records 1976]

>   Bonnie Raitt: background vocals
>   —"Here Come Those Tears Again"

Warren Zevon
Warren Zevon
  [Asylum Records 1976]
  Bonnie Raitt: harmony vocals
  —"Join Me in L.A."

Time Loves a Hero
Little Feat
  [Warner Brothers Records 1977]
  Bonnie Raitt: background vocals
  —song titles not specified in liner notes

Thanks I'll Eat It Here
Lowell George
  [Warner Brothers Records 1979]
  Bonnie Raitt: background vocals
  —song titles not specified in liner notes

Down on the Farm
Little Feat
  [Warner Brothers Records 1979]
  Bonnie Raitt: background vocals
  —song titles not specified in liner notes

No Nukes
Musicians United for Safe Energy: the Doobie Brothers, Jackson
Browne, James Taylor, Bonnie Raitt, Bruce Springsteen and the E
Street Band, Carly Simon, Nicolette Larson, Poco, Chaka Khan,
John Hall, Raydio, Jesse Colin Young, Ry Cooder, Sweet Honey in
the Rock, Gil Scott-Heron, Tom Petty and the Heartbreakers, and
Crosby, Stills and Nash
  [Asylum Records 1979]
  Bonnie Raitt: live concert solos
  —"Runaway"

—"Angel From Montgomery" background vocals
—"Power"
—"Takin' It to the Streets"

Urban Cowboy (Soundtrack Album)
Bonnie Raitt, Linda Ronstadt, J. D. Souther, Kenny Rogers,
Mickey Gilley, the Eagles, Johnny Lee, the Charlie Daniels Band,
Box Scaggs, Bob Seger and the Silver Bullet Band, Dan Fogelberg,
and others
[Full Moon Records 1980]

Bonnie Raitt: vocal solo
—"Don't It Make You Wanna Dance"
—"Darlin' "

Sippie
Sippie Wallace
[Atlantic Records 1982]

Bonnie Raitt: vocal accompaniment with Sippie Wallace
plus slide guitar
—"Women Be Wise"
—"Suitcase Blues"
—"Mama's Gone, Goodbye"

Objects of Desire
Michael Franks
[Warner Brothers Records 1982]

Bonnie Raitt: duet with Michael Franks
—"Ladies Nite"

Sun City
Artists United Against Apartheid: Bonnie Raitt, Pat Benatar,
Jackson Browne, Clarence Clemmons, Bob Dylan, Nona Hendryx,
Jimmy Cliff, the Fat Boys, Miles Davis, Peter Wolf, Ringo Starr,
Pete Townsend, Eddie Kendricks, David Ruffin, John Oates,

Darlene Love, Bobby Womack, Bono, Bruce Springsteen, Run-DMC, Little Steven, Herbie Hancock, Bob Geldof, Ruben Blades, and others
> [Manhattan Records 1985]

> Bonnie Raitt: featured and chorus vocals
>> —"Sun City"

Tribute to Steve Goodman
Bonnie Raitt, John Prine, and others
> [Red Pajama Records 1985]

> Bonnie Raitt: duet with John Prine
>> —"Angel From Montgomery"

Lives in Balance
Jackson Browne
> [Asylum Records 1986]

> Bonnie Raitt: background vocals
>> —"Candy"

Heartbeat
Don Johnson
> [Columbia Records 1986]

> Bonnie Raitt: background vocals
>> —"Lost in Your Eyes"
>> —"Heartache Away"

Let It Roll
Little Feat
> [Warner Brothers Records 1988]

> Bonnie Raitt: background vocals
>> —song titles not specified in liner notes

Stay Awake
Bonnie Raitt, Ringo Starr, and others
   [A&M Records 1988]

   Bonnie Raitt: vocal solo
      —"Baby Mine"

Free to Be . . . A Family
Marlo Thomas, with guests including Bonnie Raitt, Carly Simon,
Pat Benatar, Lily Tomlin, Jane Curtin, Gilda Radner, Whoopie
Goldberg, Bea Arthur, Steve Martin, Christopher Reeve, Amy
Grant, the Fat Boys, Robin Williams, and others
   [A&M Records 1988]

   Bonnie Raitt: vocal solo
      —"I'm Never Afraid (to Say What's on My Mind)"

A Black and White Night Live
Roy Orbison
   [Virgin Records 1989]

   Bonnie Raitt: background vocals in chorus with Jennifer
   Warnes, k. d. lang, Jackson Browne, Steven Soles, John
   David Souther
      —all cuts on album

The Healer
John Lee Hooker
   [Chameleon Records 1989]

   Bonnie Raitt: duet vocal with John Lee Hooker, and slide
   guitar
      —"I'm in the Mood"

Someone to Love
Charles Brown
   [Bullseye Blues Records 1992]

Bonnie Raitt: vocal duet with Charles Brown
—"Someone to Love" slide guitar
—"Every Little Bit Hurts"

A Very Special Christmas, 2
Bonnie Raitt, Charles Brown, Debbie Gibson, Cyndi Lauper,
Aretha Franklin, Luther Vandross, Sinéad O'Connor, Ronnie
Spector, Darlene Love, and others
[A&M Records 1992]

Bonnie Raitt: vocal duet with Charles Brown
—"Merry Christmas, Baby"

Across the Borderline
Willie Nelson
[Columbia Records 1993]

Bonnie Raitt: duet vocal with Willie Nelson
—"Getting Over You"

Harbor Lights
Bruce Hornsby
[RCA Records 1993]

Bonnie Raitt: background vocals
—"Rainbow's Cadillac"
—"The Tide Will Rise"

Elton John: Duets
Elton John
[MCA Records 1993]

Bonnie Raitt: vocal duet with Elton John
—"Love Letters"

Feels Like Rain
Buddy Guy
[Silverstone Records 1993]

Bonnie Raitt: vocal duet with Buddy Guy, and slide guitar
   —"Feels Like Rain"

Beat the Retreat
Songs written by Richard Thompson, and performed by Bonnie
Raitt, Los Lobos, REM, Graham Parker, and others
   [Capitol Records 1994]

   Bonnie Raitt: solo vocal
   —"When the Spell Is Broken"

The Tractors
The Tractors
   [Arista Records 1994]

   Bonnie Raitt: slide guitar
   —"The Tulsa Shuffle"
   —"The Little Man"
   —"The Tulsa Shuffle (Revisited)"

Grammy's Greatest Moments, Volume 1
Bonnie Raitt, Donna Summer, Marvin Gaye, Barbra Streisand, Neil
Diamond, Tina Turner, and others
   [Atlantic Records 1994]

   Bonnie Raitt: live vocal solo
   —"Thing Called Love"

Grammy's Greatest Moments, Volume 3
Bonnie Raitt, Joe Cocker, Jennifer Warnes, Don McLean, Suzanne
Vega, Aretha Franklin, and others
   [Atlantic Records 1994]

   Bonnie Raitt: live vocal solo
   —"I Can't Make You Love Me"

Aretha Franklin: Greatest Hits (1980–1994)
Aretha Franklin

[Arista Records 1994]

Bonnie Raitt: vocal trio with Aretha Franklin and Gloria Estafan
—"You Make Me Feel (Like a Natural Woman)"

Boys on the Side (Soundtrack Album)
Bonnie Raitt, Melissa Etheridge, Indigo Girls, Annie Lennox, Sheryl Crow, the Pretenders, Joan Armatrading, Stevie Nicks, the Cranberries, and others
[Arista Records 1995]

Bonnie Raitt: solo vocal
—"You Got It"

John Raitt: Broadway Legend
John Raitt
[Angel Records / 1995]

Bonnie Raitt: duet with John Raitt
—"They Say It's Wonderful"
—"Anything You Can Do"
—"Hey There"

Randy Newman's Faust
Various Artists
[Reprise Records / 1995]

Bonnie Raitt: vocal solo
—"Feels Like Home"
—"Life Has Been Good to Me"

BONNIE'S GRAMMY AWARDS

1989 (awarded in 1990)
Album of the Year
Nick of Time
Best Pop Vocal Performance, Female
Nick of Time (album)
Best Rock Vocal Performance, Female
Nick of Time (album)
Best Traditional Blues Recording
"I'm in the Mood" (album cut with John Lee Hooker)

1991 (awarded in 1992)
Best Rock Vocal Performance, Female
Luck of the Draw (album)
Best Pop Vocal Performance, Female
"Something to Talk About" (single)
Best Rock Performance, Duo or Group
"Good Man, Good Woman" (album cut with Delbert McClinton)

1994 (awarded in 1995)
Best Pop Album
Longing in Their Hearts

SOURCE NOTES

Foreword

From Mark Bego's telephone conversation with Joan Baez, August 7, 1995

Author to Reader

"Oh yes,": Bonnie Raitt to Mark Bego, February 25, 1993, at the Palace Theatre, Los Angeles cocktail reception for the Rhythm and Blues Foundation, prior to the Pioneer Awards.

"I'd love to": Bonnie Raitt to Mark Bego, March 2, 1995, at Club 555, Universal Hilton Hotel, Los Angeles, during the afternoon press conference
for the Rhythm and Blues Foundation.

1. You Got It

All quotes from the Grammy Awards, January 7, 1990.

2. Bonnie's Childhood

"From the time": *Rolling Stone*, May 3, 1990. "Bravo Bonnie—the *Rolling
Stone* Interview" by James Henke.

"My mother's": *Frets*, April 1988. "Bonnie and Slide" by Elisa Welch Mulvaney.

"She was a": *Rolling Stone*, May 3, 1990. "Bravo Bonnie—the *Rolling Stone*
Interview" by James Henke.

"I'm from": *After School Special* TV show, ABC-TV, March 16, 1995.

"I love": *Rolling Stone*, May 3, 1990. "Bravo Bonnie—the *Rolling Stone* Interview" by James Henke.

"I liked my dad's": *Rolling Stone*, April 21, 1994. "Bonnie Raitt: Q & A" by
Jancee Dunn.

"From the time": *VH1-to-One* TV show, VH1 cable TV network, October
1994.

"We would go to": *Rolling Stone*, December 18, 1975. "Ain't Gonna Be Your Sugar Mama No More" by Ben Fong-Torres.

"He was gone": *VH1-to-One* TV show, VH1 cable TV network, October 1994.

"I loved acting": *After School Special* TV show, ABC-TV, March 16, 1995.

"He wasn't around": *Rolling Stone*, December 18, 1975. "Ain't Gonna Be Your Sugar Mama No More" by Ben Fong-Torres.

"I'd never be": *People*, April 24, 1989. "Veteran Rocker Bonnie Raitt Gets Back on Track in the Nick of Time" by Kim Hubbard.

"I didn't take": *Frets*, April 1988. "Bonnie and Slide" by Elisa Welch Mulvaney.

"I took to wearing": *Rolling Stone*, December 18, 1975. "Ain't Gonna Be Your Sugar Mama No More" by Ben Fong-Torres.

"My fondest": *Frets*, April 1988. "Bonnie and Slide" by Elisa Welch Mulvaney.

"My brother": *After School Special* TV show, ABC-TV, March 16, 1995.

"I had a dream": *Rolling Stone*, December 18, 1975. "Ain't Gonna Be Your Sugar Mama No More" by Ben Fong-Torres.

"That was my saving": *After School Special* TV show, ABC-TV, March 16, 1995.

"I had a rough": *Rolling Stone*, May 3, 1990. "Bravo Bonnie—the *Rolling Stone* Interview" by James Henke.

"My old man wasn't": *Newsweek*, November 6, 1972. "Bonnie and Blue" by Hubert Saal.

"I wasn't allowed": *Rolling Stone*, December 18, 1975. "Ain't Gonna Be Your Sugar Mama No More" by Ben Fong-Torres.

"The minute that": *After School Special* TV show, ABC-TV, March 16, 1995.

"I loved Joan Baez": *Rolling Stone*, May 3, 1990. "Bravo Bonnie—the *Rolling Stone* Interview" by James Henke.

"It's really one": *Detroit News*, July 8, 1994. "Do the Raitt Thing" by Susan Whitall.

"I was going": *Rolling Stone*, May 3, 1990. "Bravo Bonnie—the *Rolling Stone* Interview" by James Henke.

"He wasn't washed up": *Rolling Stone*, December 18, 1975. "Ain't Gonna Be Your Sugar Mama No More" by Ben Fong-Torres.

"Kitty on": *Rolling Stone*, May 18, 1989. "Random Notes."

3. Bonnie Gets the Blues

"If I had to": *Frets*, April 1988. "Bonnie and Slide" by Elisa Welch Mulvaney.

"It has a strange": *VH1-to-One* TV show, VH1 cable TV network, October 1994.

"By the time": *Rolling Stone*, December 18, 1975. "Ain't Gonna Be Your Sugar Mama No More" by Ben Fong-Torres.

"John Lee Hooker": *VH1-to-One* TV show, VH1 cable TV network, October 1994.

"It took me": *Rolling Stone*, December 18, 1975. "Ain't Gonna Be Your Sugar Mama No More" by Ben Fong-Torres.

"I saw Brownie": *Rolling Stone*, April 21, 1994. "Bonnie Raitt: Q & A" by Jancee Dunn.

"We sang a": *Rolling Stone*, December 18, 1975. "Ain't Gonna Be Your Sugar Mama No More" by Ben Fong-Torres.

"I used to sing": *People*, April 12, 1982. "Sippie Wallace and Bonnie Raitt Prove That Blues Birds of a Feather Can Flock Together" by Carl Arrington and Maryanne George.

"We were just": *Rolling Stone*, December 18, 1975. "Ain't Gonna Be Your Sugar Mama No More" by Ben Fong-Torres.

"I was taking": *Frets*, April 1988. "Bonnie and Slide" by Elisa Welch Mulvaney.

"I never expected": *Rolling Stone*, May 3, 1990. "Bravo Bonnie—the *Rolling Stone* Interview" by James Henke.

"When I made $100": *High Fidelity*, June 1982. "Bonnie Raitt Lightens Up" by Steven X. Rea.

"I carried the booze": *Rolling Stone*, May 3, 1990. "Bravo Bonnie—the *Rolling Stone* Interview" by James Henke.

"I was handing": *People*, April 24, 1989. "Veteran Rocker Bonnie Raitt Gets Back on Track in the Nick of Time" by Kim Hubbard.

"I wanted": *Rolling Stone*, May 3, 1990. "Bravo Bonnie—the *Rolling Stone* Interview" by James Henke.

"I saw a rhinestone": *People*, April 12, 1982. "Sippie Wallace and Bonnie Raitt Prove That Blues Birds of a Feather Can Flock Together" by Carl Arrington and Maryanne George.

"I never heard": *Rolling Stone*, December 18, 1975. "Ain't Gonna Be Your Sugar Mama No More" by Ben Fong-Torres.

"I certainly started": Syndicated radio interview, produced by Warner Bros. Records.

"It only cost": *Rolling Stone*, December 18, 1975. "Ain't Gonna Be Your Sugar Mama No More" by Ben Fong-Torres.

"It was better than": Bonnie Raitt press bio supplied to press members with the *Home Plate* LP, September 1975.

"In the beginning": *After School Special* TV show, ABC-TV, March 16, 1995.

"It was for $200": *Rolling Stone*, December 18, 1975. "Ain't Gonna Be Your Sugar Mama No More" by Ben Fong-Torres.

"The two special": Liner notes, *Bonnie Raitt* album, Warner Bros. Records, 1971.

"I can't believe": Liner notes, *The Bonnie Raitt Collection* album, Warner Bros. Records, 1990.

"We recorded": Bonnie Raitt press bio supplied to press members with the *Home Plate* album, September 1975.

"I just think": *VH1-to-One* TV show, VH1 cable TV network, October 1994.

"I can appreciate": *Newsweek*, November 6, 1972. "Bonnie and Blue" by Hubert Saal.

"I don't like being": *People*, April 24, 1989. "Veteran Rocker Bonnie Raitt Gets Back on Track in the Nick of Time" by Kim Hubbard.

4. You Got to Know How

"I don't want to be": *Newsweek*, November 6, 1972. "Bonnie and Blue" by Hubert Saal.

"Nobody likes": *The Book of Rock Quotes*, Delilah/Putnam Books, 1982. Compiled by Jonathan Green.

"Fame is a drag": *Newsweek*, November 6, 1972. "Bonnie and Blue" by Hubert Saal.

"It was six": *People*, April 12, 1982 "Sippie Wallace and Bonnie Raitt Prove That Blues Birds of a Feather Can Flock Together" by Carl Arrington and Maryanne George.

"[Sippie] was so deeply": Liner notes, *Sippie*, album by Sippie Wallace, Atlantic Records, 1982.

"It's a connection": *People*, April 12, 1982. "Sippie Wallace and Bonnie Raitt Prove That Blues Birds of a Feather Can Flock Together" by Carl Arrington and Maryanne George.

"This album was made": Liner notes, *Give It Up* album by Bonnie Raitt, Warner Bros. Records, 1972.

"In the tradition": Liner notes, *The Bonnie Raitt Collection* album, Warner Bros. Records, 1990.

"I'm a vehicle": *Newsweek*, November 6, 1972. "Bonnie and Blue" by Hubert Saal

"I feel close": *High Fidelity*, June 1982. "Bonnie Raitt Lightens Up" by Steven X. Rea.

"This album": Liner notes, *Give It Up* album by Bonnie Raitt, Warner Bros. Records, 1972.

"I moved to L.A.": *High Fidelity*, June 1982. "Bonnie Raitt Lightens Up" by Steven X. Rea.

"I really liked": *Frets*, April 1988. "Bonnie and Slide" by Elisa Welch Mulvaney.

"I used to be sad": *Rolling Stone*, December 18, 1975. "Ain't Gonna Be Your Sugar Mama No More" by Ben Fong-Torres.

"I don't want": *The Book of Rock Quotes*, Delilah/Putnam Books, 1982. Compiled by Jonathan Green.

"*Takin' My Time*": *High Fidelity*, June 1982. "Bonnie Raitt Lightens Up" by Steven X. Rea.

"I remember the": Liner notes, *The Bonnie Raitt Collection* album, Warner Bros. Records, 1990.

"The environment changed": *Rolling Stone*, December 18, 1975. "Ain't Gonna Be Your Sugar Mama No More" by Ben Fong-Torres.
"Without them": Liner notes, *Streetlights* album by Bonnie Raitt, Warner Bros. Records, 1974.

5. Home Plate

"Paul was an": *Rolling Stone*, May 18, 1995. "Tribute: Paul Rothchild, 1935–1995" by Fred Goodman.
"I hate the sound": *Linda Ronstadt: It's So Easy*, Eakin Press, 1989 by Mark Bego.
"I don't want": *High Fidelity*, June 1982 "Bonnie Raitt Lightens Up" by Steven X. Rea.
"I heard this": Liner notes, *The Bonnie Raitt Collection album*, Warner Bros. Records, 1990.
"One of the reasons": *Frets*, April 1988. "Bonnie and Slide" by Elisa Welch Mulvaney.
"I got this": Liner notes, *The Bonnie Raitt Collection album*, Warner Bros. Records, 1990.
"They all know": *Rolling Stone*, December 18, 1975. "Ain't Gonna Be Your Sugar Mama No More" by Ben Fong-Torres.
"Between albums": Bonnie Raitt press bio supplied to press members with the *Home Plate* LP, September 1975.
"I don't think": *Rolling Stone*, December 18, 1975. "Ain't Gonna Be Your Sugar Mama No More" by Ben Fong-Torres.
"Between albums": Bonnie Raitt press bio supplied to press members with the *Home Plate* LP, September 1975.
"I don't think": *Rolling Stone*, December 18, 1975. "Ain't Gonna Be Your Sugar Mama No More" by Ben Fong-Torres.
"By the mid-seventies": *Rolling Stone*, May 3, 1990. "Bravo Bonnie—the *Rolling Stone* Interview" by James Henke.
"In Cambridge": *Rolling Stone*, December 18, 1975. "Ain't Gonna Be Your Sugar Mama No More" by Ben Fong-Torres.
"Speaking of birthdays": Author's notes taken during Bonnie Raitt's concert at Avery Fisher Hall, New York City, November 9, 1975.
"She watched me": *Rolling Stone*, December 18, 1975. "Ain't Gonna Be Your Sugar Mama No More" by Ben Fong-Torres.
"It was spring": Author's telephone interview with Deborah Mitchell, May 15, 1995.
"Our friendship": Liner notes, *The Bonnie Raitt Collection* album, Warner Bros. Records, 1990.
"that 'Runaway' ": *Village Voice*, July 11, 1977. "Bonnie Raitt Keeps on Bussin' " by Robert Christgau.

6. The Glow of Success

"I get letters": *Rolling Stone*, December 18, 1975. "Ain't Gonna Be Your Sugar Mama No More" by Ben Fong-Torres.

"I consider Bonnie": *Village Voice*, July 11, 1977. "Bonnie Raitt Keeps on Bussin' " by Robert Christgau.

"It seems like": Liner notes, *Thanks I'll Eat It Here* album by Lowell George, Warner Bros. Records, 1979.

"Lowell enlisted myself": Author's interview with Jimmy Greenspoon, May 17, 1995, Tucson, Arizona.

"Colonies of rock": *Time*, February 28, 1977. "Linda Ronstadt: Torchy Rock/Linda Down the Wind" by Jean Valley, John Skow, Edward J. Boyer, and David DeVoss.

"After 'Runaway' ": *Rolling Stone*, May 3, 1990. "Bravo Bonnie—the *Rolling Stone* Interview" by James Henke.

"Peter and I—": *Rolling Stone*, February 21, 1980. "Bonnie Raitt: Music for the Movement" by Daisann McLane.

"There are a few": *Rolling Stone*, December 29, 1977. "Peter Asher Talks About Producing" by Peter Herbst.

"I've always respected": *High Fidelity*, June 1982. "Bonnie Raitt Lightens Up" by Steven X. Rea.

"I was a little intimidated": *Rolling Stone*, February 21, 1980. "Bonnie Raitt: Music for the Movement" by Daisann McLane.

"I knew I was going": *Rolling Stone*, May 27, 1982. "Bonnie Raitt Rocks Again" by Ken Tucker.

"I couldn't sing": *Rolling Stone*, February 21, 1980. "Bonnie Raitt: Music for the Movement" by Daisann McLane.

"I guess it's a": *High Fidelity*, June 1982. "Bonnie Raitt Lightens Up" by Steven X. Rea.

"People would call": *Rolling Stone*, September 20, 1979. "Tribute to Lowell George Draws 20,000" by Daisann McLane.

"I'd like to": Liner notes, *The Glow* album by Bonnie Raitt, Warner Brothers Records, 1979.

"We're going to introduce": *Dinah!* TV Show, broadcast July 30, 1979.

"I first became": MUSE Concerts for a Non-Nuclear Future concert.

"Then the whole cast": Author's notes from the MUSE concert September 19, 1979, Madison Square Garden, New York City.

"Too powerful": *Rolling Stone*, November 15, 1979. "MUSE: Rock Politics Comes of Age" by Daisann McLane.

"The MUSE concerts attracted": Press release sent by Elektra/Asylum Records to journalists to accompany the December 1979 album *No Nukes*.

"It's about a woman": *Rolling Stone*, February 21, 1980. "Bonnie Raitt: Music for the Movement" by Daisann McLane.

"*The Glow* is about": *Rolling Stone*, September 20, 1979. "Bonnie Raitt Completes *The Glow* With Peter Asher."

"The song is a real": Liner notes, *Bonnie Raitt* album, Warner Bros. Records, 1971.

"I think": *High Fidelity*, June 1982. "Bonnie Raitt Lightens Up" by Steven X. Rea.

"I'm not Miss Party anymore": *Rolling Stone*, February 21, 1980. "Bonnie Raitt: Music for the Movement" by Daisann McLane.

"I don't think I've done": *Village Voice*, July 11, 1977. "Bonnie Raitt Keeps on Bussin' " by Robert Christgau.

7. Green Light

"I don't want a hit": *Rolling Stone*, February 21, 1980. "Bonnie Raitt: Music for the Movement" by Daisann McLane.

"Sometimes I feel like": *Rolling Stone*, December 18, 1975. "Ain't Gonna Be Your Sugar Mama No More" by Ben Fong-Torres.

"I've always been": *Rolling Stone*, February 21, 1980. "Bonnie Raitt: Music for the Movement" by Daisann McLane.

"It's true that": *High Fidelity*, June 1982. "Bonnie Raitt Lightens Up" by Steven X. Rea.

"What I wanted": *Rolling Stone*, May 27, 1982. "Bonnie Raitt Rocks Again" by Ken Tucker.

"I was a little stung": *High Fidelity*, June 1982. "Bonnie Raitt Lightens Up" by Steven X. Rea.

"I needed a break": *BAM*, March 26, 1982. "Bonnie Raitt Rocks Out!" by Regan McMahon.

"I tend": *High Fidelity*, June 1982. "Bonnie Raitt Lightens Up" by Steven X. Rea.

"This song is one": Liner notes *Bonnie Raitt* album, Warner Bros. Records, 1971.

"An all-out": *High Fidelity*, June 1982. "Bonnie Raitt Lightens Up" by Steven X. Rea.

"It's one of": *Rolling Stone*, "Bonnie Raitt Rocks Again" by Ken Tucker.

"A scorcher LP": *People*, April 12, 1982. "Sippie Wallace and Bonnie Raitt Prove That Blues Birds of a Feather Can Flock Together" by Carl Arrington and Maryanne George.

"I love it!": *High Fidelity*, June 1982. "Bonnie Raitt Lightens Up" by Steven X. Rea.

"I never thought": *Rolling Stone*, May 27, 1982. "Bonnie Raitt Rocks Again" by Ken Tucker.

"The album shocked": *High Fidelity*, June 1982. "Bonnie Raitt Lightens Up" by Steven X. Rea.

"I don't have any": *Rolling Stone*, May 27, 1982. "Bonnie Raitt Rocks Again" by Ken Tucker.

"I'm amazed": *High Fidelity*, June 1982. "Bonnie Raitt Lightens Up" by Steven X. Rea.

"Sippie has": *People*, April 12, 1982. "Sippie Wallace and Bonnie Raitt Prove That Blues Birds of a Feather Can Flock Together" by Carl Arrington and Maryanne George.

"[Her] life has been": Official Proclamation for "Sippie Wallace Day" in Detroit, Michigan.

"Sippie constantly": *People*, April 12, 1982. "Sippie Wallace and Bonnie Raitt Prove That Blues Birds of a Feather Can Flock Together" by Carl Arrington and Maryanne George.

"When Sippie had": Author's telephone interview with Jim Depogny, May 23, 1995.

"The band is James": Author's telephone interview with Peter Ferran, May 23, 1995.

"We often did": Author's telephone interview with Jim Depogny, May 23, 1995.

"I can remember when": Author's telephone interview with Peter Ferran, May 23, 1995.

"Ron Harwood": Author's telephone interview with Jim Depogny, May 23, 1995.

"I would imagine": Author's telephone interview with Peter Ferran, May 23, 1995.

"One of the things": Author's telephone interview with Jim Depogny, May 23, 1995.

8. Too Long at the Fair

"There was a corporate": *Rolling Stone*, May 3, 1990. "Bravo Bonnie—the *Rolling Stone* Interview" by James Henke.

"Nobody wants to": *Rolling Stone*, October 19, 1989. "It's Bonnie Raitt's Time" by Sheila Rogers.

"It wasn't until": *Rolling Stone*, May 3, 1990. "Bravo Bonnie—the *Rolling Stone* Interview" by James Henke.

"It was a love": *Rolling Stone*, October 19, 1989. "It's Bonnie Raitt's Time" by Sheila Rogers.

"To put it": *Rolling Stone*, May 3, 1990. "Bravo Bonnie—the *Rolling Stone* Interview" by James Henke.

"I was heartbroken": *Newsweek*, March 13, 1989. "Getting Back on Track: Bonnie Raitt" by Ron Givens.

"One of the projects": Syndicated radio interview, produced by Warner Bros. Records.

"I only got loaded": *Rolling Stone*, May 3, 1990. "Bravo Bonnie—the *Rolling Stone* Interview" by James Henke.

"In the past, I've": Syndicated radio interview, produced by Warner Bros. Records.

"As a Bryan Adams fan": Liner notes, *Bonnie Raitt* album, Warner Bros. Records, 1971.

" 'Running Back to Me' ": Syndicated radio interview, produced by Warner Bros. Records.

"I've always loved Toots": Liner notes, *Bonnie Raitt* album, Warner Bros. Records, 1971.

"I think that this": Syndicated radio interview, produced by Warner Bros. Records.

"If I was in the middle": *People*, April 12, 1982. "Sippie Wallace and Bonnie Raitt Prove That Blues Birds of a Feather Can Flock Together" by Carl Arrington and Maryanne George.

"We just couldn't": *Frets*, April 1988. "Bonnie and Slide" by Elisa Welch Mulvaney.

"What happened was": *Rolling Stone*, May 3, 1990. "Bravo Bonnie—the *Rolling Stone* Interview" by James Henke.

"It's true that": *After School Special* TV show, ABC-TV, March 16, 1995.

"For a long time": *People*, April 24, 1989. "Veteran Rocker Bonnie Raitt Gets Back on Track in the Nick of Time" by Kim Hubbard.

"I had a skiing": *Rolling Stone*, May 3, 1990. "Bravo Bonnie—the *Rolling Stone* Interview" by James Henke.

"I wasn't kicking": *People*, April 24, 1989. "Veteran Rocker Bonnie Raitt Gets Back on Track in the Nick of Time" by Kim Hubbard.

"There are people": *Rolling Stone*, May 3, 1990. "Bravo Bonnie—the *Rolling Stone* Interview" by James Henke.

"I knew that if it": *Rolling Stone*, October 19, 1989. "It's Bonnie Raitt's Time" by Sheila Rogers.

"It's one thing": *People*, April 24, 1989. "Veteran Rocker Bonnie Raitt Gets Back on Track in the Nick of Time" by Kim Hubbard.

"A couple of friends": *Rolling Stone*, May 3, 1990. "Bravo Bonnie—the *Rolling Stone* Interview" by James Henke.

"Within about two weeks": *Rolling Stone*, October 19, 1989. "It's Bonnie Raitt's Time" by Sheila Rogers.

"I just couldn't come up": *After School Special* TV show, ABC-TV, March 16, 1995.

"The basic": *Rolling Stone*, May 3, 1990. "Bravo Bonnie—the *Rolling Stone* Interview" by James Henke.

"Bonnie Raitt's going": Author's conversation with Sue McDonald, June 16, 1987, Central Park, New York City.

"I've been doing": *Frets*, April 1988. "Bonnie and Slide" by Elisa Welch Mulvaney.

"This is a night": *Rolling Stone*, March 10, 1988 "Blues for Salvador" by Michael Goldberg.

"There wasn't room on": *Musician*, July 1991. "Bonnie Raitt's Ace of Hearts" by Mark Rowland.

"The [music] industry": *Rolling Stone*, August 8, 1991. "Bonnie Raitt Keeps the Faith" by Steve Pond.

"It's time to make": *Frets*, April 1988. "Bonnie and Slide" by Elisa Welch Mulvaney.

9. Nick of Time

"I never had a hit": *Newsweek*, March 13, 1989. "Getting Back on Track: Bonnie Raitt" by Ron Givens.

"I have my own": *Frets*, April 1988. "Bonnie and Slide" by Elisa Welch Mulvaney.

"You have to find": *USA Today*, February 27, 1995. "Studio Maestro—Don Was Produces Hits for First-String Musicians" by Edna Gundersen.

"I wanted to make": *Rolling Stone*, October 19, 1989. "It's Bonnie Raitt's Time" by Sheila Rogers.

"There's less production": *People*, April 24, 1989. "Veteran Rocker Bonnie Raitt Gets Back on Track in the Nick of Time" by Kim Hubbard.

"We figured it would": *USA Today*, June 24, 1991. "Raitt Finds Lady Luck" by Edna Gundersen.

"We live near": *Rolling Stone*, May 18, 1989. "Random Notes."

"More than anyone": *Musician*, July 1991. "Bonnie Raitt's Ace of Hearts" by Mark Rowland.

"Raitt's best since": *Stereo Review*, June 1989. *Nick of Time* record review by Alana Nash.

"*Nick of Time* is her": *Newsweek*, March 13, 1989. "Getting Back on Track: Bonnie Raitt" by Ron Givens.

"For the first time since": *People*, April 24, 1989. "Veteran Rocker Bonnie Raitt Gets Back on Track in the Nick of Time" by Kim Hubbard.

"For almost any": *Rolling Stone*, April 20, 1989. *Nick of Time* record review by Fred Goodman.

"In many ways this": *Rolling Stone*, October 19, 1989. "It's Bonnie Raitt's Time" by Sheila Rogers.

"If I had to put": *People*, April 24, 1989. "Veteran Rocker Bonnie Raitt Gets Back on Track in the Nick of Time" by Kim Hubbard.

"Every song on there": *Rolling Stone*, May 3, 1990. "Bravo Bonnie—the *Rolling Stone* Interview" by James Henke.

"Raitt is at the": *Rolling Stone*, June 29, 1989. "Still Nobody's Girl" by Moira McCormick.

"Bonnie Raitt has suddenly": *New York Times*, June 11, 1989. "Bonnie Raitt Sings of Equality in Love" by John Parales.

"A soulmate to share": *People*, April 24, 1989. "Veteran Rocker Bonnie Raitt Gets Back on Track in the Nick of Time" by Kim Hubbard.

"I was single": *Rolling Stone*, May 3, 1990. "Bravo Bonnie—the *Rolling Stone* Interview" by James Henke.

"In case I won": *Musician*, July 1991. "Bonnie Raitt's Ace of Hearts" by Mark Rowland.

"I was as out": *Rolling Stone*, May 3, 1990. "Bravo Bonnie—the *Rolling Stone* Interview" by James Henke.

"Wake me up": *The Thirty-second Annual Grammy Awards* TV special, February 21, 1990, CBS-TV.

"That was just so": *Musician*, July 1991. "Bonnie Raitt's Ace of Hearts" by Mark Rowland.

"What are there": *Rolling Stone*, August 8, 1991. "Bonnie Raitt Keeps the Faith" by Steve Pond.

"Like I said": *Rolling Stone*, May 3, 1990. "Bravo Bonnie—the *Rolling Stone* Interview" by James Henke.

"I was in Europe": *Musician*, July 1991. "Bonnie Raitt's Ace of Hearts" by Mark Rowland.

"Dear friends": *Marin Independent Journal*, April 17, 1990. "Rock Fans Moved by Mandela's Message" by Sydney Rubin.

"This is the first time": *Rolling Stone*, October 19, 1989 "It's Bonnie Raitt's Time" by Sheila Rogers.

"It was so great": *USA Today*, June 24, 1991. "Raitt Finds Lady Luck" by Edna Gundersen.

"Bonnie Raitt came in": *Living Blues*, November/December 1994. "Charles Brown" by John Anthony Brisbin.

"On stage, as always": *Down Beat*, December 1990. "Bonnie Raitt/Charles Brown/NRBQ" concert review by Don Ouellette.

"I'm on the road": *Rolling Stone*, October 19, 1989. "It's Bonnie Raitt's Time" by Sheila Rogers.

"I still stay up": *Newsweek*, March 13, 1989. "Getting Back on Track: Bonnie Raitt" by Ron Givens.

"We were close": *Musician*, July 1991. "Bonnie Raitt's Ace of Hearts" by Mark Rowland.

"The music's great": *Rolling Stone*, May 3, 1990. "Bravo Bonnie—the *Rolling Stone* Interview" by James Henke.

"I'm not into clothes": *People*, April 24, 1989. "Veteran Rocker Bonnie Raitt Gets Back on Track in the Nick of Time" by Kim Hubbard.

"I don't think I'm": *Rolling Stone*, August 8, 1991. "Bonnie Raitt Keeps the Faith" by Steve Pond.

10. Let's Give Them Something to Talk About

"I don't think people": *USA Today*, June 24, 1991. "Raitt Finds Lady Luck" by Edna Gundersen.

"When I first met": *People*, May 13, 1991. "A Bonnie Day."

"I knew Bonnie": *After School Special* TV show, ABC-TV, March 16, 1995.

"I was never really": *Musician*, July 1991. "Bonnie Raitt's Ace of Hearts" by Mark Rowland.

"I stand before you": *People*, May 13, 1991. "A Bonnie Day."

"Well, you woulda": *Rolling Stone*, August 8, 1991. "Bonnie Raitt Keeps the Faith" by Steve Pond.

"I wish I had": *Frets*, April 1988. "Bonnie and Slide" by Elisa Welch Mulvaney.

"I got a couple": *Rolling Stone*, May 3, 1990. "Bravo Bonnie—the *Rolling Stone* Interview" by James Henke.

"I couldn't even": *Musician*, July 1991. "Bonnie Raitt's Ace of Hearts" by Mark Rowland.

"I had terrible dreams": *USA Today*, June 24, 1991. "Raitt Finds Lady Luck" by Edna Gundersen.

"He wrote this": *Musician*, July 1991. "Bonnie Raitt's Ace of Hearts" by Mark Rowland.

"Just because": *USA Today*, June 24, 1991. "Raitt Finds Lady Luck" by Edna Gundersen.

"I don't think there's": *Detroit News*, July 8, 1994 "Do the Raitt Thing" by Susan Whitall.

"The basic theory": *Musician*, July 1991. "Bonnie Raitt's Ace of Hearts" by Mark Rowland.

"Bonnie Raitt superbly": *Down Beat*, September 1991. *Luck of the Draw* record review by Don Ouellette.

"Raitt continues": *Stereo Review*, October 1991. *Luck of the Draw* record review by Alana Nash.

"Raitt has recorded": *Rolling Stone*, July 11–25, 1991. *Luck of the Draw* record review by Elysa Gardner

"I really like the": *VH1-to-One* TV show, VH1 cable TV network, October 1994.

"To say Bonnie had": *USA Today*, June 24, 1991. "Raitt Finds Lady Luck" by Edna Gundersen.

"I've never stopped": *VH1-to-One* TV show, VH1 cable TV network, October 1994.

"I've got an enthusiasm": *Musician*, July 1991. "Bonnie Raitt's Ace of Hearts" by Mark Rowland.

"I don't want to": *Rolling Stone*, August 8, 1991. "Bonnie Raitt Keeps the Faith" by Steve Pond.

"It really is": *Musician*, July 1991. "Bonnie Raitt's Ace of Hearts" by Mark Rowland.

"The Rhythm and Blues": *VH1-to-One* TV show, VH1 cable TV network, October 1994.

"We always considered": *Rolling Stone*, October 18, 1990. "Support for Ailing Mary Wells" by David Wild.

"When I was younger": *TV Guide*, July 11–17, 1992. "Raitt Increase" by Greg Fagan.

"I anticipated it": *People*, June 1, 1992. "A First Raitt Duo"

"I just can't believe": *USA Today*, April 29, 1993. "Aretha Serves Soul at AIDS Benefit Show" by James T. Jones.

"I don't see it": *Global Network News*, June/July 1994. "Bonnie Raitt: Something to Talk About" by Edna Gundersen.

"For anyone who's": *Musician*, July 1991. "Bonnie Raitt's Ace of Hearts" by Mark Rowland.

"I have my": *Rolling Stone*, August 8, 1991. "Bonnie Raitt Keeps the Faith" by Steve Pond.

11. Love Sneakin' Up on You

"I'm supporting": *VH1-to-One* TV show, VH1 cable TV network, October 1994.

"We start pretty": *Musician*, July 1991. "Bonnie Raitt's Ace of Hearts" by Mark Rowland.

"These songs": *Global Network News*, June/July 1994 "Bonnie Raitt: Something to Talk About" by Edna Gundersen.

"Love Sneaking . . .": *VH1-to-One* TV show, VH1 cable TV network, October 1994.

"He's a poet": *Rolling Stone*, April 21, 1994. "Bonnie Raitt: Q & A" by Jancee Dunn.

"Both times": *Detroit News*, July 8, 1994. "Do the Raitt Thing" by Susan Whitall.

"I wrote that": *Global Network News*, June/July 1994. "Bonnie Raitt: Something to Talk About" by Edna Gundersen.

"I had tried to": *New Country*, August 1994. "Beyond a Shadow of Doubt: Gary Nicholdon's Hits Keep on Coming" by Jay Orr.

"I don't see any": *VH1-to-One* TV show, VH1 cable TV network, October 1994.

"As bluesy": *Discovery*, BMG Music Service, 1994 quoting *Time* magazine.

"She's continuing": *Entertainment Weekly*. March 2, 1994 "Raitt on Track" by David Browne.

"To be able to": *VH1 Honors* TV special, June 26, 1994, VH1 cable network.

"[Al] Green's": *Los Angeles Times*, June 28, 1994. "Dream Teams Abound Except for One: VH1's First Award Show Delivers a Star-Studded Lineup" by Chris Willman.

"I've been really upset": *Detroit News*, July 8, 1994. "Do the Raitt Thing" by Susan Whitall.

"Ms. Raitt is one": *New York Times*, August 5, 1994. "Bonnie Raitt, Balladeer for the 90s" by Jon Parales.

"Roseanne asked": *TV Guide*, November 12, 1994. "Groom New Guitarists" Item from "Newsmakers" column

"I think, 'How wonderful' ": *Global Network News*, June/July 1994. "Bonnie Raitt: Something to Talk About" by Edna Gundersen.

"Because I'm a musician": *TV Guide*, November 12, 1994. "Groom New Guitarists," Item from "Newsmakers" column.

"This is one": *After School Special* TV Show, ABC-TV March 16, 1995.

"Hey, old": *Rolling Stone*, June 29, 1995. "Blues Power/Stevie Ray Vaughn Honored at Fete" by Don McLeese.

12. What Is Success?

"I love Bonnie": Author's conversation with Peggy Lee, June 24, 1995, backstage at Carnegie Hall, New York.

"To have a career": *VH1-to-One* TV show, VH1 cable TV network, October 1994.

"Being successful": *After School Special* TV show, ABC-TV, March 16, 1995.

"There's a ton": *Rolling Stone*, April 21, 1994. "Bonnie Raitt: Q & A" by Jancee Dunn.

"Girl, I never": *Rolling Stone*, June 1, 1995. "Melissa Etherige Takes the Long Hard Ride From the Heartland to Hollywood" by Jancee Dunn.

"Hitting your stride": *VH1-to-One* TV show, VH1 cable TV network, October 1994.

"Goofing off": *After School Special* TV show, ABC-TV, March 16, 1995.

"It's always been . . .": *Detroit News*, July 8, 1994. "Do the Raitt Thing" by Susan Whitall.

"I'm the recipient": *Musician*, April 1995. "If I Knew Then What I Know Now" gathered by the *Musician* magazine staff.

"Having to get": *After School Special* TV show, ABC-TV, March 16, 1995.

"The comfort level": *Musician*, April 1995. "If I Knew Then What I Know Now" gathered by the *Musician* magazine staff.

"I don't see": *Global Network News*, June/July 1994. "Bonnie Raitt: Something to Talk About" by Edna Gundersen.

"I've been asked": *Rolling Stone*, April 21, 1994. "Bonnie Raitt: Q & A" by Jancee Dunn.

"Bonnie doesn't": *TV Guide*, November 12, 1994. "Groom New Guitarists" Item from "Newsmakers" column.

"Actually, only": *Detroit News*, July 8, 1994. "Do the Raitt Thing" by Susan Whitall.

"Some of the industry": *After School Special* TV show, ABC-TV, March 16, 1995.

"Oh, those": *Rolling Stone*, October 19, 1990. "Prince Talks" by Neal Karlen.

"My own struggle": *Global Network News*, June/July 1994. "Bonnie Raitt: Something to Talk About" by Edna Gundersen.

"Everyone wants": *USA Today*, February 23, 1995. "Full Slate for Bonnie Raitt/Dad Keeps Going on With the Show" by Edna Gundersen.

"There is no time off": *Global Network News*, June/July 1994. "Bonnie Raitt: Something to Talk About" by Edna Gundersen.

"I don't care": *Rolling Stone*, March 10, 1988. "Blues for Salvador" by Michael Goldberg.

"I never liked": *VH1-to-One* TV show, VH1 cable TV network, October 1994.

"When I got": *Rolling Stone*, April 21, 1994. "Bonnie Raitt: Q & A" by Jancee Dunn.

"I don't expect to": *USA Today*, February 23, 1995. "Full Slate for Bonnie Raitt/Dad Keeps Going on With the Show" by Edna Gundersen.

"In my job": *Detroit News*, July 8, 1994. "Do the Raitt Thing" by Susan Whitall.

"Nobody's famous forever": *People*, April 24, 1989. "Veteran Rocker Bonnie Raitt Gets Back on Track in the Nick of Time" by Kim Hubbard.

"I expect to be": *Global Network News*, June/July 1994 "Bonnie Raitt: Something to Talk About" by Edna Gundersen.

"My Dad just": *Global Network News*, June/July 1994. "Bonnie Raitt: Something to Talk About" by Edna Gundersen.

INDEX